They Keep It All Hid

Trends in Classics – Supplementary Volumes

Volume 56

They Keep It All Hid

Augustan Poetry, its Antecedents and Reception

Edited by
Peter E. Knox, Hayden Pelliccia and Alexander Sens

Studies in honor of Richard F. Thomas

DE GRUYTER

ISBN 978-3-11-054417-6
e-ISBN (PDF) 978-3-11-054570-8
e-ISBN (EPUB) 978-3-11-054450-3
ISSN 1868-4785

Library of Congress Cataloging-in-Publication Data
Names: Knox, Peter E., editor. | Pelliccia, Hayden, editor. | Sens, Alexander, editor.
Title: They keep it all hid : Augustan poetry, its antecedents and reception / edited by Peter E. Knox, Hayden Pelliccia, Alexander Sens.
Description: Berlin : De Gruyter, 2018. | Series: Trends in classics. Supplementary volumes ; volume 56 | Includes bibliographical references and index.
Identifiers: LCCN 2018009487 (print) | LCCN 2018012043 (ebook) | ISBN 9783110545708 | ISBN 9783110544176 (hardcover : alk. paper)
Subjects: LCSH: Latin poetry--History and criticism. | Latin poetry--Appreciation.
Classification: LCC PA6047 (ebook) | LCC PA6047 .T43 2018 (print) | DDC 871/.0109--dc23
LC record available at https://lccn.loc.gov/2018009487

Bibliographic information published by the Deutsche Nationalbibliothek
The Deutsche Nationalbibliothek lists this publication in the Deutsche Nationalbibliografie; detailed bibliographic data are available in the Internet at http://dnb.dnb.de.

Editorial Office: Alessia Ferreccio and Katerina Zianna
Logo: Christopher Schneider, Laufen
Printing: CPI books GmbH, Leck

www.degruyter.com

Any Kiwi yachtsman would

A recent photograph from 2017 of the honorand (right) in his native habitat, coastal New Zealand, together with a colleague from childhood (left). Thomas describes the scene as follows: "We spent New Year's Eve with an old sailing friend of mine up in the Bay of Islands. Went for a spin on his boat to a couple of islands (all six of us) ... We found out that two years ago he was sailing on his own from Chile to the Caribbean, blacked out off Brazil and woke up 12 or 24 hours later (he's not sure which), eventually realizing 'Oh you've had a stroke.' His right side was paralyzed, but he could just manage to open a can, so for the next 3+ weeks he drank coffee in the am, ate a can of cold something in the evening, and sailed on to Grenada,"—and said on his return that he had done as "any Kiwi yachtsman would".

Photo: Sarah Thomas.

Table of Contents

Editors' Preface —— IX

David O. Ross
Prologue —— 1

Charles McNelis
Mythical and Literary Genealogies: Aeneas and the Trojan Line in Homer, Ennius and Virgil —— 3

Leah Kronenberg
Reading Virgil and His Trees: The Alder and the Poplar Tree in Catullus and Virgil —— 17

Peter E. Knox
A Known Unknown in Pompeian Graffiti? —— 29

Sergio Casali
Dido's *furtiuuus amor* (Virgil, *Aeneid* 4.171–2) —— 41

James O'Hara
Genre, Gender, and the Etymology Behind the Phrase *Lugentes campi* at *Aeneid* 6.441 —— 51

Julia Hejduk
***Saepe stilum uertas:* Moral and Metrical Missteps in Horace's *Satires* —— 63**

Hayden Pelliccia
The reception of Horace *Odes* 2.4 in Horace *Odes* 2.5 —— 75

Barbara Weiden Boyd
***Beatus ille qui procul ... otiis?:* Ovid's Rustication Cure (*Remedia amoris* 169–98) —— 89**

Alexander Sens
Envy and Closure in the Greek Anthology —— 101

Brian W. Breed
Some Second Poems: Theocritus, Virgil, Tibullus — 117

Charles Martindale
The Horatianism of Marvell's "Horatian Ode" — 131

Thomas Palaima
Masters of War: Virgil, Horace, Owen, Pound, Trumbo, Dylan and the Art of Reference — 147

Works Cited — 169

Notes on Contributors — 185

Index of Passages Discussed — 187

Index Rerum — 189

Editors' Preface

The papers in this volume were contributed by students and friends of Richard Thomas to celebrate his teaching, scholarship, and friendship through many years.[1] They cover the broad range of Richard's interests in Greek and Roman literature and its reception, interests that he has shared with all of us in settings both public and private, all marked by his characteristic blend of energy and wisdom. There were others who wished to contribute, but were prevented by time and circumstance; still others who would have wished to participate, if this volume could have been expanded indefinitely.

The title is taken from the lyrics of "Subterranean Homesick Blues" by Bob Dylan, the contemporary poet who marks the upper end of Richard's interests in the reception of classical literature. Poets, ancient and modern, engage with their predecessors' and contemporaries' texts in ways that open up their work to new meanings once the reader has discovered how and where they keep it all hid. Richard's career has been distinguished by his focus on uncovering such meanings in the poetry he has cherished—the poets of the Hellenistic Greek world, Catullus, the Augustans, but above all Virgil and Bob Dylan, no longer an unlikely pairing. This volume represents a token of gratitude for sharing this project with us and others.

PEK
HP
AS

1 We are all, editors and authors, indebted to Claire Healy of Georgetown University for her meticulous copy editing and bibliographical expertise; her work was supported by the Markos and Eleni Tsakopoulos Kounalakis Chair of Hellenic Studies.

https://doi.org/10.1515/9783110545708-001

David O. Ross

Prologue

Richard and I arrived in Ann Arbor in the same year: I well remember our first meeting, though Richard (how like him) has a somewhat different version of the event. We met at John D'Arms' (then department chairman) opening-of-the-year garden party, on a warm and welcoming late summer afternoon. John, saying something like "Here's someone you should meet", provided the introduction. Yes, we shared the same scholarly interests, but from the beginning it was clear that this was not all. Sartorially challenged, phonemically distinct, Richard has always been, as we all know, at his best with a cigarette in one hand and a glass in the other.

Those first years at Michigan were perhaps my happiest and most productive, and Richard had much to do with it. He soon became the center of the intellectual and social life of our graduate students, the founding member of the regular Friday afternoon Happy Hour, but also a source of scholarly energy generally. And, as I remember, it was often just plain fun. I had then been trying to make sense of the elemental physics in Virgil's *Georgics*, and in our second year I offered a seminar, hoping to get some clarity through having to present the material I had in hand. Richard signed on, and the seminar worked as a seminar is supposed to and so seldom does. He seemed to see at every point what was relevant and might be of interest and which path was not worth pursuing; he had, clearly, a remarkable scholarly instinct. From this emerged in good time his thesis and first publication, and eventually, of course, his two volumes of commentary on the poem that was not overshadowed by, but complemented, Sir Roger Mynors' distinguished commentary published shortly after.

This is not the place to review the steady stream of work that followed, but it can be easily characterized: it's honest. The big idea never precedes, the thesis never controls the argument. There's Richard (one often feels) reading simply for the pleasure of reading again a text he knows well and loves, and a word, or phrase, or passage strikes him in a way it hadn't before, and he's off and running, a hound on a scent, whether it leads to a brief but illuminating comment or to a comprehensive study of reception. It is safe to say that when he has shown us what we hadn't seen or appreciated before in Virgil, say, or Horace, it can be traced back to a specific insight into some detail of language or expression. With Richard, it's the words that count, and it's from the words that the vision emerges. This is philology at its best.

This Festschrift testifies to the loyalty and love that his students, colleagues, and friends feel for him, and this too was evident to me from our first acquaint-

https://doi.org/10.1515/9783110545708-002

ance and friendship in Ann Arbor. Richard has never been one to smile upon the undeserving, and his wit can be devastating, but we all know too that it is without academic *odium*, never *ad hominem* merely to score a point, because he has a marvelous, and rare, ability to connect with just about anyone, even with the most reclusive of scholarly introverts. Richard is a stimulating and warm companion, but his conversation is (again) just such fun. Our friendship of some 45 years now has been one of the great joys of my life. I regret that I can offer no substantial contribution to this publication, but I welcome the opportunity to present to him, and to Joan as well, this inadequate expression of my affection. Thanks, Richard.

Charles McNelis

Mythical and Literary Genealogies: Aeneas and the Trojan Line in Homer, Ennius and Virgil

After the Roman army under his command defeated the Macedonians at Cynoscephalae, Titus Quinctius Flamininus set up two inscriptions at Delphi to commemorate his grant of freedom to the Greeks (Plut. *Flam.* 12.6):

> Ζηνὸς ἰὼ κραιπναῖσι γεγαθότες ἱπποσύναισι
>   κοῦροι, ἰὼ Σπάρτας Τυνδαρίδαι βασιλεῖς,
> Αἰνεάδας Τίτος ὔμμιν ὑπέρτατον ὤπασε δῶρον,
>   Ἑλλήνων τεύξας παισὶν ἐλευθερίαν.

O sons of Zeus, who take pleasure in nimble horsemanship, O children of Tyndareus, rulers of Sparta, Titus, a descendant of Aeneas, bestowed to you a great gift when he brought about freedom for the children of the Greeks.

> Τόνδε τοι ἀμβροσίοισιν ἐπὶ πλοκάμοισιν ἔοικε
>   κεῖσθαι, Λατοΐδα, χρυσοφαῆ στέφανον,
> ὃν πόρεν Αἰνεαδᾶν ταγὸς μέγας. ἀλλ', Ἑκάεργε
>   ἀλκᾶς τῷ θείῳ κῦδος ὄπαζε Τίτῳ.

It is right for this shiny golden wreath to lie on your ambrosial hair, O son of Leto. The great leader of the children of Aeneas gave this wreath, so to god-like Titus, Far-shooting Apollo, give the glory of valour.

Delphi, like other Panhellenic athletic venues,[1] was a traditional and essential location for the display of victories—both martial and athletic—achieved by communities and individuals from all over the ancient world (e.g. Hdt. 1.14; 1.31; 1.92). The motivations to dedicate gifts at Apollo's sanctuary were manifold, but the oracle, which communicated parts of a divine plan to humans and thus seemed to sanction success (as well as defeat), must have influenced decisions to make offerings. Livy, for example, provides an anecdote about a situation similar to and nearly contemporaneous with Titus' inscriptions: after the disastrous defeat at Cannae in 216, the Romans sent an embassy to Delphi. When Fabius Pictor, the leader of that expedition, returned to Rome, he revealed that the oracle outlined the proper way to pray to specific gods. The oracle also

---

1 Plutarch also indicates that Titus himself also utilized the Isthmus to herald Rome's military accomplishments (*Flam.* 10.3).

https://doi.org/10.1515/9783110545708-003

declared that the Romans would win the war, and it added that after that victory gifts should be sent to Apollo. Finally, the oracle ordered Fabius not to remove the laurel crown that he had worn during his performance of sacred rites at Delphi until he reached Rome. Upon reaching Rome, Fabius dedicated the crown on Apollo's altar in Rome (Livy 23.11.1–7), and the Romans went on to defeat Carthage. Fabius' laurel crown, a traditional token of victory for a general as well as for an athlete, symbolically presages Rome's conquest. The clear connection between Roman victory and Apollo's oracle at Delphi is subsequently rounded off by a dedication credited to Titus of a similar crown at that very prophetic source of recent Roman success.

Against this backdrop, it is intriguing that one inscription refers to Titus as a 'descendant of Aeneas'. The Aeneas myth was important for Rome's representation of itself—especially to the Greek world—during Titus' lifetime,[2] and the language of the inscription is unlikely to have been casual. Whatever may have motivated the diction of Titus' inscription, the concern with the 'children of Aeneas' taps into a tradition that ultimately stems from a prophetic statement found in Homeric poetry. In *Iliad* 20, Poseidon intervenes to save Aeneas from Achilles' onslaught, claiming that it is fated for Aeneas and his children to rule (20.300–308). As early as Homer, then, the 'children of Aeneas' were thought to be fated to govern, and the particular status of Aeneas—as well as his ancestors and descendants—plays a key role in shaping the overall dynamics of the *Iliad*. In fact, as will be discussed, the *Iliad* tightly links Aeneas' domestic past with the promise of his children ruling in the future. Far from being 'unmemorable',[3] Aeneas and his family play a strategic role in the Homeric epic.

In *Aeneid* 3, Virgil alludes to and rewrites the Homeric prophecy from *Iliad* 20. Mark Edwards, for example, rightly notes that Virgil translates part of the Homeric lines in his rendition of the prophecy.[4] Yet, more complex literary dynamics are in play with the Virgilian recasting of the Homeric prophecy. Alessandro Barchiesi has already shown that Callimachus' *Hymn to Delos* mediates the Virgilian rewriting of the Homeric prophecy,[5] and Alexander Sens and I have argued that Lycophron's *Alexandra* is another important intermediary.[6] In this paper I want to expand the discussion of antecedent texts to include Ennius' *Annales*, a poem which addresses Rome's rise to power within the context

2 Galinksy 1969, 171–173; Erskine 2001, 36 f. for the importance of the myth in the Greek world. See Erskine 2001 and Casali 2010 for recent overall treatments of the Aeneas legend.

3 Horsfall 1986, 17.

4 Edwards 1991, 326.

5 Barchiesi 1994

6 McNelis and Sens 2016, 167 f.; 201–217.

of the Homeric prophecy and its attendant issue of Aeneas' lineage. The *Annales*, roughly contemporaneous with Titus' dedications, shares with those inscriptions the rhetorical aim of both connecting Aeneas and his lineage with Rome's military success and appealing to divine influence as a way to explain the rise of Rome.[7] The re-workings of the Homeric prophecy about Aeneas and his descendants in this period in turn influenced, at least in broad terms, the depiction of Aeneas' lineage and the problem of interpreting divine will as expressed in the *Aeneid*.[8] In this sense, Virgil's reworking of the Homeric prophecy varies the phenomenon, noted and well explained by Richard Thomas, of the "window allusion".[9] Here, instead of rewriting a more immediate literary passage by reaching back to a remote third text, Virgil looks back to the archaic past through a Hellenistic window. Moreover, in this case, Virgil's allusion to his predecessors involves literary tactics as well as cultural importance: in the *Aeneid*, the Homeric prophecy about Aeneas and his children ruling the world is filtered through poetry whose very focus and themes included and even took as their content Rome's conquest of the Greek world. In that sense, Virgil's allusions to Homer and earlier writers generate a literary genealogy as a well a 'political' history that explains Rome's rise to power.

Fate and the Family

In *Iliad* 20.300 – 308, the enraged Achilles is on the verge of killing Aeneas when Poseidon steps in and saves the Trojan hero.

> ἀλλ' ἄγεθ' ἡμεῖς πέρ μιν ὑπὲκ θανάτου ἀγάγωμεν
> μή πως καὶ Κρονίδης κεχολώσεται, αἴ κεν Ἀχιλλεὺς

---

7 Ennius was of course not unique in his literary treatment of the rise of Rome. Lycophron's *Alexandra*, a text I believe to be from this period (see McNelis and Sens 2016, 10 f.), also covers the rise of Rome. If Melinno is properly dated to the second century BCE (for conflicting views of date, see Bowra (1957) and *SH* 541), her poem is another example of the importance of fate for Roman success (*SH* 541.5). Polybius attempts to explain by what means and under what kind of governance the inhabited world was conquered and brought under Roman dominion within 53 years (1.1.5); Carneades and Panaetius seemingly engaged in philosophical disquisitions stemming from Aristotle and others about empire as the reward of virtue and how that pertained to Rome's rise to power. Roman conquest thus stimulated a great deal of intellectual activity.

8 As we see, for example, from Servius' comment on Varro's treatise entitled *de familiis Troianis* (cf. Servius on *Aen.* 5.704), the lineage of Trojan families interested a host of ancient authors. My point here is not to establish direct connections within the complex mythographic tradition but rather to illustrate strategic possibilities and similarities.

9 Thomas 1986a, 188 – 190.

τόνδε κατακτείνῃ· μόριμον δέ οἵ ἐστ' ἀλέασθαι,
ὄφρα μὴ ἄσπερμος γενεὴ καὶ ἄφαντος ὄληται
Δαρδάνου, ὃν Κρονίδης περὶ πάντων φίλατο παίδων
οἳ ἕθεν ἐξεγένοντο γυναικῶν τε θνητάων
ἤδη γὰρ Πριάμου γενεὴν ἔχθηρε Κρονίων
νῦν δὲ δὴ Αἰνείαο βίη Τρώεσσιν ἀνάξει
καὶ παίδων παῖδες, τοί κεν μετόπισθε γένωνται.

But come, let us lead him away from death so that Zeus not get angry if Achilles kills this man. For it is destined that he will survive so that the race of Dardanus, whom Zeus loved more than all sons whom mortal women bore to him, not die, blotted out without seed. For Zeus has cursed the generation of Priam, and now the might of Aeneas will rule over the Trojans, and his sons' sons, and those born in the future.

Hera immediately responds that it is for Poseidon to decide whether or not to save Aeneas (*Il.* 20.310–312). The scene in *Iliad* 20, inasmuch as it deals with Zeus' special offspring and features a reaction from Hera about saving a human, invites comparison with *Iliad* 16.431–461, where Hera cautions Zeus against saving his dear son Sarpedon and thereby violating fate.[10] In the case of Sarpedon, the beloved child of Zeus dies, but in the case of Aeneas, the line and the individual himself survives. Indeed, the exceptional status of Aeneas' family is reinforced in a similar scene in which Achilles' pursuit of Hector prompts Zeus to ask whether or not Hector should be saved instead of perishing at the hands of Achilles (*Il.* 22.175 f.). Athena responds that since Hector's death is fated the gods will not approve of any intervention (22.180 f.). She also speaks of the necessity to adhere to fate, and, once again, Zeus declines to intervene. The stark differences between Poseidon's rescue of a human and Zeus' obedience to fate—even when dealing with those he loves—establish the exceptional position of Aeneas within the poem itself.[11] As Poseidon declares, Aeneas and that branch of Dardanus' line will survive, while Priam and his branch are cursed.

---

10 Janko 1994, 374 f.

11 Smith, 1981 notes Aeneas' singular status in the poem by comparing him with Hector. In particular, Smith argues that Aeneas' willingness to come forth and face Achilles for a fight that he cannot win prepares for Hector's decision to do battle, but the divine intervention that saves Aeneas is inverted in Hector's climactic duel when Athena abandons Hector and no god intervenes to help. The poignant contrast between the two heroes is further enhanced by the awareness that Aeneas needed encouragement to go face Achilles, whereas Hector advances against Achilles on two occasions only to be warned not to do so. In Smith's view, Hector's greatness is defined in part by his contrasting behavior with Aeneas. However that may be, the overall point is that Aeneas serves as a marked foil to Hector and the current ruling house at Troy. See also the discussion of Alden 2000, 170–172 for divine favor as displayed in a genealogy.

The contrasting fates of the branches of Dardanus' family develop larger internal dynamics found in the *Iliad*. Before Poseidon utters his prophecy, Achilles and Aeneas exchange words (20.177–258). At one moment, Achilles taunts Aeneas by saying that even if Aeneas should prevail, Priam would not honor him because the king has sons (20.182–184):

> ἦ σέ γε θυμὸς ἐμοὶ μαχέσασθαι ἀνώγει
> ἐλπόμενον Τρώεσσιν ἀνάξειν ἱπποδάμοισι
> τιμῆς τῆς Πριάμου;
>
> Does your spirit drive you to fight in the hope that you will command Priam's power among the horse-breaking Trojans?

Achilles' insult, however, is revealed as empty in some sense when Poseidon uses similar language to confirm that Aeneas will indeed rule over the Trojans (20.307 ἀνάξει). Achilles has limited knowledge of the divine plan, but his taunt is not entirely baseless. After all, in *Iliad* 13, the narrator says that Aeneas held back from battle because he always resented Priam's failure to honor him (*Il.* 13.459–461):

> ...τὸν δ' ὕστατον εὗρεν ὁμίλου
> ἑσταότ'· αἰεὶ γὰρ Πριάμῳ ἐπεμήνιε δίῳ
> οὕνεκ' ἄρ' ἐσθλὸν ἐόντα μετ' ἀνδράσιν οὔ τι τίεσκεν.
>
> He found Aeneas standing at the periphery of battle, for he was always angry at brilliant Priam because Priam didn't honor him, though he was noble, among the people.

Moreover, when Aeneas himself recites his genealogy at *Il.* 20.213–241 he notes that his family may be noble, but it is not ruling over the Trojans. Indeed, though he implies there is a close connection between the branches of the house of Dardanus (*Il.* 20.232 Ἶλός τ' Ἀσσάρακός τε καὶ ἀντίθεος Γανυμήδης), he clearly divides his branch, stemming from Assaracus (20.239), from that of Ilos. His genealogy concludes by distinguishing between him and Hector, the two most important offspring of their generation. The exchange between Aeneas and Achilles synecdochically captures crucial issues having to do with lineage, survival, and power within the Trojan line.

The Homeric interest in Aeneas and his family is taken up in the *Annales*. The scanty remains of the poem limit our understanding of large sections of Ennius' work, but a tantalizing note on the phrase *Assaraci proles*, found in *Georgics* 3.35, is recorded by Servius Danielis. In an attempt to explain the family tree behind the Virgilian phrase, which, as Richard Thomas has noted, highlights the Julian clan,[12] Servius records that Ennius wrote (*Ann.* 1.28 f. Skutsch):[13]

> Assaraco natus Capis optimus isque pium ex se
> Anchisen generat...
>
> Capys, the best of men, was sprung from Assaracus and from his loins he begot devoted Anchises...

The line reworks *Iliad* 20.239, in which Aeneas explains to Achilles the distinct branches of the Trojan household (Ἀσσάρακος δὲ Κάπυν, ὃ δ' ἄρ' Ἀγχίσην τέκε παῖδα). Two points are significant here. The first is that the identification of Capys as Aeneas' grandfather was not unambiguous or inevitable. Authors such as Livy (1.3) and Virgil (*Aen.* 6.768) make a Capys one of the Alban kings. For his part, Coelius Antipater, roughly a contemporary of Ennius, makes the Trojan Capys a cousin of Aeneas who then goes on to found Capua.[14] So while there were various figures from Roman lore with the name Capys, Ennius avoids any possible confusion and simply draws upon Homeric authority to establish the genealogical relationship between Assaracus, Capys, Anchises, and ultimately Aeneas himself. Capys, as in Homer, is Aeneas' grandfather.

Despite the lack of any larger context for Ennius' reworking of the Homeric line, it seems plausible to connect it with the kind of larger interest in Aeneas' genealogy that we see in the *Iliad.* After all, the Homeric verse about Anchises' descent from Capys looks backwards to Aeneas' ancestors; within close compass, Poseidon steps in to save Aeneas and utters his prophecy that looks forward to the descendants of Aeneas (20.308). The Homeric genealogy thus covers past and present, but its suggestion of the future is understandably limited.

A second point emerging from Ennius' adaptation of the Homeric line is that, as Skutsch argues, the speaker in the *Annales* may be Aeneas—just as he was the speaker of the words in the *Iliad*—and that he addresses the Alban king.[15] If this incorporation of Homeric genealogy occurs at the moment Aeneas

12 Thomas 1988 on *G.* 3.35; Casali 2007, 113 f. Goldschmidt 2013, 51–53 discusses the Ennian line in light of literary history and aesthetics.

13 The fragment fits into the pattern, well discussed by Elliott 2013, 75–134, of Ennian fragments that are preserved by sources whose primary interest is Virgil.

14 See Harrison 1990 on *Aen.* 10.145.

15 Elliott 2013, 330 soberly notes there is no solid evidence for the location of the fragment. However that may be, the genealogy clearly hearkens back to *Iliad* 20. Skutsch 1985, 187 argues the verses in which Aeneas lists his ancestry must be spoken to the king of Alba. Skutsch also posits that Ennius' interaction between Aeneas and the king of Alba influenced *Aeneid* 8 where Aeneas speaking to Evander, another king, also lists his ancestry (though it is an ancestry that is

strikes an agreement with the Alban king to marry his daughter, the genealogical implications are clear: when the princess gives birth to a girl who in turn will bear Romulus, she extends Aeneas' line.[16] While this reconstruction of the poem's narrative is necessarily speculative, it is certain that Aeneas, in Ennius' version, is Romulus' grandfather, a striking relationship that keeps within a single family the beginning stages of the unfurling of Roman history.[17] Ennius' mythography thus establishes unity within Rome's earliest royal household—in a pointed departure from the distinctions within the Trojan ruling house found in the *Iliad*. That ideal will be destroyed once the poem reaches Romulus' murder of Remus, but Ennius' representation of Aeneas as Romulus' grandfather (a relationship that was not universally accepted in the third and second centuries)[18] strategically integrates Rome's first family. Moreover, from a literary historical perspective, Ennius' recasting of the words of the Homeric ancestry of Aeneas directs the reader back to the genealogy in *Iliad* 20, yet in the *Annales*, the phrase supplements that genealogy by specifying the origin of Aeneas' offspring. In this way, the *Annales* constructs its own literary lineage by showing itself to be a 'descendant' of the Homeric forecast.

Homeric prophecy provides a broader backdrop for the depiction of Aeneas' family in other ways too. The rape of Ilia is modeled, as is well noted,[19] upon the Homeric scene in which Poseidon, after raping Tyro, predicts that her offspring will be glorious (*Od.* 11.235–259). In Ennius' rendition of the rape of Ilia, the prophetic backdrop also highlights the coming glory of the children who will result from the rape. For instance, when Ilia reports to him what had happened, Aeneas responds in prophetic terms, telling his daughter that misfortunes are to be en-

---

markedly different than that offered in *Annales* 1). That Virgilian alliance between Aeneas and Evander is presaged by Aeneas' alliance in the *Annales*.

16 We cannot tell from the remains of the *Annales* who this king of Alba is, but Dionysius Halicarnassus (1.57 f.) and Cato (fr. 8) suggest that the king who granted land to Aeneas and the Trojans was named Latinus. In other versions, of course, Aeneas and Latinus engage in conflict (e.g. Livy 1.3). Against the backdrop of this interaction, Aeneas' encounter with the local king raises important issues of integration or conflict. In the *Annales*, however, Aeneas and his troops are integrated through marriage, perhaps another indication of the unity that attaches to the house of Aeneas.

17 Erskine 2001, 30–39 outlines that the Romulus myth was prevalent in Rome at the expense of the Aeneas legend; conversely the Aeneas myth was used in the Greek world and outside of Rome, while the story of Romulus was 'unfamiliar' (p. 37). Ennius' conflation of the two founders nicely and notably reflects a combination of Greek and Roman mythography.

18 See, e.g., Feeney 2007, 52–57 for the intellectual background of the Aeneas and Romulus relationship.

19 See Skutsch 1985, 194. Connors 1994, 103–108 examines Homeric influence on Ennius' scene; Krevans 1993 illustrates the importance of tragedy for Ennius' treatment of Ilia.

dured, and that afterwards her fortune will gain a solid footing from the river (*Ann.* 1.44–46):

> ... o gnata, tibi sunt ante gerendae
> aerumnae, post ex fluuio fortuna resistet.'
> Haec ecfatus pater.
>
> Daughter, hardships are to be borne by you first; afterwards, fortune will gain a firm footing from a river. These things the father declared.

That the exact sense of Aeneas' statement is not clear may reflect the ambiguity typical of oracles.[20] For certain, *ecfatus* belongs to the solemn language of augury.[21] Similarly, the use of the verb *resistet* instead of a form like *resurget* may, in Skutsch's view, also reflect oracular language. Moreover, in subsequent verses, Venus, whose prophetic skills had been endorsed earlier in the poem when she is treated as the source of Anchises' prophetic knowledge (*Ann.* 1.15),[22] seems to be the speaker who replicates Aeneas' language when speaking to Ilia about the rape and its consequences. Whoever the speaker is, the phrase *aerumnas tetulisti* (*Ann.* 1.60) puts in the past the very difficulties that Aeneas had foretold for his daughter (*Ann.* 1.45 *sunt ... gerendae / aerumnae*) and thus confirms the prediction. The unfolding of the narrative, which reports the accomplishments of descendants like Romulus and subsequent Roman leaders, likewise authorizes Aeneas' vision, and in this way Rome's history as described in the poem proves the prophecies to be right. In turn, the divine predictions about the future that is realized in the course of the poem imbue Ennius' version of events with sacral authority. History, prophecy, and the poetic narrative all partake in a triangulated relationship predicated upon truth and divine authority.

The rape scene also operates within the tradition in which childbirth was a standard moment of prophecy. Aulus Gellius (3.16.9 f.), for example, records that Varro explained the names of the Parcae by saying that

> The ancients ... gave names to the three Fates, deriving them from *pariendo* and from the ninth and tenth months. "In fact", says Varro, "Parca comes from *partus*, 'birth,' with the change of one letter; Nona and Decima come from the period of timely delivery".

---

20 Skutsch 1985, 200. The most famous case of ambiguity involves Pyrrhus' decision to fight the Romans; see *Annales* 6.167.

21 *TLL* 5.2.199.23–42.

22 Casali 2007, 115n.25 discusses the tradition of Anchises as prophet.

In Ennius, of course, the moment at which Aeneas makes his statement about his grandchildren is not the moment of birth per se, but strict parturitional chronology is irrelevant. After all, the Homeric Poseidon predicts the glory of Tyro's children as soon as their sexual union is over (*Od.* 11.249 f.), and Hecuba has her prophetic dream that she will give birth to a firebrand while she is pregnant with Paris (Pind. *Pae.* 8.10–14). Most significantly, in the Homeric *Hymn to Aphrodite,* the goddess, immediately after the sex act in which Aeneas is conceived, foretells that Anchises' son will rule over the Trojans (196 f.):

> σοὶ δ' ἔσται φίλος υἱὸς ὃς ἐν Τρώεσσιν ἀνάξει
> καὶ παῖδες παίδεσσι διαμπερὲς ἐκγεγάονται
>
> And you will have a dear son, who will rule among the Trojans, and children will continually be born to children.

The topic and language obviously recalls the Iliadic prophecy. The phrase καὶ παῖδες παίδεσσι recalls the Homeric line: like it, the verse begins with καὶ and has the same polyptoton, and the line ending Τρώεσσιν ἀνάξει replicates a Homeric line ending Τρώεσσιν ἀνάξει. The hymn, however, shifts the prediction from the mouth of one divinity (Poseidon) to another, the *genetrix* of Aeneas and his descendants. In the *Annales,* Aeneas' prediction to his pregnant daughter repeats the process for the next generation and passes along prophecies from one generation to the next. As Ennius' poem proceeds through Roman history—and through the generations—archaic Greek predictions are rewritten and confirmed.

In the *Annales*, prophecies and thus a divine plan persistently figure in Rome's earliest moments.[23] Homeric poetry is the backdrop for this divine involvement, and the verse that Ennius took over from *Iliad* 20 allusively marks the importance of the Homeric genealogy for a scene that, arguably, concerns the production of children for Aeneas' family. In so doing, the allusion not only provides specifics on the names and identities of the children that were (necessarily) left vague in Poseidon's Homeric prophecy but also establishes genealogical unity in Rome's ruling family. The *Annales* fills in Homeric gaps, and simultaneously links the authority of Homeric verse to the Roman historical process. Against this backdrop, the opening of the *Annales,* where Homer ap-

23 Divine concern for Rome reappears at subsequent crucial junctures such as the augury of birds with Romulus and Remus and when Jupiter predicts the destruction of Carthage (Serv. on *Aen.* 1.20). The extent to which the gods were depicted as directly involved in the later so-called 'historical' parts of Roman history is debated; see Elliott 2013, 45–50 for the attractive argument that the gods were likely involved throughout the epic.

pears to Ennius in a dream and Ennius ends up, in the words of Lucilius (1189 M), as a 'second Homer', foreshadows strategies of *Annales* 1 in beginning a broader transference of power from the Homeric world of Troy to a new Roman political—and literary—context.[24] Indeed, the very structure of Ennius' poem reinforces the significance of that early lineage for Roman history. Ennius seems to have innovated in utilizing a year-by-year structure to cover Roman history,[25] but primacy need not be not the point here so much as the overall effect of his unrelenting account of the march of Roman history, which takes as its starting point the lineage of Aeneas himself. The inexorable march throughout Roman history from the days of its founder down to Fulvius Nobilior tightly connects periods of history stemming back to the Trojan—and Homeric—past.

The Trojan past and future as depicted in *Iliad* 20 features prominently in the *Aeneid*. In *Aeneid* 3, for example, when the refugee Trojans arrive at Delos, a voice delivers a prophecy (94–98):

> Dardanidae duri, quae uos a stirpe parentum
> prima tulit tellus, eadem uos ubere laeto
> accipiet reduces. antiquam exquirite matrem.
> hic domus Aeneae cunctis dominabitur oris
> at nati natorum et qui nascentur ab illis.

> Hardy sons of Dardanus, the land which first bore you from the stock of your parents will welcome you back with a rich bosom. Seek out your ancient mother. In this place the house of Aeneas will rule over all shores, and his children's children and those who will be born from them.

The prophecy from *Iliad* 20 is a fundamental intertext for this prophecy in *Aeneid* 3.[26] The Homeric phrase Αἰνείαο βίη has become *domus Aeneae*. The phrase *et nati natorum* recalls καὶ παίδων παῖδες, with a reversal of the nominatives and genitives, and Virgil's *dominabitur* corresponds to the Homeric ἀνάξει. The Virgilian prophecy pointedly starts by addressing the Trojans as *Dardanidae*, evidently a nod to a phrase in the Homeric prophecy that the line of Dardanus must not perish (20.303 f. γενεὴ καὶ ἄφαντος ὄληται | Δαρδάνου). Finally, we know from Strabo that some ancient texts had a slight variant for the ending of *Il.* 20.307 that read γένος πάντεσσιν ἀνάξει (13.1.53). It would seem that Virgil's

---

24 For a good discussion of ways in which Ennius adapts Homeric elements, see Gildenhard 2007, 79 f.

25 Rüpke 2012, 169.

26 McNelis and Sens 2016, 211.

cunctis oris, with *cunctis* picking up the Homeric πάντεσσιν, reflects that variant reading of the text.[27]

Virgil also picks up on the genealogical interest in Aeneas and his family evinced by Homer and Ennius. To be sure, the *Aeneid* does not borrow the same line from Homer that Ennius does. Rather, Virgil takes over a Homeric verse that appeared just before the Homeric line about Capys that Ennius borrowed. At *Aen.* 6.650, the narrator identifies characters in the underworld and points out figures from the deep past of Troy (*Ilusque Assaracusque et Troiae Dardanus auctor*); the line is modeled on one mentioned earlier, *Iliad* 20.232 Ἶλός τ' Ἀσσάρακός τε καὶ ἀντίθεος Γανυμήδης. Indeed, Virgil's connectives (*-que...-que et*) perfectly correspond to the Homeric diction (τ'...τε καί), and the sequence of proper names matches up in the first half of the verse. The Homeric backdrop is clear. In the remainder of the verse, however, Virgil alters the Homeric model. Ganymede, who occupies the second half of the Homeric verse, is absent in the *Aeneid* since mythology precludes his presence in the underworld.

Virgil's choice to replace Ganymede is significant: Dardanus. He, the founder of Troy, Ilus, and Assaracus form an integral whole, a point reinforced elsewhere in the poem with nearly formulaic language (cf. *Aen.* 3.503, 4.365). When Ilus and Assaracus are introduced in the Homeric lineage, as discussed above, the line ends up in divergent branches of the Trojan household, but in the *Aeneid* the two are mentioned in a context that represents the origins of Aeneas' line as harmonious.[28] That sense of accord persists throughout the poem, as multiple characters equate Anchises and Priam as well as Hector and Aeneas. Ilioneus, for example, offers Latinus both a golden vessel used by Anchises in libation and the golden clothes that Priam wore (*Aen.* 7.245 f.). The gesture implies equivalency between the two branches of the Trojan household. Diomedes explicitly equates Aeneas and Hector as warriors (*Aen.* 11.289–91), and Aeneas holds himself and Hector up as models of martial valor for Ascanius (*Aen.* 12.440). In Buthrotum, Andromache sees in Ascanius the likeness of her Astyanax, the dead prince of Troy (*Aen.* 3.489). The former Trojan princess is an authoritative voice for this articulation of the close connection between the lines of Anchises and of Priam, as well as for the transfer of power between the two branches. After all, her offspring is dead, but she sees in Ascanius the future that her princely son could have realized. In fact, Hector himself explicitly passes the line of Trojan authority to Aeneas (*Aen.* 2.293). Virgil's treatment of the close relationship within the Tro-

27 For discussion of the text and variant, see Horsfall 2006, 108.

28 Gildenhard 2007, 96–98 helpfully analyzes the role of genealogy and the construction of national myth.

jan royal household, then, follows, at least indirectly, a strategy that Ennius had already adopted with his version of familial bonds within the early Trojan house.

In other regards, however, Virgil seems to diverge from Ennius' strategies. Whereas Aeneas has prophetic skill in the *Annales*, prophecies in the *Aeneid* challenge Aeneas' comprehension.[29] In particular, Aeneas does not understand that of *Aeneid* 3.94–98. Sens and I have argued that Virgil's adaptation of the *Iliad* 20 prophecy here was mediated through Lycophron's *Alexandra*.[30] Aeneas and his companions are told to seek out their ancient mother, and that from this spot (*hic*) they will rule the world. No one properly comprehends the location that the voice refers to (3.100 f. *cuncti quae sint ea moenia quaerunt, quo Phoebus uocet errantis iubeatque reuerti*), and the revered Anchises of course gets the answer wrong when he tells the Trojans to head to Crete. It is only after the journey to Crete when the Penates tell Aeneas that they need to head for Italy that the Trojans understand their real destination.

Yet confusion about Aeneas' destination was not limited to characters in the *Aeneid*. Indeed, we know from multiple sources that the locale of Aeneas' domain, as suggested by the Homeric prophecy, was debated even in the Augustan age. Strabo, for example, vehemently argues against three different accounts and unambiguously states that Aeneas ruled in Troy after the family of Priam was destroyed. Further, Dionysius of Halicarnassus rejects claims that Aeneas settled his people in Italy, subsequently returned home, ruled over Troy, and bequeathed this sovereignty to Ascanius and future generations (1.53.4 f.). In this regard, the misunderstanding of the prophecy in *Aeneid* 3 by Anchises and the Trojans makes them meta-characters.[31] Their initial failure counterpoises the limits on human comprehension of divine predictions to the claims, found for example in the *Annales*, that Anchises and Aeneas are prophetic figures who can accurately assess fate. In the *Aeneid*, Anchises and his fellow travelers are made to play meta-roles in the ancient debate about the *Iliad* 20 prophecy and where it foretells Aeneas will rule. The substantial gulf between the depictions of Aeneas' awareness of prophecy and divine plans calls attention to the nature of the interaction between humans and the gods in each poem.

As Rome's military dominion was being established in the third and second centuries BCE, its apparent destiny prompted a variety of written responses, including the inscriptions that Titus set up at Delphi. In the literary world, however, the presence of the Homeric prophecy afforded poets of that era—such as En-

---

29 For prophecies and limited understanding, see O'Hara 1990.
30 McNelis and Sens 2016, 211–216.
31 McNelis and Sens 2016, 212.

nius—the opportunity to recast, supplement and augment parts of the Aeneas myth while strategically drawing upon the power and authority of the Homeric tradition to validate and strengthen their account of that military control. The *Aeneid*, in turn, also reworks Poseidon's prophetic declaration about the children of Aeneas, but simultaneously rewrites Ennius' earlier handling of Homeric material. For Ennius and others like Flamininus, the "children of Aeneas" eventually became a broad term that included the Romans more generally, but for Virgil, writing in a world dominated by the Julian clan, the relationship between the Roman present and Trojan past mattered deeply. By equating the Homeric prophecy about Aeneas and his descendants to the word of the gods, Virgil appeals to the literary authority of Homer. But when Anchises and Aeneas fail to understand divine plans—a point highlighted against the backdrop of their earlier incarnations in the *Annales*—as articulated through prophecy, even Homeric authority becomes subject to misinterpretation and reconsideration.

Leah Kronenberg

Reading Virgil and His Trees: The Alder and the Poplar Tree in Catullus and Virgil

If readers learn one thing from Richard Thomas' seminal article on Catullan intertextuality, "Catullus and the Polemics of Poetic Reference (Poem 64.1–18)",[1] it is that Catullus knew his trees, and he knew them in both Greek and Latin. But in fact, we learn many things about Catullus and his intertextual strategies in this article, which starts with an example of Virgil's masterful conflation of his poetic sources in *Eclogue* 6.52 and then weaves together an intricate argument about Catullus' polemical use of his sources in the opening lines of Catullus 64, which utilize different types of tree wood and competing etymologies of the Argo to position Catullus in a literary tradition stretching from Euripides, to Apollonius of Rhodes, to Ennius. The article ends by circling back to Virgil and his own effortless incorporation of all of the above into the *Aeneid*, and then by providing a quick glance at Ovid's attempt to one-up everybody with his "all-inclusive instance of multiple reference and conflation on this theme".[2] In homage to Thomas' groundbreaking work on Catullan and Virgilian intertextuality, I offer a minor contribution to solving a puzzle involving trees in *Eclogue* 6—one that sends us back to Catullus 17 and 64, and then further back to Homer and Theocritus, before returning, in good Thomas-fashion, to Virgil again (with a brief glance at Ovid).

The puzzle is this: in *Eclogue* 6.62f., Tityrus[3] recounts how Silenus sang of the Heliades and their transformation into trees. Of course, in good Alexandrian fashion, he does not quite call them that, but instead uses the adelphonymic Phaethontiades.[4] More surprising than their name, however, is the tree they

1 Thomas 1982.
2 Thomas 1982, 163.
3 Thomas 1998 teaches us the importance of not conflating Tityrus with Virgil in *Ecl.* 6.
4 Cf. Thomas 1982, 148 (*ad* Catull. 64.4–9): "In good Alexandrian fashion, Catullus refrained from mentioning the Argo by name". Huyck (1987) revives the interpretation of *Phaethontiadas* as a true patronymic based on the use of Phaethon as a name for Helios and specifically its use as such in Eur. *Hipp.* 740. Huyck's suggestion is convincing, though Virgil's choice of name may be intended to evoke simultaneously their relationship to their father and brother. I will return to discussion of this name when I consider Virgil's allusions to Catullus 64.

https://doi.org/10.1515/9783110545708-004

turn into (62f.): *tum Phaethontiadas musco circumdat amarae / corticis atque solo proceras erigit alnos* ("Then he surrounds the Phaethontiades with the moss of bitter bark and raises tall alders from the ground"). As commentators note, in every other version of the tale, including in Virgil's own (*Aeneid* 10.190), the sisters turn into (black) poplar trees.[5] For example, Wendell Clausen writes:

> In all other accounts, Phaethon's sisters, weeping over their brother's charred remains on the banks of the Eridanus, are turned into poplars distilling tears of amber. Ancient readers, understandably, were puzzled: 'quidam alnos poetica consuetudine pro populis accipiunt' (DServ.). But. V. remembered the alder-fringed Po, the mythical Eridanus, of his youth, *G.* 2.451–2 'nec non et torrentem undam levis innatat alnus / missa Pado'. It is rare for a Latin poet to prefer personal experience to literary tradition, and V. may have regretted his youthful originality, for he later took pains to 'correct' it, *A.* 10.189–91...[6]

Did Virgil really prefer personal experience to literary tradition in his decision to substitute or conflate the alder tree with the poplar tree? In his account of the literary figures lying behind Virgil's Old Man of Tarentum, Thomas has shown us that even when Virgil "remembers having seen" (*memini...uidisse*, *G.* 4.125–27) an old Corycian, we should be careful not to privilege personal experience over literary memory.[7] I would argue that the same caution applies to Virgil's placement of alder trees around the Po, and that Virgil does so not because of personal experience but because Catullus did so first when he subtly conflated the alder and the poplar tree in Poems 17 and 64.[8]

Before I show *how* Catullus conflates these two trees through allusions to Theocritus and Homer, I will first posit *why* he may have done so. One answer might be found in the Celtic language, which Catullus is fond elsewhere of referencing, particularly in connection with his home region of Cisalpine Gaul.[9]

---

5 E.g., Ap. Rhod. *Argon.* 4.604. Pausanias calls the black poplar tree the "nursling of the land of the Celts and of the Celtic Eridanus" (τὴν δὲ αἴγειρον γῆς τῆς τῶν Κελτῶν καὶ Ἠριδανοῦ τοῦ Κελτικοῦ θρέμμα εἶναι, 5.14.3).

6 Clausen 1994, 199 (*ad Ecl.* 6.63).

7 Thomas 1992.

8 Cf. Huyck's (1987, 228) suspicion that Virgil's use of *alnos* in *Ecl.* 6 suggests a missing Greek source. Harrison (2007, 54) proposes that Parthenius' *Metamorphoses* could be the source. My argument that the immediate source is Catullus does not, of course, preclude a Greek source, as well.

9 Cf. *ploxeni* in Catull. 97.6, a word that Quintilian (*Inst.* 1.5.8) explains as belonging to the region around the Po and which scholars have deemed likely Celtic in origin (e.g., Garrod 1910, 203f.; Krostenko 2001, 283). On Catullus' witty use of Celtiberian speech patterns in Catull. 39.20, a poem in which Catullus embraces his Transpadane roots (*Transpadanus, ut meos quoque attingam*, 39.13), see Katz 2000. On other uses of Celtic in Latin texts, see Adams 2003, 185–200.

In Celtic, the word for "alder tree" is **alisā* (f.) or **aliso-* (m.), which is cognate with the similar-sounding Greek word ἄλιζα ("white poplar"), as well as the Latin *alnus* ("alder").[10] While we cannot be sure that Catullus knew that the Celtic word for "alder" was phonetically similar to a rare Greek (or Macedonian) word for "white poplar", the use he makes of alder and poplar trees in Poems 17 and 64 suggests that he may have been and that he enjoyed flaunting his erudition by drawing connections between the two trees.

Catullus uses *alnus* ("alder tree") in this conflationary manner in Catullus 17, a poem with a strong Cisalpine setting and which would thus be at home with a reference to the Celtic language.[11] Catullus does not name the *Colonia* to whom he addresses the poem (17.1), but most commentators assume it is Verona or a nearby town since he mentions in the poem "a certain fellow townsman of mine" (*quendam municipem meum*, 8) and also the Cisalpine region of Liguria (*Liguri...securi*, 19).[12] The thrust of this poem in Priapean meter involves the speaker's desire to throw this certain townsman off *Colonia*'s bridge due to his sluggish impotence and inability to guard his wanton *puella*, a state of lethargy that Catullus compares to a fallen alder tree in a ditch (17.14–20):

---

10 On the relation between the Celtic, Greek, and Latin words, see Mallory and Adams 1997, 11 (s.v. "alder"). On the meaning of ἄλιζα, see the gloss of Hesychius, who attributes it to the Macedonians: ἡ λεύκη τὸ δένδρον. Μακεδόνες. While ἄλιζα is attested only in Hesychius, it is easy to imagine that obscure tree names would have attracted the attention of other ancient scholars and scholar-poets. Tree and plant names in multiple languages and dialects may also have been preserved in recipes and medico-magical texts. As Adams (2003, 191–196) notes, Marcellus of Bordeaux gives many examples of plants named in both Latin and Gaulish in his own medico-magical text *De medicamentis*.

11 In addition, I would note that modern scholars (see Koch 2006, 1.41, s.v. "Alesia / Alisia") connect the Celtic town Alesia etymologically to **alisā* (f.) / **aliso-* (m.) ("alder tree"). According to Diod. Sic. 4.2, Alesia was founded by Heracles and is the "hearth and mother-city of all of Celtica". While Diodorus himself derives Alesia from the Greek for "wandering" (ἄλη) (4.1–2), due to the wandering of Heracles' campaign, if Catullus was familiar with the Celtic word for alder tree, he may have made the connection to Alesia. This connection between the alder tree and the "mother-city" of Celtica could further explain Catullus' focus on the alder tree as a symbol of Cisalpine Gaul. I would also add that Heracles himself is closely associated with the white poplar tree, and so the mythical origins of Alesia, combined with its etymology, could strengthen the nexus between the poplar and the alder tree. On Heracles and the white poplar tree, see *Ecl.* 7.61, *G.* 2.66 (and Thomas 1988, 1.168, *ad* 2.66). Finally, it may be relevant to Catullus 17 to note that after Heracles founds Alesia, he travels to Liguria (Diod. Sic. 4.19 f.).

12 E.g., Ellis 1889, 61 f.

cui cum sit uiridissimo nupta flore puella
et puella tenellulo delicatior haedo,
Adseruanda nigerrimis diligentius uuis,
Ludere hanc sinit ut lubet, nec pili facit uni,
Nec se subleuat ex sua parte, sed uelut alnus
In fossa Liguri iacet suppernata securi,
tantundem omnia sentiens quam si nulla sit usquam.

Although a girl was married to him of freshest bloom, and she is more wanton than a tender little kid, who must be guarded more diligently than the blackest grapes, he permits her to play as she pleases, neither does he care one bit, nor does he bestir himself on his own behalf, but just like an alder that lies in a ditch having been felled by a Ligurian ax, feeling everything just as if it did not exist at all.[13]

There are three ways in which Catullus conflates the poplar and alder tree in this passage by substituting in Latin an alder where in the Greek we would expect a poplar. The first is through allusion to Homeric similes. Commentators note that Catullus' depiction of an alder tree felled by an ax evokes *Iliad* 4.482–487.[14] In these lines, Homer describes how Telamonian Ajax slays Simoesius, who falls to the ground "like a black poplar tree, which has grown smooth in the riverside meadow of a great marsh" (αἴγειρος ὣς / ἥ ῥά τ' ἐν εἱαμενῇ ἕλεος μεγάλοιο πεφύκει, / λείη, 482–484), but is cut down by the ax of a chariot maker (485 f.). Catullus may also allude to another simile comparing fallen soldiers to trees cut down by axes, occurring twice in the *Iliad* (13.389 f. = 16.482–485): Asius killed by Idomeneus, and Sarpedon by Patroclus, are said to fall "like an oak, or white poplar, or tall pine" (δρῦς ἤριπεν ἢ ἀχερωῒς / ἠὲ πίτυς βλωθρή, 13.389 f.), felled by the axes of ship builders. This time, the simile includes the white poplar, which more directly connects to the Celtic word for alder tree through its alternative Greek name ἄλιζα. By utilizing these grand Homeric similes for his not-so-grand subject matter, Catullus does not just add bathos to his sordid northern Italian tale, but may mirror the importation of the Greek epic world into Cisalpine Gaul by translating the Greek poplar into the Latin alder by way of the Celtic alder.

There is one other word for "white poplar" in Greek—indeed, the most common one—namely λεύκη. I argue that Catullus alludes to this word, as well, once

13 I am using the Mynors OCT for both Catullus (1958) and Virgil (1969). Translations are my own.

14 E.g., Ellis 1889, 65. Fordyce (1961, 144, *ad* 17.18 f.) notes, "The elaborate Homeric simile of the felled poplar (*Il.* iv. 482–487) to which editors refer, has nothing in common with the vivid local colour of Catullus' image, in which the proper name calls up a picture of the forest-jungle of the wet Ligurian highlands..."—but that disjunction between high epic and Cisalpine swamp is precisely the point.

again through allusion to Homer. While Homer never uses this word for "white poplar", there is a well-known acrostic in *Iliad* 24.1–5 (*LEUKĒ*), which Eustathius interpreted as either "leprosy" or "white poplar tree" (and accordingly dismissed as accidental).[15] Even though most modern scholars agree with Eustathius that the Homeric acrostic was accidental, there is evidence that many ancient readers were intrigued by Homeric riddles and wordplay, including acrostics.[16] In addition, Thomas has shown that Catullus had knowledge of Hellenistic debates on the Homeric text,[17] while Walter Schmid has specifically demonstrated Catullus' interest in acrostics.[18] I would propose that Catullus alludes to Homer's "white poplar" acrostic by creating an acrostic of his own, namely *ALNI* ("alder trees" or "of the alder tree") in 17.16–19, and thus furthers the conflation between alder and poplar trees in this poem.

As scholars of acrostics note, ancient authors frequently include signposts in the text to help the reader find the acrostic or understand its intentional nature, and Catullus includes several in Poem 17. One of the most common clues to the vertical acrostic word is the repetition of the word (either in the same or different case) horizontally. While frequently the repeated word occurs at the beginning of the first line containing the acrostic, such as in Aratus' famous *LEPTĒ* acrostic (*Phaen.* 783–787), a so-called "gamma-acrostic", there are in fact a variety of ways and places in which the acrostic word may be repeated.[19] In Poem 17.18, the line-end placement of *alnus*, in a case different from the acrostic version of the word, and occurring in the second to last line of the acrostic, finds a precise parallel in Virgil's *MARS* acrostic in *Aeneid* 7.601–604, which contains *martem* at the end of line 603.[20] Alexei Grishin has also discovered the acrostic

15 On Eustathius' discussion of the acrostic, which likely derives from Athenaeus or the Homeric scholia (though it is not in their extant texts), see Jacques 1960, 48–50; Damschen 2004: 105; Korenjak 2009: 393; Hilton 2013: 88f.

16 See Jacques 1960, 48–50; Levitan 1979, 57; Hilton 2013.

17 See Thomas 1979.

18 See Schmid 1974. Admittedly, not all of Schmid's many examples of Catullan "Kryptogramme" are convincing, but his discovery (102f.) of the acrostic/telestic *NATU CEU AES* in Catull. 60 has (I think rightly) found acceptance. E.g., Goold 1983, 248; Damschen 2004, 99; Hawkins 2014, 569 n. 23 (with further bibliography).

19 Jacques (1960) first discovered the *LEPTĒ* acrostic and related it to Homer's *LEUKĒ* acrostic. The most recent contribution on Aratus' acrostic (Danielewicz 2015) outlines five different ways in which the word λεπτή may be found in *Phaen.* 783–787. Levitan (1979) proposes another acrostic in Aratus, *PASA* (*Phaen.* 803–806), which is reinforced by the acrostic word in a different case at the start of line 803 (πάντα).

20 On the *MARS* acrostic, see Fowler 1983.

UNDIS in *Eclogue* 9.34–38, which is reinforced by *undis* at the end of line 39.[21] Catullus' vertical and horizontal alder trees also nicely offer a visual pun in these lines, representing the literal falling over of the vertical tree that ends up lying horizontal in a ditch (*in fossa*). The placement of *in fossa* in 17.19 is also witty: it follows directly not just on the horizontal *alnus* but on the vertical *ALNI*, which literally collapses into the ditch by sharing the "i" with the word *in*.[22]

Grishin notes that Virgil's use of *ludus* ("game") in *Eclogue* 9.39 might be a marker of the wordplay in these lines.[23] I would similarly suggest that Catullus' use of *ludere* in 17.17 could point to the ludic nature of the acrostic. In addition, acrostic authors frequently use verbs of seeing to direct the reader to "see" the acrostic: Catullus' *adseruanda* in line 16, while modifying the *puella*, also initiates the acrostic and could indicate that in addition to the *puella*, Catullus' lines of poetry must be carefully watched.[24] Finally, Ted Somerville has suggested that Virgil's use of *nigrum* ("black") in *G.* 1.428, amid his acrostic homage to Aratus' *LEPTĒ* acrostic, could simultaneously allude to Homer's *LEUKĒ* acrostic by suggesting (by its opposite) the color "white" (another possible meaning of the *LEUKĒ* acrostic).[25] Perhaps Catullus' *nigerrimis* (16) functions in a similar way, though it could also call attention to the black poplar of the Homeric simile

21 Grishin 2008. Grishin (2009) wrote an excellent MA thesis on acrostics in Virgil under the direction of Richard Thomas.

22 For another possible iconic acrostic, cf. Thomas (2011, 104, *ad* 2.1–4): "As John Henderson notes *per litteras*...the opening *PINDARUM* begins to generate an acrostic (PIN, of the type most famous at Arat. *Phaen.* 783–7...), but instead creates incomplete PINN-, an iconic image of what is going on in the lines, the crash of Icarus into the sea".

23 Grishin 2009, 39 f. See also Katz 2016, 75 on the use of *ludere* to point to wordplay.

24 For similar signposting words in Virgil's acrostic in *G.* 1.429–433, see Feeney and Nelis 2005; Somerville 2010. As Katz (2016, 73 n. 13) has noted, Richard Thomas' support in his *Georgics* commentary (1988, 1.139, *ad* 1.427–437) for Brown's (1963) discovery of the *MA-VE-PU* acrostic in *G.* 1.429–433 did much to gain attention for this important acrostic (and acrostic studies, in general).

25 Somerville 2010, 207 f. In his discussion, Somerville mentions Thomas' oft-cited term "window reference" and his fundamental work on Virgil's use of conflation or multiple reference (Thomas 1986) as providing a useful framework for understanding what Virgil is doing with his allusions to Aratus and Homer in his *Georgics* acrostic. It is also possible that Catullus himself combines allusions to the *LEPTĒ* and *LEUKĒ* acrostics in his play on *ALNI*/*alnus:* Aratus' *LEPTĒ* acrostic occurs during discussion of the moon, and *luna* ("moon") is contained in anagram form within *ALNUs*. On Lucretius' acrostic allusion to the *LEPTĒ* and *LEUKĒ* acrostics amid his discussion of the *luna* (5.712–715), see Kronenberg forthcoming. Hayden Pelliccia has also pointed out to me that there is a near-anagram of *alnus* in *si <u>nulla s</u>it* (17.20), as well as a telestic (*SI SIM*) in lines 16–20.

in *Iliad* 4.482, as well as the black poplar trees into which the Heliades traditionally transform.

Indeed, there is one more possible allusion to the poplar tree by way of the Heliades in Catullus' lines about the alder: he specifies in 17.19 that the ax that cuts down the alder is a Ligurian one (*Liguri...securi*). Beyond noting that Liguria has a lot of trees, commentators have not known what to do with this geographical reference,[26] but Liguria is closely connected to the myth of Phaethon through the figure of Cycnus, the King of Liguria, who becomes a swan after mourning for him (e.g., Ov. *Met.* 2.367–380). Indeed, after *Eclogue* 6, the next time that Virgil mentions the Heliades (and associates them with their proper tree: *populeas inter frondes*, 10.190), he does so precisely because he has just mentioned the Ligurians (10.185–197).[27] Thus, Catullus' use of *Liguri* in conjunction with an alder that has been conflated with the poplar could function as an indirect allusion to the Heliades and the Phaethon myth.[28]

More confirmation of Catullus' conflation of the alder and the poplar tree can be found in Poem 64.288–291, in a description of the trees that Peneus brings to the wedding of Peleus and Thetis:

> ...namque ille tulit radicitus altas
> fagos ac recto proceras stipite laurus,
> non sine nutanti platano lentaque sorore
> flammati Phaethontis et aerea cupressu.

> For he bore by the roots tall beech trees and lofty laurels with straight trunks, together with the swaying plane and the pliant sister of burnt Phaethon and the airy cypress.

Catullus intentionally leaves the precise type of tree that Phaethon's sisters turn into unnamed, but through allusions to Theocritus and Homer, he once again conflates the alder and the poplar tree. As commentators note, Catullus' selec-

26 E.g., Ellis (1889, 65, *ad* 17.19), who quotes Strabo 4.2, in which he notes that the Ligurians have a lot of timber suitable for building ships. Thomson (1997, 255, *ad* 17.19) compares Virgil's use of alders for the Phaethon legend in *Ecl.* 6.63 and adds, "But there seems little reason why C. should locate his simile at such a distance".

27 On these lines, cf. McCallum (2015, 31–33), who, building on Ahl (1985, 33), O'Hara (1996a, 223 f.), and Paschalis (1997, 350 f.), concludes that "both name and nationality connect the Ligurians with the Apollonian account of Phaethon's grieving sisters" (33).

28 Of course, *Liguri* in Catull. 17 could have other resonances, as well, unrelated to the Phaethon myth or poplar theme. For example, given the theme of sexual inadequacy in Catull. 17, Thomas' suggestion (2011, 100 f.) that Ligurinus in Hor. *Carm.* 4.1.33 could bring to mind *ligurrio* ("lick") (he compares Catull. fr. 3 *de meo ligurrire libido est*) may apply to *Liguri* in Poem 17, as well.

tion of trees in these lines picks up on Theocritus 22.41: λεῦκαί τε πλάτανοί τε καὶ ἀκρόκομοι κυπάρισσοι ("white poplars and plane trees and cypresses with leafy crown").[29] Boris Kayachev adds that Theocritus' "white poplar" does not fit the mythical tradition regarding the Heliades, who are transformed into black poplars.[30] However, the "white poplar" is a perfect tree for Catullus to reference if his purpose is to conflate the poplar and the alder tree through the trilingual play on **alisā* ("alder") / ἄλιζα ("white poplar") / *alnus* ("alder"). The allusion to Theocritus' λεῦκαι may also bring to mind Catullus' conflation of the alder and poplar in Catullus 17 through allusion to the *LEUKĒ* acrostic with his own acrostic *ALNI*.

As Kayachev has also noted, Catullus' replacement of Theocritus' "white poplars" with the (implied) black poplars of the Heliades myth may be a reference to the Homeric model for Theocritus 22.41, namely *Odyssey* 5.64.[31] Or, as Thomas might say, Catullus is correcting Theocritus with this window reference. But a look at the Homeric line, which describes the trees around Calypso's cave, will reveal that Catullus is doing even more (*Od.* 5.64): <u>κλήθρη</u> τ' <u>αἴγειρός</u> τε καὶ εὐώδης κυπάρισσος ("<u>alder</u> and <u>black poplar</u> and sweet-smelling cypress"). Catullus' unnamed Heliadic tree in Poem 64 does not just allude to the white poplar of Theocritus and the black poplar of Homer, but also to the alder tree, which appears in close conjunction with the black poplar tree both times it is mentioned by Homer.[32] Thus, it is not just the Celtic and Greek languages that bring together the alder and poplar tree: Homer does, as well.

With this Catullan background in mind, we can now return to Virgil and put the pieces together. Commentators note that Virgil alludes to Catullus in his depiction of the *proceras...alnos* in *Eclogue* 6.63, but they see allusion only to the word *proceras* in Catullus 64.289, which modifies Catullus' laurels and leads into mention of the unnamed tree of the "sister of Phaethon" (*sorore...Phaethon-*

---

29 E. g., Ellis 1889, 328, *ad* 64.291. Partly on the basis of the close comparison between Catullus' trees and Theocritus', Kayachev (2016b) has recently argued that Catullus wrote *cyparisso* instead of *cupresso*.

30 Kayachev 2016b, 3 n. 21.

31 Kayachev 2016b, 3 n. 21. On *Od.* 5.64 and Theoc. 22.41, see Sens 1997, 109. Kayachev suggests that Catullus may also be motivated to conflate the white and black poplar in Greek since the same word in Latin is used for both of them (*populus*). This may be the case and would fit with the sort of linguistic play I argue Catullus is engaging in by alluding to the various words for poplar and alder in Latin, Greek, and Celtic. Catullus may also have been aware of the belief that the white poplar can change into the black (Theophr. *Caus. pl.* 2.16.2, 4.5.7; Plin. *HN* 17.242)—a metamorphosis that he achieves on the level of literary allusion.

32 The alder shows up again in another description of trees on the island of Calypso, though this time the cypress is replaced by a tall fir (κλήθρη τ' αἴγειρός τ', ἐλάτη τ' ἦν οὐρανομήκης, *Od.* 5.239).

tis, 290 f.). I agree that Virgil alludes to this passage, and even his choice of name *Phaethontiadas*, which suggests "sisters of Phaethon" despite its patronymic form, closely maps onto Catullus' designation of the Heliad in Poem 64 as "sister of Phaethon". But what has not been noticed is that with his use of alders in *Eclogue* 6, Virgil also alludes to Catullus' conflation of the alder and the poplar in Poems 17 and 64. In the one other passage that Virgil mentions the Heliades, namely the lines from *Aeneid* 10 that I have already discussed, he reverts to calling their tree the poplar, but only after mentioning the Ligurians—a reference that sends the reader back to Catullus 17 and his Ligurian ax.[33]

The next poet to mention the Ligurians is Ovid, again in conjunction with the myth of the Heliades. Incidentally, Ovid avoids any mention of the type of tree the Heliades turn into and focuses instead on the drops of amber that come from their tears. It is not hard to imagine that Ovid's silence on the matter is itself a form of allusion to the shifting nature of the Heliades' arboreal identity in Catullus and Virgil. However, perhaps Ovid does reference the "correct" tree through a pun on *populus* ("people") and *pōpulus* ("poplar tree") when he describes Cycnus as ruling over the "people of Liguria" (*Ligurum populos*, *Met.* 2.370).[34] Perhaps Ovid also subtly alludes to the "white poplar" tree when he calls Lampetie, one of the Heliades, *candida* ("white") just as she is turning into a tree (3.349). While of course *candida* is an appropriate adjective to describe someone named Lampetie ("the shining one"), Virgil uses *candida* to specify the "white poplar" in *Eclogue* 9.41 (*candida populus*). In addition, the adjective "white" and "white poplar" are spelled identically in Greek, so *candida* could function as a bilingual pun on "white poplar tree".

I would like to conclude by returning to Clausen's suggestion that Virgil replaced poplars with alders in *Eclogue* 6 because he "remembered the alder-fringed Po, the mythical Eridanus, of his youth"—an assertion which he supports by quoting Virgil's association of the alder with the Po in *Georgics* 2.451 f.: *nec non et torrentem undam levis innatat alnus / missa Pado* ("moreover the light alder, sent onto the Po, swims in the impetuous wave"). While it is of course possible that Virgil remembers alders on the Po, I would submit that what is more important for Virgil's poetry is the alder tree of his fellow poetic denizen of the Po, Catullus. Indeed, those inclined to metapoetic readings, which is usually a good inclination when water or ships are involved, might interpret *levis alnus*

---

33 Before Virgil, Catullus is the only other surviving Latin poet to mention Liguria or the Ligurians.

34 Ahl (1985, 105, 196) notes Ovid's puns on *populus*, *pōpulus*, and *populari* in the story of Phaethon but does not quote the example in *Met.* 2.370. Isid. *Etym.* 17.7.45 derives *pōpulus* from *populus* (because a "multitude can be born from a heel cutting").

as connoting the light, neoteric style of Catullus, while *torrentem undam* could capture the raging passion of his poetry. The fact that the alder tree is "sent" onto the Po could even reference Catullus' intentional decision to place the alder—and not the poplar—on the swampy banks of the Po.[35] Like Catullus, Virgil, too, might be symbolically like his alder tree: a poet of the Po attempting to combine learned "light" poetry with the sublime poetry of passion. That Virgil could conceive of the alder as a metapoetic symbol is also suggested by his comparison of his growing love for Gallus to a young, growing shoot of an alder tree at the start of spring in *Ecl.* 10. 74 (*quantum vere novo viridis se subicit alnus*, "as much as a green alder shoots up at the start of spring"). John Henkel nicely connects the shade that the alder tree provides its young shoot, as well as the shade in the next line, which is "burdensome for singers" (*gravis cantantibus umbra*, 75), to the shadow of Gallus' poetic influence on Virgil, which is both nourishing and potentially stifling.[36] I would add that the shade of Catullus, perhaps himself the parent tree of Gallus' alder shoot, may be present in these lines, as well.[37]

Richard Thomas has cast a large shadow on Virgilian studies, but it is one that has been purely nourishing and never stifling. Thanks to Thomas, we recognize and value the fact that Virgil shared the same obsessions with obscure allusions and wordplay as his Hellenistic and neoteric predecessors. We can also better appreciate the hidden allusive polemics that animate Catullus' poetry every bit as much as the more obvious polemics on the surface of his text. I hope to have shown that even a poem like Catullus 17, that appears to be concerned primarily with the sordid and shameful life of a resident of Cisalpine Gaul, utilizes intricate allusions and wordplay to reenact through tree-choice the importation of the Greek epic world into the swamps of Cisalpine Gaul. Catullus returns to the same alder-poplar conflation in Catullus 64, a minor example of the many ways in which Catullus provides threads of unity through the labyrinth of his varied oeuvre. Virgil, too, references the Heliades and their indeterminate tree in both his youthful *nugae* (the *Eclogues*) and his mature epic, and he found in Catullus a model for creating unity across his generically diverse poems. Richard Thomas always taught the importance of reading Virgil's three

35 Perhaps Virgil's placement of alders in the swamp in *G.* 2.110 (*paludibus alni*) is also in homage to the swampy atmosphere of Catullus 17, and not just a reflection of reality.

36 Henkel 2014, 40 f., building on Kennedy 1983.

37 Catullus and Gallus are possibly brought together again, this time under the shade of a poplar tree, in a simile from *Georgics* 4.511–515, which compares Orpheus' (Gallus?) grieving to that of a nightingale (Catullus? Cf. Catullus' nightingale simile in 65.13 f.) beneath the shade of a poplar (*qualis populea maerens philomela sub umbra*, 511). On the connections between Gallus and the Orpheus epyllion, see Thomas 1988, 1.15 f., 2.226.

works together and alongside the texts that inspired them. While Thomas has focused much of his work on explicating the intricate intertextual games poets such as Catullus and Virgil play, he never loses sight of the overall goal of finding larger meaning in their work, of seeing the forest through the trees.

Peter E. Knox

A Known Unknown in Pompeian Graffiti?

In the first of two poems addressed by Propertius to Ponticus—an epic poet, his friend, and his straw man—the elegist constructs a rather specific image of the readership that he wants for his work (Prop. 1.7.11–14):[1]

> me laudent doctae solum placuisse puellae,
> Pontice, et iniustas saepe tulisse minas;
> me legat assidue post haec neglectus amator,
> et prosint illi cognita nostra mala.

> Let my praise be that I alone pleased a learned girl, Ponticus, and often suffered her unjust threats; and in the time to come may the abandoned lover read me assiduously, and may it help him to learn of the wrongs I've suffered.

Propertius pivots from claiming as his exclusive audience his "learned girl", a pose that he adopts elsewhere,[2] to designate as his audience neither scholars nor readers steeped in learned Greek and Latin poetry; the readership he constructs here is decidedly less elite, lovers who have suffered disappointments like his.[3] This sentiment is echoed somewhat more expansively by Ovid in the programmatic opening poem of the second book of the *Amores*, where he, like Propertius, implicitly contrasts his anticipated audience with the more sophisticated readership that he imagines for epic poetry (*Am.* 2.1.5 f.):

> me legat in sponsi facie non frigida uirgo
> et rudis ignoto tactus amore puer.

> For my reader I want the girl who is not left cold by the good looks of her betrothed, and the untaught boy touched by a passion he did not know.

As latter-day readers of Roman poetry who are well aware of the extent to which it was influenced by the traditions of Hellenistic Greek verse, we are so accus-

---

1 Text as in Barber 1960, with these couplets in the sequence of the paradosis. Heyworth 2007b transposes 11–12 to follow 14 and emends *laudent* to *laudet*, perhaps rightly; cf. Heyworth 2007a, ad loc.

2 Cf. esp. 2.13.11 *me iuuet in gremio doctae legisse puellae*, 2.3.20, 2.11.6; Fordyce 1961, 178.

3 It would be difficult to assume that Propertius here implies only lovers steeped in learned poetry. The sentiment is repeated elsewhere at Prop. 3.3.19 f. *ut tuus in scamno iactetur saepe libellus, / quem legat exspectans sola puella uirum*, and 3.9.45 *haec urant pueros, haec urant scripta puellas*; cf. Fedeli 1985 ad locc.

https://doi.org/10.1515/9783110545708-005

tomed to programmatic appeals to an elite, highly literate readership in the Callimachean vein that it is easy to underestimate this kind of reference made by the surviving elegists to readers of a different sort suffering in everyday life from the kind of experiences the poets have elevated to literature.

The elegists' claim to exercise practical effect in matters of the heart is, of course, a convention of the genre as we know it from the works of the surviving Roman elegists.[4] There are good reasons for supposing that the trope of targeting the poet's love interest as a reader figured also in the poetry of the genre's earlier practitioner, Cornelius Gallus. In Virgil's Tenth Eclogue, the poet wishes to offer his verses as a gift not only to Gallus, but to Lycoris (*Ecl.* 10.2): *quae legat ipsa Lycoris* ("that Lycoris herself might read").[5] It is entirely likely that Lycoris, like Cynthia, was fashioned as an ideal reader, who might empathize with the experiences described by Virgil and, by extension, Gallus. This thought probably also lies behind the snippet found in the celebrated papyrus fragment of Gallus (145.6 f. Hollis): *fecerunt carmina Musae / quae possem domina dicere digna mea* (the Muses have fashioned songs that I can say are worthy of my mistress").[6] The fragmentary context renders interpretation uncertain, but if there is a connection with *Ecl.* 10.2, as seems likely, Gallus might well have set up his Lycoris as a foil for his other intended readers. What if the other readers portrayed by Propertius and Ovid actually existed, anonymous lovers who unrolled their elegies and found in them something that resonated with their experiences? And what if they read not only Propertius and Ovid, but other poets, such as Gallus, now lost to us?

The possibility that such references were grounded in the realities of a reading public that to at least a measurable extent included non-elites finds some validation in the surviving evidence of Pompeian graffiti and painted inscriptions. And that body of evidence also supplies meaningful evidence for the broad dissemination of non-canonical literature among that reading public, an aspect of Roman literary culture that has often been played down by classical scholars. At least 78 graffiti have been found in Pompeii that demonstrate some

4 Clearly formulated by Stroh 1971 and see, esp., 204–228. Cf. Conte 1986, 124 f.

5 On the ever-tantalizing relationship between the Tenth Eclogue and the lost poetry of Gallus, Ross 1975, 85–106 is still fundamental. *Ecl.* 10.42–63 is included as a "fragment" of Gallus by Courtney 1993, 268–270. For more recent discussion of *Ecl.* 10 as a testimonium to Gallus' poetry, see Hollis 2007, 237–240.

6 Thus Hinds 1983, following the original interpretation of the papyrus by Nisbet in Anderson / Parsons / Nisbet 1979, 144, pace Courtney 1993, 267 and Hollis 2007, 247. Cf. Barchiesi 1981, 155; Cairns 2006, 91–93.

familiarity with surviving Latin poets, either as quotations or adaptations.[7] The overwhelming majority of these quotations, 48 in total, come from Virgil's works, with the opening lines of Books 1 (12 times) and 2 (14) accounting for over half of them. Most of these graffiti probably reflect the boredom or the mischievousness of Pompeian schoolchildren.[8] Ennius' *Annales* is represented, hardly a surprise since it was a staple in the schools until it was replaced by the *Aeneid*. Nor is it a surprise to find Lucretian tags among the Pompeian graffiti, given the association of the region with adherents of Epicureanism.[9] What is surprising is the relatively high number of graffiti that demonstrate familiarity with Tibullus, Propertius, and Ovid, 17 in total. Unlike the scribblings of tags from the *Aeneid* by schoolchildren, for example, these graffiti indicate a high level of personal interest and engagement with their source texts. Scholars interested in general levels of literacy and the penetration of literature into Roman popular culture have not taken sufficient notice of the presence of elegiac poetry—Propertius and Ovid in particular, but perhaps others too—on the walls of Pompeii.[10] Unlike Virgil, none of these authors was read in the schools, and so knowledge of their poetry could only have come from books in circulation and from word of mouth. Bits of Virgil remembered from school were slapped on the walls by schoolboys, but the elegiac poets were actually present in the minds of these readers. And the evidence that they were well versed in non-canonical texts that they did not study in school should encourage us to find in some of their scribblings snippets of lost works, other poets who once were read but now are lost. One of these would be the "known unknown" to which my title refers as an invitation to consider that we may have access to some glimpses into that lost world of poetry by the likes of Cornelius Gallus, Varius Rufus, or Varro of Atax, poets who are mere names to us, but once were widely known and admired.[11] There are several cu-

---

7 The evidence is conveniently assembled in a table at Cooley / Cooley 2013, 292f.

8 Cf. Franklin 1996/7; Harris 1989, 261. Christopher Wordsworth, the nephew of the poet, visited the site in 1835 and wrote a short monograph about the graffiti that he had seen. In it, he rhapsodized about the cultural literacy of the denizens of Pompeii, adding a curious pitch in favor of graffiti (1937, 6): "I should much question whether all the walls of all the country towns in England would, if Milton were lost, help us to a single line of the Paradise Lost. *Our* Pompeiis do not yet exhibit the words of *our* Virgils, nor does it seem probable that they soon will".

9 Cf. D'Arms 1970, 55–61; Gigante 1995, 1–13; Sider 1997, 12–24.

10 It does not figure in Harris 1989, but cf. Franklin 1991, 98: "The frequent appearance of elegiac couplets and quotations from the poets indicates education (though perhaps closer to the level of copybook, or a good ear in an oral society, than to true familiarity)".

11 Cf. Spal 2016, 11 on the hypothesis, occasionally mooted, that many of the verse graffiti are at least attempts at quotation.

rious aspects to the six graffiti that show an affinity with Propertius and Ovid,[12] which suggest that they may reflect familiarity with a well-known author whose works have been lost.

The most extensive example comes from a house in Region VI, known as the "House of the Scientists" (VI 14, 43) excavated in 1845. On the wall of the atrium someone wrote on the plaster two hexameters (*CIL* IV.1520; *CLE* 354 = Courtney 96):

> Candida me docuit nigras odisse puellas.
> Odero si potero; si non, inuitus amabo.
>
> A fair girl taught me to spurn dark ones.
> I shall spurn them if I can, if not, I shall love them unwillingly.

Unlike the quotations from Virgil,[13] this has been considered to be a creative composition, not a recall of specific passage. It is generally thought that this couplet draws on Propertius and Ovid, combining a line from each to say something new,[14] although a different line of development will be suggested here. The first line appears to echo the opening elegy of Propertius' first book, in which he says that Love personified, *Amor*, kept him under foot, "until he taught me to spurn chaste girls" (1.1.5): *donec me docuit castas odisse puellas.* The second line is found in the manuscripts of Ovid's *Amores*, where it has stood in many editions in spite of the suggestion by Nicolas Heinsius that it should be deleted (*Am.* 3.11.35 f):[15]

> Odero, si potero; si non, inuitus amabo:
> nec iuga taurus amat; quae tamen odit, habet.
>
> I shall hate, if I can; if not, I shall love against my will:
> the ox does not love the yoke, but what he hates he bears nonetheless.

---

12 *CIL* IV.1520, 1523, 1526, 1528, 3040, 9847.

13 With the exception of a spoof scribbled on the door of a fullery (IX.12.5) belonging to Marcus Fabius Ululitremulus, near a painting of Aeneas leading Anchises and Ascanius to safety (*CIL* IV 9131): *fullones ululamque cano, non arma uirumque.* The pun on the fuller's name probably pokes fun at his ostentatiousness in featuring a scene from the *Aeneid*, one of the very few discovered in Pompeii, on the façade of his building.

14 Cf. Gigante 1979, 188 f.; Varone 2002, 54; Milnor 2014, 92 f.; Spal 2016, 89 – 100. Courtney 1995, 309 f., accepting that Ov. *Am.* 3.11.35 f. is an interpolation, argues that "in that case the author of the Pompeian distich, after adapting a line from Propertius, will have quoted a line from another unknown poet".

15 "Distichon hoc Ovidianum non videtur esse" is Heinsius' lapidary comment in his edition of 1658.

The two lines are securely transmitted in the medieval manuscript tradition of Ovid's *Amores*, so if they are an interpolation, they must be ancient. And if they were known to the author of *CIL* IV.1520 as Ovidian, they must be very ancient indeed to have entered the text prior to the eruption of Vesuvius in 79 CE. A minority of modern editors of the *Amores* have athetized this couplet, though without supplying the detailed argument that would vindicate Heinsius' judgement, which was primarily based on its awkwardness in its position in the poem.[16] This was supplied in E. Courtney's detailed discussion of the metrical irregularity in the scansion of *oderŏ*, in which the shortened *–o* would be wholly inconsistent with Ovid's practice.[17] But as the examples examined by Courtney demonstrate, while Ovidian authorship of this couplet is dubious at best, its actual author need not be post-Ovidian, because others among Ovid's contemporaries and predecessors, including Catullus, Horace in the *Satires*, Tibullus, and Maecenas (fr. 3 Courtney), were less fastidious. And that is to say nothing about still others whose works are lost. If it is an interpolation, then Courtney's further conclusion is inescapable: "it is an illustration of the general sentiment of the poem, taken from another poet who did not observe Augustan restrictions on the use of – *ŏ*".[18] If that is the case, it leaves open the question of who that other poet was, as well as the question of the source of the first line in *CIL* IV.1520.

The relationship of the first hexameter in the graffito to Propertius 1.1.5 is different. Clearly one line must be an adaptation of the other, or of some common source. And in either case, the adaptation is apt, for the distich makes a paradoxical point of the sort that we not infrequently find in Roman erotic poetry: immediately after professing his desire to give up on dark-complexioned girls, the writer of the graffito professes the opposite intention. But are these lines the work of a local poet, as most have supposed, who adapted one line from Propertius and pilfered another from some other poet (or Ovid) to make up a new sentiment? Other evidence makes it unlikely that the author was the graffitist. The opening phrase, *candida me docuit*, was apparently striking enough to be reinscribed as graffiti in the same house four times (CIL IV.1523; 1526; 1528; 3040).[19] In one in-

16 Thus E. J. Kenney in both editions of his Oxford Classical Text (1961 and 1994); cf. Kenney 1962, 13, where he merely notes that the couplet was "rightly condemned by Heinsius". He is followed by Ramírez de Verger 2003. For the most part other editors have retained the two lines in the text: e.g. Munari 1951, Goold 1977, and McKeown 1987.

17 Courtney 1987, 7–9, with reference to the data assembled in Platnauer 1951, 50–53.

18 Courtney 1987, 9.

19 A motive for such repetitions could well have been the fact that *Candida* was also a proper name: thus *TLL Onom.* s.v. 134.25

stance, the graffitist seems to have struggled with the rest of the line, since it trails off in gibberish after *docuit.*[20] In another the graffitist misspells the first word as *canda.*[21] And in another he (or she) got no further than *candida* and only made a start on the following *me.*[22] So it is more likely that persons other than the author were inspired by the full couplet to write out a few of its opening words.[23] But it is also likely that that graffito was not the only source from which those hexameters were known, since the same hexameter distich was later discovered in a different district of the city.

On the other side of town these two lines were written in full beneath a picture of the god Priapus by the entrance to a *taberna* (I 11, 11) in the connecting vineyard garden (I 11, 10).[24] Now the question becomes, did these lines circulate in some form so that another person, an admirer of the local bard, copied them out again? Possible. Or did the original author like them so much that he repeated them in another venue? Also possible. But the more plausible explanation for the appearance of this couplet in two disparate locations is that the graffitists who wrote them out knew them from some work of literature, a poem that inspired not only the author of the elegiac couplet that was inserted into Ovid's *Amores* 3.13, but also Propertius in his opening programmatic poem. In other words, what if this couplet is not a composition *per se*, but a quotation, or an attempt at one? The context in Ovid's poem doesn't offer much in the way of guidance for anyone interested in frivolous speculation, but Propertius' poem does. It has long been suspected and argued from various points of view that the opening poem of the first book is replete with reminiscences of Propertius' predecessor, Cornelius Gallus.[25] Gallus, of course, is best known as an elegist, but the evidence is far from conclusive that he wrote only elegies.[26] The evidence of the graffiti, which suggest a deep and engaged familiarity with the non-canonical texts, makes it rather tempting to consider that some snippets of verse actually derive from the lost works that we wish we had, among which there might have been... Gallus.

---

20 *CIL* 4.1526 *Candida me docuit nigxtT*

21 *CIL* IV.3040.

22 *CIL* IV.1523

23 It is possible, but just possible, that *CIL* IV.1528 went on to include more verses, since Zangemeister's accompanying illustration (Tab. XXIX 26) shows possible traces of indecipherable writing after the opening phrase. Cf. Spal 2016, 90, n. 419.

24 *CIL* 4.9847. Cf. Varone 2002, 54.

25 Most notably Ross 1975, 51–70.

26 Cf. Hollis 2007, 238–240.

There is another case that merits inquiry for the possibilities it offers of attaching a name to an unknown poet whose words are repeated on the city's walls. In the House of L. Caecilius Iucundus (V 1, 23–26) someone scratched an elegiac couplet into the plaster wall of a triclinium (*CIL* IV.4091 = *CLE* 945 = Courtney 88):[27]

> quis]quis amat ualeat, pereat qui nescit amare;
> bis tanto pereat quisquis amare uetat.
>
> Good luck to whoever loves, damn whoever doesn't know how to love;
> double damnation to whoever forbids love.

This particular couplet was apparently quite well known in Pompeii, since graffiti with its opening words *quisquis amat ualeat*, or some close variation, have been found at least eight other times in the city.[28] One school of thought holds that *quisquis amat* is merely "a stock phrase in Pompeian graffiti writing".[29] Even if this were the case—and it is not clear what it would mean to think of this as a phrase that is specific to this community—it does not address the source of the phrase, its relationship to the couplet found in the House of Caecilius Iucundus, or that couplet's resonances in surviving Latin poetry. The likelihood that the couplet comes from a literary source is strengthened by its appearance in an entirely different context, not as a graffito.

In early excavations at Pompeii a painting was discovered, perhaps in the House of Fabius Secundus (V.4.13),[30] depicting a still-life scene with a scraper, an open codex, an inkpot, a reed pen, and an open papyrus roll with 16 lines of writing on it.[31]

Only the first eight lines have been deciphered with any degree of certainty (*CIL* IV.1173 = *CLE* 946):[32]

> quisquis | amat, ualeat; | pereat qui n | escit amare; |
> bis tanto pe | reat, quisqu | is amare | uetat.

27 Text and translation reproduced from Courtney 1995, 96; cf. Spal 2016, 46–61.
28 *CIL* IV.3200 *quisquis amat*; 4659 *quisquis amat pereat*, followed by an illegible word; 4663 *quisquis amat perea(t)*; 5186 *quisquis amat per(eat)*; 5272 *quisquis amat u(aleat)*; 8745 *quisquis ama(t)*; 9130 *quisquis amat ualeat pereat*; Giordano 1966, no. 24 *quisquis amat.*
29 Milnor 2014, 186, who goes on to remark that it is "not one, it should be added, which is ever found in canonical Latin poetry". Similar views at Wachter 1998, 77; Busch 1999, 545 f.
30 On the location, see Meyer 2009, 591, n. 108.
31 Now in the Museo Archeologico Nazionale di Napoli (Inv. no. 4676). Cf. Helbig 1868, no. 1724.
32 Text as restored by Courtney 1995, 304 for *CIL* IV.4091.

Fig. 1: Naples, Museo Archeologico Nazionale. Photo: Archivio dell' Arte – Pedicini Fotografi.

The text is clearly the same as the graffito in the House of Caecilius Iucundus, but this is not the work of a graffitist, but an artist, presumably working on commission and under instructions from a patron. Illustrations of writing materials are not uncommon among the frescoes recovered in Campania, and it has been forcefully argued that ensembles such as this were intended to communicate the owner's seriousness as a literate person active in the world of affairs.[33] It seems most likely that the writing on the scroll reflects the patron's liking for amatory elegy, and it is worth considering whether any connections with surviving poetry can be teased out of these two lines.

Propertius formulates the same theme in his first book, in a poem that elaborates on the topos that a life of love, difficult though it may be, is preferable to the alternative (1.6.12):[34]

> a pereat, si quis lentus amare potest!
>
> Damn the man who can be indifferent in love!

The phrasing—the mock imprecation in *pereat* and the generalizing *si quis*—evoke the Pompeian couplet, as does another passage where Propertius inverts the topos, cursing lovers who persist in pursuing an unwilling girl (2.23.12):

---

33 Meyer 2009, 574 argues that the inclusion of this poem on the papyrus in the painting was "a tiny painterly joke", reversing the expectation that the document in the picture should represent business accounts. This seems unlikely, but even if it were true, it would not affect the identification of the work on the scroll.

34 The parallel is noted by Gigante 1979, 210 f.

a pereant, si quos ianua clausa iuuat!

Damn those men whom a closed door delights!

Variations on the opening words of the Pompeian line are found in all of the surviving elegists: Tib. 1.2.29 *quisquis amore tenetur*; Prop. 3.6.13 *quisquis amator erit*; 4.5.77 *quisquis amas*; Ov. *Rem. am.* 579 *quisquis amas.*[35] Another variant is found twice in Ovid's *Remedia amoris* (13 *si quis amat* and 613 *si quis amas*),[36] and it is found in yet another Pompeian graffitist's misremembered quotation in the House of the Mysteries: *si quis amat ualeat; quisquis uetat male pereat.*[37] The recent publication of a graffito from the baths of Trajan, postdating the eruption of Vesuvius, also militates strongly against the hypothesis that this was a local Pompeian product, rather than a literary work in general circulation.[38]

In the painted version of this couplet, it is followed by eight lines that form another couplet, which has thus far proved indecipherable (*CIL* IV.1173):[39]

felices | abias mia | pupa a | martia | si te
vidi | de nobis | maxima | cura mage

The underlined words are those on which there is consensus among the many attempts to make sense of this couplet; there is wildly divergent opinion about how to interpret the other remaining traces of writing.[40] A full and accurate transcription would be welcome, but even from the available evidence, it is possible

35 Cf. Lissberger 1934,123; Gigante 1979, 210, n. 56; Varone 2002, 62f. Wachter 1998, 76f., followed by Milnor 2014, 187 attributes these parallels to a process of popular "oral" composition. Given the distribution of the phrase in Campania and elsewhere, that seems unlikely.

36 As B. W. Boyd remarks *per litteras*, both of these passages may contain fuller evocations of the anonymous author of *CIL* IV.1173. In the first passage, "*si quis* is repeated at the beginning of the next hexameter (15), and the following pentameter begins with *ne pereat*". And in the second, "there is a good bit of Propertius in the background: the pentameter 578, *ignotas cogor inire uias*, is modeled on Prop. 1.1.28; and the repetition of *loca sola* in 379 very likely recalls Prop. 1.18.1 *deserta loca* (not to mention *Ecl.* 10)–behind all of which is likely to stand Anonymous again".

37 *CIL* IV, Suppl. 3.9202; cf. *AE* 2009 (2012) no. 216.

38 Cf. *Bulletinio della Commissione archeologica comunale di Roma* 115 (2014) 201: *Quisquis amat ualeat pe/reat qui nescit amare / bis tanto pereat quis amare uetat.* Likewise, the hexameter *uenimus huc cupidi, multo magis ire cupimus*, which is found in some form eleven times in Pompeii (*CIL* IV.1227, 2238, 2995, 4880, 6697, 8114, 8231a, 8231b, 8891, 9849, 10065a) and once in Herculaneum (*CIL* IV.10640), has also been found in Narbonne: cf. *AE* 1997 (2000) no. 1068 [*uenimus huc cupi*]*di multo magis ire cupimus.* It is difficult to square this with the theory that the line did not originate in a textual context, as argued by Milnor 2014, 183f.

39 The text reproduced here is adapted from Spal (2016) 46.

40 See the extensive discussion by Spal 2016, 54–60, with summary of earlier views.

to draw some inferences about the provenance of this poem. First, the simple fact that there actually *is* a second couplet is in and of itself suggestive that the oft-repeated couplet formed part of a larger work known to the painter or his patron. Second, the words that can be detected would be consistent with the theme of the first couplet, representing some group as fortunate (*felices*) probably in contrast with the poet, perhaps because they are, or are not, going to war: in line 12 of the painting, *martia* is probably not a proper name, but the adjective.[41] And finally, although its sense here cannot be guessed, the phrase *maxima cura* is attested in this position in the pentameter three times in the surviving elegists: Prop. 2.16.2, Ov. *Her.* 17.198, *Tr.* 3.11.70. Without further evidence, the most reasonable inference is that the painter depicted four lines from a well-known literary source.[42]

That *quisquis amat* became a tag line as ubiquitous as (for other reasons) *arma uirumque* leaves open the possibility that it could be appropriated to other contexts, as happened, too, to the opening line of the *Aeneid*, which was reworked in a humorous context on the wall of a cleaner's shop in Pompeii.[43] But this need not be true of *all* of the other attestations in Pompeian graffiti. An example: (*CIL* IV.1898 = *CLE* 948 = Courtney 90):

> quisquis amat, calidis non debet fontibus uti,
> nam nemo flammas ustus amare potest.
>
> Whoever is in love ought not to use hot springs, for no one who has been burned can like flame.

The familiar play on the theme of fire and love has affiliations in Greek epigram,[44] and while it could be a non-literary composition, it is more plausible that the graffitist is here quoting a text known to him, as he did elsewhere on

41 Thus Spal 2016, 57 f., rightly.

42 The same inference may be made about the only other depiction of a papyrus roll with writing on it held by a Cupid in a painting uncovered before 1877 (IX.V.11). In Zangemeister's reconstruction (*CIL* IV Suppl. 3691 = CLE 951) it appears to consist of hexameters or an elegiac couplet: [*non e*]*go tam* [c]*ur*[*o*] *Venerem* [*d*]*e marmor*[*e*] *factam ... carmina.* Reports of the other components of the painting are conflicting, but like Meyer 2009, 578, n. 43, I am inclined to trust the report in *CIL* that it contained a papyrus roll, not a wax tablet. The "Venus made of marble" may refer to Julius Caesar's temple of Venus Genetrix (dedicated on 26 September 46 BCE), with its statue of the goddess by Arcesilas; cf. Ov. *Ars am.* 1.81 f. *subdita qua Veneris facto de marmore templo / Appias expressis aera pulsat aquis.*

43 Cf. n. 13 above.

44 Courtney 1995, 305 cites *Anth. Pal.* 5.82 (cf. Page (1981) 45) of uncertain date and authorship: ὦ σοβαρὴ βαλάνισσα, τί μ' οὕτως ἔμπυρα λούεις; / πρίν μ' ἀποδύσασθαι τοῦ πυρὸς αἰσθάνομαι.

the same wall of the basilica, quoting a couplet each from Ovid and Propertius.[45] If so, it might well have originated in the same poem as the two couplets of *CIL* IV.4091.

The same hypothesis might apply to another verse fragment, also found in the basilica (*CIL* IV.1824 = *CLE* 947 = Courtney 89):

> quisquis amat, ueniat. Veneri uolo frangere costas
> fustibus et lumbos debilitare deae.
> si potest illa mihi tenerum pertundere pectus,
> quit ego no possim caput i[ll]ae frangere fuste?

> Whoever is in love, let him come. I want to break Venus' ribs with sticks and cripple the goddess' backside. If she can pierce my delicate heart, why should I not be able to break her head with a stick?

Much of the context eludes us, for example in the sense of *ueniat.*[46] The meter begins to dissolve in the third line, which, as Courtney notes, "perhaps points to defective reproduction of a model".[47] The opening of the first couplet has been found in at least one other location in Pompeii, in the House of the Silver Wedding (V 2, 1), where the graffitist begins to slip in the first line (*CIL* IV.4200): *quisquis amat, ueniat. Veneri lumbos uo*[lo.[48] The most plausible explanation for his failure here is that his memory leapt to *lumbos* in the following pentameter before he gave up. That again suggests that his source was a text, not another graffito or a 'popular' verse, and a plausible context would be a poem that took its theme, and perhaps its refrain,[49] from the opening *quisquis amat.*[50]

---

45 *CIL* IV.1893 (Ov. *Am.* 1.8.77 f.) and 1894 (Prop. 4.5.47 f.); cf. Milnor (2014) 151–157, who inclines to the view that this is *not* a quotation.

46 Perhaps a euphemism for a sexual encounter, in which it often has a female as subject, although it is also used of males; cf. Adams 1982, 176.

47 Courtney 1995, 305; cf. Gigante 1979, 204–208 on the literary affiliations of this fragment, which may not fully merit the lavish praise of Maiuri 1964, 143 f., who called it "degno d'esser collocato al primo posto fra le invettive nella poesia d'amore". A different view is taken by Milnor 2014, 186, who argues that "the author is embarking upon writing an erotic epigram in a 'popular' mode", the view to which Spal 2016, 70–82 also inclines, albeit with some equivocation.

48 We cannot know which couplet the graffitist of *CIL* 4.5272 had in mind: *quisquis amat u*[.

49 Gigante 1979, 210, n. 58 compares the refrain-like qualities of the phrase to the *Pervigilium Veneris.* There are grounds for further speculation on this score in the appearance of the phrase in the House of Marcus Fabius Rufus (VII 16, 17.20–22), excavated in the 1960s (cf. Solin 1975, 254–256): *uasia quae rapui quaeris, formosa puella; / accipe quae rapui non ego solus, ama. / quisquis amat ualeat.*

Who was the original author of the hypothetical elegy that began *quisquis amat ualeat?* The same sentiment is echoed, not closely, to be sure, but clearly, in Propertius and Ovid. So, was there an influential elegist known to them whose works have been lost...? One of the great attractions in reconstructing lost works is that, once reconstructed, they tend to cooperate quite nicely with one's hypotheses. And Cornelius Gallus has always been among the most cooperative of lost poets in this respect. In Pompeii and throughout the Roman world, epic poetry, like the *Aeneid*, was what was read in school. It's what people thought about when engaged in serious reflection on the human condition. Or what students scribbled on the wall on their way home from school. But in the everyday life of traveling salesmen, young men and young women, it was elegiac love poetry that was on the brain. And common readers did not limit themselves to school texts; there is ample evidence that they knew works that were not introduced to them by their teachers.[51] The evidence from Pompeii offers a tantalizing glimpse into the Roman world of literature that is otherwise opaque to us. It suggests that at least within the 15 % or so of Romans who were literate—if we adopt the most conservative estimates of Roman literacy rates in this period[52]—there were readers who integrated into their daily lives authors known to us whose works, alas, are largely unknown. And we might be reading some of these known unknowns in the graffiti of Pompeii.

---

50 It would, of course, then be an open question whether the three graffiti that read *quisquis amat pereat* (*CIL* 4.4659, 4663, and 5186) reflect a different couplet, or a graffitist's ironic twist on the well-known line.

51 On the material evidence for familiarity with Ovid's *Metamorphoses*, which was never a school text, see Knox 2014.

52 Harris 1989, but cf., in addition to Franklin 1991, Keegan 2014, 59–66.

Sergio Casali

Dido's *furtiuuus amor* (Virgil, *Aeneid* 4.171–2)

In this paper,[1] I would like to address the difficulties which are in my view contained in the narrator's words at *Aeneid* 4.171 f., *nec iam furtiuum Dido meditatur amorem: / coniugium uocat, hoc praetexit nomine culpam* "and Dido no longer thinks of a clandestine love–affair" (if this, as I will argue, is the right translation), "she calls it a marriage, and with this name she cloaks her *culpa*". There are a number of unclear issues here:

(i) what is the *culpa* of line 172?

(ii) when Dido cloaks her *culpa* with the name of marriage, does she do so publicly, or only in her own heart?

(iii) is Dido sincerely convinced that she is married to Aeneas? – a question with important consequences for our reading of the whole problem of Dido and Aeneas's "marriage"; and, finally, my main question,

(iv) what is the exact meaning of *furtiuus amor* in line 171?

Whereas one cannot attain complete certainty about the "solution" to any of these issues, the third has important consequences for our reading of the whole problem of Dido and Aeneas's "marriage", while I think at least the fourth, my chief interest here, can be satisfyingly answered, even if in a manner different from that usually given by translators and commentators.

At *Aeneid* 4.160–168, the storm foretold by Juno at 120–125 breaks out; the hunters scatter; Aeneas and Dido reach the same cave together. Earth and Juno as *pronuba* give the signal, lightning bolts flash, aether/Aether stands as a witness to the wedding, and the Nymphs howl on the mountain–top.[2]

Both Dido and Anna have always spoken of the potential relationship with Aeneas as a marriage (16–18, 33, 48, 59); Juno has envisioned an actual wedding

---

1 For constructive criticism and advice I wish to thank Luigi Galasso, Emily Gowers, Philip Hardie, Stephen Oakley, Alessandro Schiesaro, Fabio Stok, and above all Jim O'Hara, discussion with whom helped me enormously in the construction of my argument.

2 On *Aen.* 4.160–172, and the problems of Dido's "marriage", see Quinn 1963, 37 f., G. Williams 1968, 377–389, Monti 1981, 45–48, Feeney 1983, 204 f. = Harrison 1990, 167 f., Moles 1984, 51 f., Green 1986, 411–417, Moles 1987, 155 f., Cairns 1989, 47–49, Harrison 1989, 14 f., Desmond 1994, 28–30, Horsfall 1995, 126–128, Bowie 1998, 68–70, Nelis 2001, 148–152, Thomas 2001, 186–189, Hardie 2012, 84–86, Seider 2013, 113 f.

https://doi.org/10.1515/9783110545708-006

(125–127), and the repetition of Juno's words at 161 and 165 f. underlines the accomplishment of the will of the goddess.[3] Lines 166–168 might legitimately suggest that an actual wedding has taken place (*Aen.* 4.165–168):

> speluncam Dido dux et Troianus eandem
> deueniunt. prima[4] et Tellus et pronuba Iuno
> dant signum;[5] fulsere ignes et conscius Aether
> conubiis summoque ulularunt uertice Nymphae.
>
> The Trojan chief and Dido come to the same cave. First Earth and Juno as pronuba give a sign; fires flashed, together with Aether, witness to the wedding, and the Nymphs screamed on the mountain-top.

Aether[6] is a witness "to the wedding" (*conubiis*, 167): "The word... should not be dismissed, forgotten, or ignored. It provides the greatest stumbling block for those who do not believe that a marriage of any kind took place. Modern writers can speak of a 'marriage', but although ancient analogies to the modern use of quotation marks may exist in speeches, it is unthinkable in narratives. Virgil seems to be emphasizing that a marriage occurred, albeit one shrouded in am-

---

3 At 161 *insequitur commixta grandine nimbus* echo the words of Juno in 120 *his ego nigrantem commixta grandine nimbum*; at 165 f. *speluncam Dido dux et Troianus eandem / deueniunt* repeat Juno's words at 124 f. (with *deuenient*). How Juno's pronouncing the union a marriage (126, *conubio*; cf. 168) can be disregarded or even subverted by the narrator at 4.171 f. is one of the major mysteries surrounding the issue of Dido's "marriage".

4 It is not clear whether *prima* means "first", referring to the order of the actions (so Heyne, who also recalls Heinsius' conjecture *primae Tellus et pr. I.*, and many translators), or "primal", Earth being the oldest of the divinities, cf. 7.136 f. *primamque deorum / Tellurem* (so, after Henry 1878, 646–648, the majority of the commentators). The first possibility is more natural.

5 It is not easy to decide whether Tellus and Juno "give a sign", which *consists* in the *ignes* flashing in the sky and in the shrieking of the nymphs (168) – to be interpreted as good or bad omens; or whether they "give the signal" for the "ceremony" to begin, a signal, that is, which is to be imagined as something *different* from the *ignes* and the shrieking of the nymphs; for example, Servius thinks that Tellus gives her signal through an earthquake (an ominous event for a wedding *secundum Etruscam disciplinam*), and Juno *per tempestatem... et pluuias, quae de aere* (Juno's element) *fiunt*. Henry, instead, imagining that "[t]he signal was either a note of the *tibia* or some such instrument, or it was the first strain of the *hymenaeus* raised by the *pronuba* to be taken up from her and continued by the whole procession", thinks of some sort of unspecified signal given by the two goddesses, Tellus and Juno, personally present at the wedding (Henry 1878, 649).

6 With Thomas 2001, 187 I would prefer to follow Henry and Page in reading *Aether* (as in *G.* 2.325), in order to underline the effective presence of another "authoritative divine witness" to the union.

biguity".[7] There is Juno herself as *pronuba*, a sign "as if for the bridal procession" (Austin 1955), lightning bolts as wedding torches, Nymphs who sing the wedding song.[8] Obviously that would be a strange "rite": the storm itself is an ominous setting, there are no human witnesses, and the howling of the nymphs could be a ritual cry but also a cry of horror.[9] But nevertheless it would be easy for the reader to understand from all this that "the gods, in a way as inexplicable as if it were magic, accomplished what they had planned" (G. Williams 1968, 379).

Yet the narrator's observations in 169–172 contradict this implication:

ille dies primus leti primusque malorum
causa fuit; neque enim specie famaue mouetur
nec iam furtiuum Dido meditatur amorem:
coniugium uocat, hoc praetexit nomine culpam.

That day was the first of death and the first cause of sorrow; Dido is no longer influenced by what people see or hear, nor does she any longer think of a clandestine love–affair, but calls it marriage, and with this name she cloaks her crime.

---

7 Green 1986, 411.

8 The union in the cave is reminiscent of the marriage of Jason and Medea in a cave in Corcyra in Ap. Rhod. 4.1128–1169; see Nelis 2001, 148 f. The Nymphs and Hera also attend Jason and Medea's wedding (Nymphs: 4.1143–1155, 1196 f.; Hera: 4.1151, 1184 f., 1199 f.), but between the two passages there are many significant differences: see Cairns 1989, 47–49. According to Henry 1878, 644, "there is a union taking place at the same time between Dido and Aeneas and between the air and the earth" (cf. e.g. *G.* 2.325–327), a notion accepted by Page and O'Hara ad loc.; see Thomas 2001, 187; contra, see Pease on 160.

9 The shriek of the Nymphs corresponds to the marriage song of the Nymphs on the morning after the wedding of Jason and Medea at Ap. Rhod. 4.1196 f. (Virgil's words recall also Ap. Rhod. 3.1218 f., where the nymphs howl when Jason sacrifices in honour of Hecate: Nelis 2001, 148 n. 104.) Some commentators take this howling as a sinister sign (Heyne, Pease); others as a joyful song (Henry, Conington). In fact, Virgil has, in *ululo*, chosen an ambiguous word. As already noted by Servius and DServius, the verb (and the noun *ululatus*) is a *uox media* whose meaning depends on the context: it can refer to a ritual cry (DServ. ad loc.: *non nulli ita accipiunt, quod ululare ueteres etiam in sacris dicebant ex Graeca consuetudine. ergo ulularunt nymphae quasi nuptiarum sacra celebrarunt*) or to an ominous cry of sorrow or horror (cf. e.g. 667, the cries at Dido's death). As an example of *ululo* in a non–mournful context Servius quotes Luc. 6.261 *laetis ululare triumphis*, and DServ. the howling of the Amazons in battle at *Aen.* 11.662 *magnoque ululante tumultu*; *ululatus* is also used by Virgil of cries in the worship of Bacchus (7.395); Dido herself in her curse invokes Hecate *nocturnis... triuiis ululata per urbes* (4.609). (The same is true for the corresponding Greek verb ὀλολύζειν which can be a cry both of joy and of sorrow.) Ovid in *H.* 7.95 f. clearly takes Virgil's words as implying a positive ritual cry of the nymphs: *audieram uoces: nymphas ululasse putaui; / Eumenidum fati signa dedere mei* (see Knox 1995, 22 f.).

That was the first day of death and sorrow; Dido is no longer concerned about appearances or renown; "she no longer thinks of a *furtiuus amor*, but calls it marriage, with this name she cloaks her *culpa*" (171 f.). This implies that the relationship that begins in the cave was not a *coniugium* at all, and that the whole scene is to be reconsidered as "an elemental and demonic parody of the Roman marriage ceremony" (Hardie 1993, 90).

But the narrator's comment in 169 – 172 is far from being straightforward. Especially problematic are the crucial lines 171 f. Let us begin with line 172: "she calls it marriage, with this name she cloaks her guilt".[10] A preliminary issue to be clarified is the meaning of *culpa*. According to Pease, "In 4.19 and here the *culpa* involves unfaithfulness to the memory of Sychaeus".[11] But in 19 what Dido considered as a *culpa* was exactly her being married to Aeneas, that is, what she uses here to "cloak" her *culpa*. So, from a strictly logical point of view, the *culpa* in 172 must be different from the *culpa* in 19, and must refer to a sexual relationship that was not a marriage, a "sexual misdeameanour".[12] In other words, the *culpa* corresponds to the *furtiuus amor* of the preceding line: if *furtiuus amor* is, as we shall see, an illicit love–affair, then Dido no longer thinks of an illicit love–affair; she calls it marriage; with this name cloaks her misdeed (i. e. the fact of being involved in an illicit love–affair).[13] But one cannot altogether exclude that the line is (also?) focalized through Dido, with *culpa* suggesting "her previous sense that her marriage to Aeneas would have involved *culpa*" (O'Hara), in a contradiction with line 19 which we have to accept as such.[14]

It is not specified if Dido calls her relationship a marriage in public or in her own heart. In the first case, there is a slight contradiction with 170, as Dido would show some concern over her reputation after all. Furthermore, if the mar-

---

10 For the problems of line 172, see O'Hara 2011, ad loc.: "Does the narrator condemn what she is doing, or is the line 'focalized' through Dido (or looked at her from her perspective or point of view), so that she is overcoming her previous sense that marriage to Aeneas would have involved *culpa?* Does Dido 'call' (*uocat*) the relationship a marriage openly, or only in her mind? Does she 'cover over' a fault, or her previous sense that her marriage to Aeneas would have involved *culpa?*"

11 So for example also G. Williams 1968, 384, Agrell 2004, 101.

12 See Monti 1981, 106 f. n. 29, Moles 1984, 51 – 53, Horsfall 1995, 126 – 128.

13 For *culpa* "de amore illicito" see *TLL* 4.1302.67 – 1303.18.

14 See also, similarly, Harrison 2015, 167 f.: "On the famous crux of *culpam* at 4.172, S[eider 2013, 113 f.] takes it as the narrator's negative moral judgement, but it is equally well worth considering it as Dido's own exaggerated self–condemnation (neither party is currently married, and Dido's devoted attachment to the dead Sychaeus might be excessive even from a Roman perspective)".

riage is publicly declared as such, it is difficult to understand Aeneas' position: why did he not clarify from the beginning that he did not see their union as a marriage? On the other side, the contrast between 170 f. and 172 seems to imply that Dido is indeed talking *publicly* of her relationship as a marriage. We must remain uncertain, regarding it perhaps as slightly more probable that Dido *calls* her relationship a marriage only in her own heart: what she offers to people to see and hear (170) is her cohabiting with Aeneas (never expressly characterized as such, but obviously implied by the narrative), and in any case the public parading of the relationship; for this she does not have to make open statements about its legal status. For her the relationship is a marriage, and she behaves, publicly and privately, as if it is, but she does not necessarily declare it to be such explicitly. Obviously, how Aeneas could first accept all this, and then deny that he is married to Dido, remains an open question.

Also debatable, and clearly more important, is whether Dido, when she cloaks her *culpa* with the word *coniugium*, is sincerely convinced she is married to Aeneas, i. e., is she cloaking her guilt from *her own* eyes, or is she lying?[15] It is again impossible to reach a definite conclusion, but the first possibility is by far the most probable; in fact, from this point on Dido always refers to her relationship with Aeneas in terms of marriage (307 *data dextera quondam*, 314–316, 324, 431, 495 f., 550, 597 *en dextra fidesque*), and there is nothing in the text to suggest that she is not sincerely convinced that this is its true nature.

In fact, it is possible to think that what at the beginning is not a marriage, as stated in 172, later evolves, through prolonged cohabitation and because of Aeneas' behavior (think of his involvement in the construction of Carthage at 260 and of the word *uxorius* used by Mercury at 266), into what Dido can even *legitimately* think of as a real marriage.[16]

In sum, notwithstanding the narrator's explicit declaration that what happened in the cave was no *coniugium*, Dido can still be sincerely convinced

---

15 For the first possibility see for example G. Williams 1968, 380: "the decisive fact is that Virgil always portrays Dido as really convinced that she is married to Aeneas"; for the second one, Moles 1984, 53: "at this point Dido knows that she is not married to Aeneas but pretends to the world that she is to avoid disgrace".

16 For this position see Monti 1981, 45–48; on the possible ambiguity of the legal status of relationships in Roman society see G. Williams 1968, 378–383, Treggiari 1981, 59 f. (with reference to Dido and Aeneas). Hardly relevant for this issue is the fact that Aeneas can be seen as a proto-Roman and Dido as a *peregrina*, as maintained by Cairns 1989, 48, Horsfall 1995, 128. At 192 *cui se pulchra uiro* ("as a husband") *dignetur iungere Dido* it is not clear whether Fama depicts Aeneas as the *real* husband of Dido (so e. g. O'Hara 2011, ad loc.: "Rumor describes the union as a marriage"), or whether *uiro* represents Dido's point of view (= *tamquam uiro* "considering him as a husband"; so e. g. Paratore 1947, ad loc.).

that she is married to Aeneas; Aeneas, on the other side, is surely right when he points out that there has been no formal ceremony (338 f. *nec coniugis umquam / praetendi taedas*); but we are not given any clue about the sincerity of his claim that on his part there has been no consent or *maritalis affectio* (339 *aut haec in foedera ueni*): we are given a peek into Dido's "consciousness", but never into Aeneas', and we do not know what Aeneas has said in the cave or during his subsequent cohabitation with Dido, or how he reacted to Dido's public presentation, or (possibly) even declaration, of their relationship as a marriage.

Let's now turn to 171, *nec iam furtiuum Dido meditatur amorem*. A translation along the lines of "and Dido does not think anymore of (or does not practice anymore) her love as a secret one" is supported by the glosses of Heyne ("nec iam clam amat, non celat amorem"), West ("no longer kept her love as a secret in her own heart"), and Hardie ("no longer kept her love a secret in her heart").[17]

---

17 Hardie 2012, 84, but see below. See Buscaroli 1932, ad loc.: "Didone non nutre piu segretamente in cuor suo (*furtiuum* non è, come sembra ad alcuni, attributivo!) l'amore per Enea, ma lo chiama, perché lo considera, vero e proprio connubio [...]. *Meditatur* è "cogitando persequitur" (Forbiger), 'vagheggia'" (notice, however, that Forbiger seems to intend the line in a different way: see below); La Penna in La Penna / Grassi 1971, ad loc.: "'né ormai Didone coltiva l'amore nascondendolo nel suo animo'. *Furtivum... amorem* si riferisce al precedente amore non dichiarato"; G. Williams 1968, 379: "Then he [sc. the narrator] says that Dido is now acting openly – where previously she had kept her love for Aeneas a secret known only to her sister. (It should perhaps be said explicitly that, when Virgil speaks here of a "secret love", he does not mean that Dido had been secretly making love with Aeneas, but that she had been feeling love for him and not talking about it.)"; he translates: "it is not a secret love she now practices". De la Cerda 1612, 411 (in his "Explicatio") explains: "Itaque non iam furtim exercet amores suos, sic explico *meditatur*, sed vocat coniugium": this evidently means that Dido no longer nourishes a feeling of love for Aeneas in the secret of her heart (i.e. the usual explanation). Those who interpret the line in this sense usually take *meditatur* in the sense of *exercet* "nourishes", "practices her love in secret" (cf. La Cerda's *exercet*, Buscaroli's "nutre", La Penna's "coltiva"); for this sense of *meditatur* cf. already Servius: *'meditatur': exercet; sic Horatius* (*Carm.* 4.14.27 f.) *'et horridam* [sic] *cultis / diluuiem meditatur agris'. nec incongrue dictum: actus enim est in ipsa meditatione, nam exercitium est meditatio.* Horace's passage means that "Tiberius as river is plotting a deluge against cultivated fields", where *meditatur* "involves actual planning" (Thomas 2011, ad loc.), so perhaps it is not the best parallel for *meditor* = *exerceo* (saying that "Dido no longer secretly plans a love" with Aeneas does not seem to be what those who follow the usual explanation want to mean); but otherwise this seems a possible extension of the meaning of *meditor* (cf. *OLD* s.v. 5a "To rehearse, practise (an action, part, etc.)"), even if in the only other instance of the phrase, Hor. *Carm.* 3.6.23 f. *incestos amores / de tenero meditatur ungui* (a difficult passage owing to the uncertain meaning of *de tenero ... ungui*) the sense is probably "goes over in contemplation" (Nisbet in Nisbet–Rudd 2004, ad loc.). It goes without saying that "[t]o contemplate as a possible course of action, have in mind, intend" (*OLD* s.v. 2a, which so catalogues our passage) is the most natural sense of *meditor* here. But this meaning can be adapted also to the usual explanation of the line: "she no longer thinks of her love as a secret in her heart"; so,

However, *furtiuum... amorem* clearly suggests "the secret elegiac (or iambic, lyric) liaison" (Hardie 2012, 86).[18] *Furtiuus* in this erotic sense normally refers to a relationship kept secret from others but also consummated, while in this case, if we were to accept Heyne's interpretation, it should exceptionally refer to a love kept secret *from the other partner*. I cannot find any parallel for such a meaning of *furtiuus amor*. Clearly right is that minority of interpreters who understand: "she no longer thinks of a secret love–affair" (Green 1986, 414),[19] "[Dido] no longer thinks of enjoying a secret liaison" (Ahl).[20] This is actually the inevitable meaning of this line: "Dido is not moved by appearances or what people say; and she no longer thinks of a clandestine love–affair [i.e. no longer thinks of

---

for example, if I correctly understand, Day Lewis: "the love she brooded on now was a secret love no longer"; Lombardo: "She no longer thinks to keep the affair a secret" (where, however, the use of the term "affair" probably points towards the interpretation we will consider next). – I am not sure of how Conington interprets the line: "It is not on a concealed love that Dido's heart is any longer set".

18 Cf. Catull. 7.8, Tib. 1.5.75, and see O'Hara 2011, ad loc.: "the phrase suggests the clandestine affairs of Latin love poetry (which Dido thinks she is not pursuing); cf Catullus 7.8, Tib. 1.5.75, Ov. *F.* 6.573", *TLL* s.v. *furtiuus* 6.1644.42–63; for *furtum* in reference to a clandestine love affair, see Thomas 1981, 372 and n. 7 = 1999, 302 and n. 12 (with reference also to *Aen.* 4.171), Pichon 1966, 158.

19 Green 1986, 414: "The phrase *nec iam* should be given its full force, indicating that the situation has changed in an important aspect. She no longer thinks of a secret love–affair, which is the plain sense of *furtiuum* in such contexts", with reference to Catullus and Tibullus quoted above. Green does not see the problem which arises from the contradiction with Dido's previous thinking of her relationship with Aeneas always as a marriage, on which see below.

20 See also Forbiger 1873, ad loc.: "*furtivum*, celatum, tectum; vox propria de hac re. [...] *meditatur*, cogitando persequitur; non iam furtivo amori se indulgere putat"; Agrell 2004, 100 f. (on which see below, n. 22). I take for granted that the translation of Ahl 2007 does not refer to a love–affair that is kept "secret" from *Aeneas himself*; that would be an absurd way of expressing oneself in English. The same I would think of Seider's translation (2013, 111): "nor does she any longer think of her love as clandestine". Often, however, the translators reproduce the Latin text with all its ambiguity (Canali 1978 is an extreme case: "ormai non medita un amore furtivo"), so that we cannot understand how exactly they interpret the line. For example, the translations of Fairclough ("no more does she dream of a secret love"), followed by Goold, Mandelbaum ("she no longer thinks of furtive love"), R. D. Williams ("nor does she any longer think of a hidden love"), Clausen 2002, 46 ("nor thinks now of a secret love"), Scarcia ("né più quale furtivo considera il suo amore"), and Fo ("né piú immagina ormai, Didone, un amore furtivo") would seem most naturally to agree with our explanation, but in the absence of an explicit discussion one cannot be completely certain (anyway, my impression is that, when the translators do not think too much about the implications of the line, they instinctively tend to translate *furtiuum ... amorem* in its most natural sense, that is as "clandestine love–affair"). Nor is it clear to me from Rudd's translation (1976, 40) how he understands the line: "Nor does she engage in a clandestine love–affair", which seems to omit *iam* (cf. Perret's explanation in the following note).

being involved in a clandestine love–affair]; she calls it [sc. this love which in fact remains a clandestine love–affair] marriage and with this name she cloaks her crime [sc. her being involved in a clandestine love–affair, with the other possible implications we have seen above]".

Nevertheless, this entails a big problem: saying that Dido "*no longer* thinks of a clandestine love–affair" implies that *at a certain point* she did think of it as such, and this contrasts with the fact that Dido has always spoken of her possible relationship with Aeneas only in terms of marriage (15 – 19): that she ever envisioned that relationship as a "clandestine love affair" seems out of character.[21]

So either we accept this anomaly (which is of course a possible decision), or we have to find a different way of explaining how Virgil can say of Dido that, after the encounter in the cave, she no longer thinks of her relationship with Aeneas as a *furtiuus amor*, a clandestine love–affair. There seems to be only one way of applying the words in this meaning to the evolution of Dido's attitude towards her relationship with Aeneas. That is, if it is true that Dido has always thought of that relationship as a (possible) marriage, there must have a moment, during, or immediately after, the love–making in the cave, when she did "think" of that union as a *furtiuus amor:* making love in a cave during a storm interrupting a hunt can most plausibly be seen as a "clandestine love–affair". It is difficult to imagine that she was thinking of her union with Aeneas as a marriage the moment *before*, or *during*, their love–making, and it is difficult to think that before, or even during, their love–making Aeneas can have said or done anything that might have made her think of their relationship in terms of marriage. It is

21 Perret, seeing this contradiction ("Il nous paraît douteux que *iam* soit ici employé pour opposer deux époques et doive être traduit: "Didon ne songe *plus* à un amour clandestine". On ne voit pas, en effet, qu'elle y ait jamais songé: dès les premiers vers du livre (v. 16) c'est sur un mariage qu'elle s'interrogeait", Perret 1977, 184 n.), but at the same time rightly considering that *furtiuus amor* can only mean "clandestine love–affair", vainly tries to explain away *iam* by giving it an implausible emphatic sense, so translating: "et elle ne pense certes pas à un amour furtif". According to Paratore 1947, ad loc. the line means that Dido "non si limita più a *ricercare un'occasione* per congiungersi nascostamente a Enea" (his emphasis); this implies that Dido was actively seeking an occasion to seduce Aeneas, but of this plan of seduction on Dido's part there is no trace in the text – which does not mean that we could not integrate the narrative in such a way; indeed, Dido's behavior as described in lines 74 – 79 can legitimately imply attempts at seduction on Dido's part. *furtiuum ... amorem*, however, seems more naturally to refer to a "clandestine *relationship*" (cf. the opposition with *coniugium*), rather than to an "*occasion* for furtive love–making". In any case, Paratore's interpretation, which probably lies beneath at least some of the translations cited in the preceding note, is well worth considering.

only *after* her intimacy with Aeneas that she begins to think of their union as a "marriage".[22]

We can imagine Dido's psychological process as hinted at by Virgil as a moment of blurring of reason (she and Aeneas in the same cave together, the love–making: the *furtiuus amor*), followed by a gaining of awareness, with *iam* marking the moment in which Dido rationalizes what just happened as a marriage, presumably helped by something that Aeneas does or says: "and she by now (already, immediately, or shortly, after the fact; when she leaves the cave) does not think of what happened in the cave as a clandestine love–affair; she calls it marriage, and with this name cloaks her guilt" – that is, her being involved in an irregular sexual relationship.

22 Agrell 2004, 100 f., who well sees both that language cannot support the usual interpretation of *furtiuus amor*, and that *furtiuus amor* = "clandestine love-affair" contrasts with the preceding presentation of Dido's thoughts about her relationship with Aeneas, sustains that the phrase "can hardly refer to the proceedings in the cave, since the separate arrivals of Dido and Aeneas seem to rule out a planned seduction, and thereafter Dido had no doubt that she was married". On the contrary, I think that *furtiuus amor* does refer to the proceedings in the cave, and that it covers a short phase of Dido's thoughts about herself only hinted at by Virgil. For the developing of a *furtiuus amor* in the cave there is no need of presupposing perforce "a planned seduction": they arrive into the same cave "by chance"; they indulge in a *furtiuus amor*; and shortly after Dido is convinced that she is married to Aeneas. For this formulation I am especially indebted to discussion with Jim O'Hara.

James O'Hara

Genre, Gender, and the Etymology Behind the Phrase *Lugentes campi* at *Aeneid* 6.441

nec procul hinc partem fusi monstrantur in omnem
Lugentes campi; sic illos nomine dicunt.
hic quos durus amor crudeli tabe peredit
secreti celant calles et myrtea circum
silua tegit; curae non ipsa in morte relinquunt.
his Phaedram .... *Aen.* 6.440–445

inter quas Phoenissa recens a uulnere Dido
errabat silua in magna .... 450 f.

per sidera iuro,
per superos et si qua fides tellure sub ima est,
inuitus, regina, tuo de litore cessi. 458–460

...respondet curis aequatque Sychaeus amorem.
nec minus Aeneas casu percussus iniquo
prosequitur lacrimis longe et miseratur euntem 474–476

In *True Names: Vergil and the Alexandrian Tradition of Etymological Wordplay* (O'Hara 1996), I discussed at length one line in the *Aeneid* where I was sure the poet was engaging in etymological wordplay, but could not figure out what it was. I think I have it now, and that the answer both complements interesting recent work on this section of *Aeneid* 6, and also tells us more about what is going on in some poems of Horace, Ovid and Apollonius that all seem to allude to the same etymology.[1]

I said in 1996 that *Aeneid* 6.441 *Lugentes campi; sic illos nomine dicunt*, "The Mourning Fields; thus they call them by name", offered "a puzzle I cannot quite

---

1 I have described my answer briefly at the start of a new Introduction to the expanded paperback reprint of *True Names* (O'Hara 2017, xvii) but did not review the extensive evidence for the wordplay in a variety of authors as I do here.

I am happy to offer this piece on etymological wordplay to Richard Thomas, since I first learned about poetic etymologizing not only from our teacher David Ross, but also from pieces now collected in Thomas 1999 on Catullus 64 (12–32), gadflies (305–310), and on "suppression" (323–327), as well as of course his *Georgics* commentary (1988).

For comments on drafts of this piece I thank Micah Myers, Alexandra Daly, and the participants in the June 2017 Vergilian Society Symposium Cumanum on "Vergil and Elegy", at Cuma, Italy, where I read a version of this paper.

https://doi.org/10.1515/9783110545708-007

solve, but I can outline the interesting problem". The key is that "*Nomine dicunt* looks like an etymological signpost", which is to say the kind of naming construction that often points to etymological wordplay in Virgil and other Greek and Roman authors.[2] But I had to confess that it was "not clear exactly what kind of etymologizing might be involved". Norden, comparing four other uses of *nomine* in the fifth dactyl, had called attention to *nomine dicunt* as a sign that Virgil is drawing upon a lost source, and I added that all four of Norden's comparanda seem to involve etymologizing: *Aeneid* 7.607: *sunt geminae Belli portae (sic nomine dicunt)*; *Georgics* 3.280: *hippomanes uero quod nomine dicunt*; Lucretius 2.629f.: *Curetas nomine Grai / quos memorant*; Cicero *Aratea* fr. xiii S: *quem claro perhibent Ophiuchum nomine Graii.* I mentioned two not very attractive suggestions about possible etymologizing:

> Servius glosses the phrase *Lugentes campi* as *lucis egentes,* and Isidore repeats the gloss with a bit more information, namely that this is the origin of *luctus* as well. De la Cerda explains *Lugentes campi* by reference to the Cocytus River, whose name is commonly derived from κωκύειν, 'mourn' (see Servius on *A.* 6.132[3] and Maltby s.v.); de la Cerda explains that the fields next to the Cocytus could thus similarly be called Mourning Fields. By itself these observations do not provide a satisfactory motivation for Vergil's phrase, but I think we have improved upon Norden's suggesting of a Hellenistic source by tentatively specifying a Hellenistic or Roman-Alexandrian source that featured an etymology of the *Lugentes campi* or that connected them either with lack of light or with the Cocytus.

This, as some reviewers and commentators have noted, was a pretty good description of the problem, but not much of a solution.[4]

I no longer posit one extensive source text, but argue that the name *Lugentes Campi*, marked by the etymological signpost *nomine dicunt*, points to the genre of love elegy, and to the fairly common etymology that connects Greek and Latin words for elegy with mourning, as if from Greek ἒ ἒ λέγειν ("to say ah, ah") or ἔλεος ("pity"). The etymologizing helps introduce a section of *Aeneid* 6 that, as recent work has shown, is much concerned both with genre and with gender.

Most of the explicit references to the etymology come from either a little later (Ov. *Am.* 3.9.3f.) or from much later,[5] but the sheer number of these, and other

---

2 Cf. O'Hara 1996/2017, 75–82, Maltby 1993, 257–275; Cairns 1997, 24–59 and 2003, 239–242, Michalopoulos 2001, 4–6, esp. 4 n. 9.

3 Servius on *Aen.* 6.132, *cocytusque sinu labens circumfluit atro fluvius inferorum est, dictus* ἀπὸ τοῦ κωκύειν, *id est lugere.*

4 Wills 1997, Horsfall 2013, 318f.

5 Sources gathered from Maltby 1991, Janko 2011, 490, Kannicht 1969, 73: Ovid *Amores* 3.9.3f.: *flebilis indignos, Elegia, solue capillos! / a, nimis ex uero nunc tibi nomen erit!* Porph. Hor. *Carm.* 1.33.2f. *nomen ipsum elegiorum* παρὰ τὸ ἒ ἒ, *quae uox est lamentium, dictum putant*;

pieces of evidence, have led scholars to assume widespread knowledge of the derivation, probably dating back to fifth-century Athens.[6] E.L. Bowie, citing Pausanias' discussion of the dedicatory epigram of the victor in the aulos competition of 586 BCE, explains that "To Pausanias, as to the Hellenistic and Graeco-Roman world as a whole, *elegoi* were by definition—and perhaps etymology—

Diom. *GL* 1.484 f. *elegia dicta siue* παρὰ τὸ εὖ λέγειν τοὺς τεθνεῶτας..., *siue* ἀπὸ τοῦ ἐλέου, *id est miseratione, quod* θρήνους *Graeci uel* ἐλεεῖα *isto metro scriptitauerunt. cui opinioni consentire uidetur Horatius, cum ad Albium Tibullum elegiarum auctorem scribens ab ea quam diximus miseratione elegos miserabiles dicit hoc modo, "neu miserabiles / decantes elegos"*; Sacerd. *GL* 6.509, 31 *elegiacum metrum dictum est, quod* ἒ ἒ *sonat interiectionem flentis, et hoc metro mortuis fletus componebant antiqui*; Mar. Victorin. *GL* 6.110. 17 *elegiacum metrum ... dictum ex eo, quod maerori rebusque tristibus modus eorum aptior esse uideatur,* ἀπὸ τοῦ ἐλεεῖν. *alii uero* παρὰ τὸ εὖ λέγειν *elegos dictus arbitantur*; Isid. *Orig.* 1.39.14 *elegiacus ... dictus eo, quod modulatio eiusdem carminis conueniat miseris.*

An etymology from εὖ λέγειν is mentioned in fragments of the *On Lyric Poets* of Didymus Chalcenterus, a contemporary of Virgil and Horace whom Horace seems to cite at *Ars P.* 75 f. (p. 387 Schmidt; the fragment is a testimonium from Orion's *Etymologicum*) and in a fragment of Varro (*De poem.* fr. 303 Funaioli = Diom. *GL* 1.484, 17); see Janko 2011, 489 f., as well as (much later!) Procl. ap. Phot. Bibl. 319b8 τὸ γὰρ θρῆνος ἔλεγον ἐκάλουν οἱ παλαιοὶ καὶ τοὺς τετελευτηκότας δι' αὐτοῦ εὐλόγουν.

The derivations from ἒ ἒ λέγειν and/or ἐλεεῖν, often with mention also of εὖ λέγειν, appear in: Schol. Ar. *Av.* 217 τοῖς σοῖς ἐλέγοις: Ἀντὶ τοῦ τοῖς θρήνοις. εἴρηται δὲ ἀπὸ τοῦ ἒ ἒ λέγειν; *Etym. Mag.* 326, 47 Ἔλεγος: Θρῆνος ὁ τοῖς τεθνεῶσιν ἐπιλεγόμενος. Εἴρηται δὲ παρὰ τὸ ἒ ἒ λέγειν ἐν τοῖς τάφοις. Ἢ ἀπὸ τοῦ εὖ λέγειν δι' αὐτοῦ τοῦ θρήνου τοὺς κατοιχομένους. Καὶ ἐλεγεῖα, παρὰ τὸ ἐλεεῖν τὸν τετελευτηκότα· ἢ ἐλέγεα, παρὰ τὸ εὖ λέγειν τὸν ἀποβιώσαντα; *Suda* 774 Adler Ἔλεγος: θρῆνος. ἀπὸ τοῦ ἒ ἒ λέγειν; Schol. Dion. Thrax 21, 1 Hilg. διὸ καὶ καλεῖται ἐλεγεῖα, οἱονεὶ ἐλεεῖα, τοῦ γ ἐκθλιβομένου, παρὰ τὸ ἐλεεῖν τὸν τετελευτηκότα· ἢ ἐλεγεῖα οἱονεὶ εὐλεγεῖα, παρὰ τὸ εὖ λέγειν τὸν ἀποβιώσαντα· ἢ παρὰ τὸ ἔλεγος, ὃ δηλοῖ τὸν θρῆνον· τοῦτο δὲ παρὰ τὸ ἒ λέγειν· ὥσπερ ἐλεοῦντες γὰρ τοὺς ἀποιχομένους τοῦτο ἐφεῦρον τὸ μέτρον;.

6 Nisbet / Hubbard 1970 on Hor. *Carm.* 1.33.2 ("The ancients frequently derived the name of elegy from ἔλεος and took lament to be its primary function"), Nagle 1980, 22 f. on *Tristia* 5.1.5 *flebile carmen* and 48 *tibia funeribus conuenit ista meis*, Hinds 1987, 103 ("From the time of Aristophanes and Euripides ancient opinion is unanimous in connecting elegy with mourning. The etymology from ἔλεος is frequently offered, or the ἒ ἒ λέγειν of funereal lament") and 1992, 105–107 (sees allusion to the etymology at Ovid *Fasti* 3.213 f. and elsewhere in elegy), Rudd 1989 on Hor. *Ars P.* 75 f. (discussed in my text), Keith 1992, 334 f., 2011, 2 ("From the start Roman elegists seem to have accepted the Greek etymology deriving elegia from funerary lament, ἒ ἒ λέγειν (to cry 'woe, woe'), and/or ἔλεος (pity)"); Knox 1995 on *Epistula Sapphus* 7 = ([Ov.] *Her.* 15.7) *flendus amor meus est—elegiae flebile carmen* ("an allusion to the connection between elegy and lamentation, which ancient scholars tried to find in the etymology of elegy from Greek ἔλεος 'pity' or εὖ λέγειν 'eulogize' or the like"; see also Davis 2005, 175 on this poem.

mournful".[7] Bowie points to a unique cluster of fifth-century uses of the Greek word "in the seven or eight years following 415 BC"[8] and suggests that

> one of Euripides' contemporaries with an interest in etymology and the history of music advanced the theory that *elegos* ought to mean 'lament', presumably adducing the fact that (by the late fifth century) the elegiac couplet was regularly used for sepulchral epigrams and the further hypothesis that elegos was to be derived from ἒ ἒ λέγειν.

Evidence does not allow this attractive suggestion to be proven beyond a doubt, but it accords well with the Roman evidence, which I shall now briefly review, before returning to *Aeneid* 6. Along the way, we shall see several examples in that Roman evidence of the characteristic features of etymological wordplay discussed in *True Names.*

The first use in extant Latin of *elegi* for the well-known Greek *elegoi*[9] is at Horace *Odes* 1.33.1–4:

> Albi, ne doleas plus nimio memor
> inmitis Glycerae neu miserabilis
> decantes elegos, cur tibi iunior
>   laesa praeniteat fide.
>
> Do not grieve too much, Albius, when you think
> of bittersweet Glycera, nor drone out

---

7 Bowie 1986, 23; Gerber 1997, 94–96 summarizes and endorses Bowie's suggestion. Bowie updates Harvey 1955, 170–172, West 1974, 4f.

8 Bowie 1986, 25, citing, with dates, "Euripides *Troades* 119 in 415, Aristophanes *Birds* 217 in 415/4, Euripides *Helen* 185 in 412, *Orestes* 968 (restored by conjecture) in 408, with *Hypsipyle* I iii 9 probably in 409 or 407 and *Iphigenia in Tauris* within the period 413–408". Cf. also Kannicht 1969 on *Helen* 185.

9 Mayer 2012 ad loc.; as Mayer notes, a different loan-word, *elegeum*, is used earlier to describe erotic graffiti associated with the paraclausithryon, at Plautus *Mercator* 409 *impleantur elegeorum meae fores carbonibus.* Wheeler 1911, 67 n. 1 says the whole passage "Undoubtedly" (more recent scholars might not be so confident) "... is taken from the Greek original of Philemon, as the word *elegeorum* with the familiar early Latin shortening of the penult (cf. platĕa: πλατεῖα) indicates". This form of the word, which would not fit elegy or the hexameter, does not occur again in extant Latin until the Fragmenta Bobiensia, *De Versibus* of uncertain date (*GL* 6.624).

Catullus uses no name for his elegiac verse, but in what is in our manuscripts the first of his elegies, may allude to the etymology at 65.10–12. Cf. Wiseman 1969, 17 f.: "addressing his dead brother, the poet promises *semper maesta tua carmina morte canam...* The promise is not to keep writing about the brother's death, but to keep writing elegiacs. And of course, the rest of our collection is elegiacs". Cf. too Wiseman 1979, 176, Hinds 1987, 103, Bleisch 1999, 214, Skinner 2003.

> pitiful elegies about why her promises were broken
> and a younger man outshines you.

Here, at perhaps its first occurrence, the word *elegi* comes equipped with an adjective that functions as a gloss of both its meaning and etymology,[10] as often in both Greek and Roman etymologizing from Homer onwards: *miserabilis* points both to the basic association of elegy with lament, and to the etymology. I think it has not been noticed by commentators either on Horace or Apollonius that Apollonius of Rhodes provides a precedent for Horace's phrase, and may also allude to the etymology as well, at *Argonautica* 2.782: οἰκτίστοις ἐλέγοισιν ὀδύρεται ἐξέτι κείνου, "mourn ever since with most sorrowful dirges/elegies" (although there are no other features of the Apollonian passage that call attention to etymology).[11] For Horace Porphyrio appropriately cites the etymology in his note on the line: Porph. Hor. *Carm.* 1.33.2f. *nomen ipsum elegiorum* παρὰ τὸ ἒ ἔ, *quae uox est lamentium, dictum putant*, "They think that the very name of elegies is derived from 'ah, ah,' which is what is said by those who lament"; the grammarian Diomedes (quoted in n. 5) cites Horace's words as proof that Horace agreed with the etymology. The Albius here addressed is naturally thought by most (though not all; more on this below) scholars to be Albius Tibullus the elegist, and Horace's ode is one of many Augustan poems that play both in general with the notion of the differences between genres, and in particular with the difference between elegy and the other genres.[12] Stephen Harrison's *Generic Enrichment* sums up much recent work when he notes of this ode that "elegy is seen here as the poetic of excess—excessive emotion and lamentation, alluding to the traditional origin of elegy in lament of the dead".[13]

---

10 Cf. O'Hara 1996/2017, 8f., 64f. on "the single-adjective gloss" or, to use the title of McCartney 1927, "modifiers that reflect the etymology of the word modified". Cf. *Aen.* 1.744 = 3.516 *pluuiasque Hyadas*, 3.693 *Plemyrium undosum*, 6.570f. *ultrix ... Tisiphone*, 7.740 *maliferae ... Abellae*, 8.340 *uatis fatidicae*, 8.663 *exsultantis Salios*, *Ecl.* 7.29f. *paruus ... Micon*, *G.* 1.75 *tristisque lupini*.
All translations in my text are adapted from those of the Loeb Classical Library.

11 The scholia do gloss the word, on 2.780 – 83 c: ἐλέγοισιν: θρήνοις· τὰ γὰρ ἐλεγεῖα ἐπὶ ἐπιτυμβίοις ἐχρῶντο οἱ παλαιοί.

12 Cf. Hor. *Epode* 11 and its relationship to elegy, epigram and lyric (Harrison 2007, 119 – 130, Watson 2003, 358 – 363), Verg. *Ecl.* 10 (Conte 1986, 100 – 129, Harrison 2007, 49 – 74, Henkel 2009, 95 – 132), *Georgics* 4 (Conte 1986, 130 – 140, 2007, 123 – 149) as well as the elegists' own staking out of their territory by contrasting their work to epic and encomium. It was while reading Henkel 2009 that I first began to think that genre and the etymology of elegy might be the solution to *Lugentes campi*.

13 Harrison 2007, 175; cf. Lowrie 1994, 381: "In telling Albius not to grieve, Horace implies not only that elegy is excessively single-minded but also that lyric is different".

A similar complex of ideas, and allusion to the etymology, appear also in *Odes* 2.9, though there the word *elegi* is not used (to use a term used by Servius of wordplay, the word perhaps is "suppressed")[14], and the generic associations are broader, and include love poetry and laments for dead lovers in elegy and other genres. The poem is addressed to the poet Valgius, named at Horace *Serm.* 10.82 along with Virgil and others as those whose opinions Horace values, and of whose elegiac verse seven fragments survive (Courtney 1993, 287–290). The poem criticizes Valgius' incessant mourning for the lost Mystes—whether a lost or dead lover we cannot be sure, though death seems likely (9–12):

tu semper urges flebilibus modis
Mysten ademptum nec tibi uespero
  surgente decedunt amores
    nec rapidum fugiente solem.

You always pursue your lost Mystes
with tearful verses; your love does not subside
when the evening star rises or when it
flees before the on-rushing sun.

Both *flebilibus modis* and the surviving fragments of Valgius urge us to think here of both elegy,[15] and the etymology to which Horace has called attention in 1.33. But Roman generic play is often complex: the description of Valgius as mourning from dawn to sunset in lines 10–12 interacts intertextually with both an epyllion by Cinna (a fragment probably describing Smyrna's love for her father), and a portion of Virgil's *Georgics* that shares features with epyllion (the description in *Georgics* 4 of Orpheus' song of mourning for the lost Eurydice).[16] Horace's poem thus evokes both elegy and the broader corpus of love poetry that includes hexameter verse describing distraught lovers.[17]

---

14 O'Hara, 1996b, 79–82, Servius on *G.* 2.126: *apud Medos nascitur quaedam arbor, ferens mala, quae medica uocantur: quam per periphrasin ostendit, eius supprimens nomen.*

15 Courtney 1993, 287: "*flebilis* is the standard epithet of elegy". Cf. Ov. *Am.* 3.9.3 quoted in text below, *Epistula Sapphus* 7 and *Tr.* 5.1.5 (quoted above n. 6).

16 Cinna fr. 6 Courtney (from the *Zmyrna* praised by Catullus 95 by contrasting it with poetry in another genre, the *Annales* of Volusius) describes someone, probably Smyrna who fell in love with her father and tricked him into having sex with her, whose weeping is seen by both the morning and evening star: *te matutinus flentem conspexit Eous / et flentem paulo uidit post Hesperus idem.* The lines likely describe some aspect of "Smyrna's anguish at her emotional conflict" (Courtney). It may well be, as Courtney suggests, that Valgius' poetry alluded to the lines of Cinna, who is mentioned by name in another fragment of Valgius, 2 FPL. But Horace's lines also clearly evoke Virgil's description in *Georgics* 4.464–466 of Orpheus' song of mourning for the lost Eurydice: *ipse caua solans aegrum testudine amorem / te, dulcis coniunx, te solo in*

A third Horatian allusion to the etymology cannot be securely dated. Some scholars put the *Ars Poetica* in the period 23–17 and so possibly before the death of Virgil and the publication of the *Aeneid*, but many would put it a decade or so later.[18] In his survey of genres and their meters at *Ars P.* 73–98, Horace describes the invention of elegy for "complaint" (*Ars P.* 75–78):

> uersibus inpariter iunctis querimonia primum,
> post etiam inclusa est uoti sententia compos;
> quis tamen exiguos elegos emiserit auctor,
> grammatici certant et adhuc sub iudice lis est;

> In verses yoked unequally first came lamentations,
> later also the sentiment of granted prayers:
> yet who first put forth humble elegiacs,
> scholars dispute, and the case is still before the court.

There is no explicit reference here or elsewhere in the *Ars* to contemporary love elegy,[19] but often words like *querela* function as a standard term for elegy,[20] or for love poetry more broadly in a way that associates it with elegy. For example, when Horace at *Carm.* 2.13.24 describes Sappho in her capacity as love poet as *querentem*, in contrast to Alcaeus who describes the hardships of exile and war, he associates her with elegy and other types of love poetry, without actually implying that she literally wrote elegy.

---

litore secum, / te ueniente die, te decedente canebat. Cf. Lowrie 1994 on Horace's allusions to Cinna, *Georgics* 4, and perhaps, in the section of the ode on encomium (17–24), even the unpublished *Aeneid.*

17 On 2.9 cf. Conte 2007, 142 f., Lowrie 1994, 380: "Orpheus' inability to let go of his mourning becomes [in Horace's *Ode*] paradigmatic for one kind of poetry. The elegiac quality of Orpheus' poetry [in *Georgics* 4] is marked by the repetition of the vocabulary of mourning: *flesse* (509), *flet* (514); *maerens* (511), *maestis* (515); *queritur* (512), *questibus* (515), *querens* (520). It is this kind of repetition that Horace criticizes in the elegy of Albius and Valgius: the former's *miserabilis elegos* (C. 1.33.2 f.) recalls *miserabile carmen* (Georg. 4.514), the latter recalls Orpheus through allusion.... Does Horace criticize Vergil too?"

I would also ask, as I have above n. 9 regarding Catullus 65, whether *miserabile carmen*, used at *G.* 4.514 to describe Orpheus' song, might also allude to the etymology of *elegi.* But there is probably not enough evidence there pointing to etymology.

18 Rudd 1989, 19–21 surveys the evidence and prefers the later date.

19 Whether this is meant as an insult to elegy (cf. Brink 1963, 205, Clark 1983), or simply reflects that Horace's concerns in this odd poem (which focuses on drama and even satyr plays) are elsewhere, is not clear to me.

20 Cf. Kennedy 1993, 32: "the verb 'to bewail' (*queri*) becomes discursively constructed to signify the act of writing elegy", as well as James 2003, 108–121 on *querela*, citing the etymology.

As I noted earlier, the first explicit poetic reference to the etymology of words for elegy is securely dated after Virgil's death, but it also clearly interacts with some of the pre-*Aeneid* examples we have seen. Ovid *Amores* 3.9, which in the final version of the *Amores* appeared around the turn of the millennium but which doubtless appeared much earlier when the original five books of the *Amores* were published,[21] laments the death of Tibullus, who is probably the addressee of Hor. *Odes* 1.33, and who of course died around the same time as Virgil. Lines 3–4 call the personified Elegia *flebilis*, and notes that she is well-named, which is to say, with the common etymological signpost of referring to a name as *uerus*, that she is named for lament (1–6).

> Memnona si mater, mater plorauit Achillem,
>   et tangunt magnas tristia fata deas,
> <u>flebilis</u> indignos, Elegia, solue capillos!
>   a, nimis ex <u>uero</u> nunc tibi <u>nomen</u> erit! –
> ille tui uates operis, tua fama, Tibullus
>   ardet in extructo, corpus inane, rogo.

> If Memnon was bewailed by his mother, if a mother bewailed Achilles,
>   and if sad fates touch great goddesses,
> <u>in tears</u>, O <u>Elegy</u>, loose your undeserving hair!
>   Ah, all too <u>truthful</u> now will be your <u>name</u>! –
> he, that singer of your strain, that glory of yours, Tibullus,
>   burns on the high-reared pyre, an empty mortal frame.

That Ovid explicitly refers to the etymology of the name Elegia in an elegy for Tibullus is of particular interest. In discussing Virgilian etymologizing I have shown elsewhere, with many examples, that Ovid often comments on Virgil's implicit etymological wordplay, either by making his own subtle allusions to etymology at the same time as he is alluding to a Virgilian instance, or by explicitly giving an etymology to which Virgil has merely alluded.[22] He does the latter here, but with Horace. By explicitly referring to the etymology of Elegia in his lament for Tibullus, Ovid shows that he has noticed Horace's gloss of the loan-word *elegi* in *Odes* 1.33's description of Albius as singing *miserabilis* ... *elegos*. Ovid's acknowledgement of Horace's etymological gloss is also another piece of evidence, a decisive piece I would say, that the Albius of *Odes* 1.33 must be Tibullus. Note too that *Amores* 3.9 is another poem much concerned with different genres. It starts with two mourning figures from epic (Aurora and Thetis, the mothers of

---

21 McKeown 1987, 79: "the lament in 3.9 would have been written most appropriately within a short time after Tibullus' death".
22 O'Hara 1996b.

Memnon and Achilles), and "not only buries an elegist and his themes but also reclaims elegy for one of its original functions, lamentation".[23] Throughout the poem Ovid not only reworks lines from Tibullus' own verse, especially Tibullus 1.3, which combines lamentation with clear references to Homer's *Odyssey.*[24] As Reed has shown, Ovid also weaves in material from two late Hellenistic hexameter poems, Bion's *Lament for Adonis* and the anonymous poem known as [Moschus] 3 or the *Epitaphion Bionis*, a lament for Bion himself.[25]

To sum up: we have seen considerable evidence for broad Greek and Roman knowledge of the derivation of words for elegy from Greek words like ἒ ἒ λέγειν ("to say ah, ah") or ἔλεος ("pity"). The Roman evidence shows both knowledge of the etymology, and frequent allusion or reference to it in poems discussing genre.

This context allows us to see that Virgil is alluding to the etymology of *elegi* and so to elegy and to love poetry more generally in 6.441 *Lugentes campi; sic illos nomine dicunt*. Both this passage of the *Aeneid*, and indeed the whole story of Dido in the poem, are much concerned with genre, and especially with connections between genre and gender. Some of this attention to genre is apparent even in Book 1,[26] but it is particularly prominent in Book 4, in whose first line the reference to Dido as *saucia cura* evokes the poetry of love as it appears or is discussed in Ennius' *Medea*, Lucretius' denunciation of romantic love, and Catullus.[27] Book 4 blends features from Homeric and Apollonian epic (drawing on Apollonius' erotic Book 3), Greek and Roman tragedy (especially Medea and Alcestis, but also Ajax), Catullan epyllion's lovesick Ariadne, and "the intricate devices required by a love-plot" in comedy.[28] It also employs a great many motifs from love elegy and related genres, as Francis Cairns has dis-

---

23 Harrison 2002, 81. Domitius Marsus, fr. 7 Courtney pairs epic and elegy in one poem lamenting the deaths of both Tibullus and Virgil. Myers 2013 has discussed this poem together with Virgil's *Lugentes Campi*, and I thank him for sharing with me a copy of his unpublished paper.
24 Cf. Bright 1971, Cairns 1979, 44–46, Maltby 2002, 183, 185 f., Huskey 2005.
25 Reed 1997.
26 Cf. e. g. Hinds 2000, 230: "whereas the Carthaginian episode in *Aeneid* I and 4 boasts the full paraphernalia of epic divine machinery, the agent of that machinery [in *Aen.* 1.657–722] is none other than Cupid, the divine player stereotypically associated with erotic elegy; remember [Ovid] *Rem. am.* 379 *blanda pharetratos Elegia cantet Amores*".
27 Cf. Ennius, *Medea* fr. 216 Jocelyn *amore saeuo saucia*, Lucr. 4.1048 *saucia amore*, and Catullus 64.250 *multiplices animo uoluebat saucia curas*.
28 These words are from the discussion in Anderson 1981, 115 of Servius' introduction to *Aen.* 4, which Anderson is paraphrasing: *sane totus in consiliis et subtilitatibus est; nam paene comicus stilus est: nec mirum, ubi de amore tractatur.*

cussed at length and Stephen Hinds and others more briefly.[29] Hinds' paragraph is part of his valuable discussion of how women, though always a part of Greek and Roman epic, are also always depicted as out of place in epic, or as violating the essence of male heroic epic.[30] In the *Aeneid*, as opposed to in the passages from Horace, Tibullus, and Ovid mentioned above, the generic contrast between epic and elegy is often depicted as a conflict between male epic concerns and female amatory concerns.

Neither the brief treatment of Hinds, nor Cairns' extensive catalogue of elegiac motifs associated with Dido, include any discussion of Book 6, but the attention called to the name *Lugentes campi* at 641 is the first of many features pointing to elegy and to erotic poetry more generally; we may even think of *Lugentes campi* as not only an "etymological signpost", as I have called it, but a generic "signpost" marking the start of inclusion of material from other genres in the poem, to adapt Horsfall's use of the term "segnali per strada" or "signposts by the wayside" for other passages in the *Aeneid.*[31] The six women mentioned before Dido in 445–449, Phaedra, Procris, Eriphyle, Euadne, Pasiphae, Laodamia and Caeneus, correspond, at times imprecisely, to various aspects of Dido's own story (overwhelming love, divine interference, death by wound and/or on a pyre, playing male and female roles).[32] They are not primarily women from extant Latin love elegy (though Propertius at least briefly mentions Phaedra, Eriphyle, Euadne and Pasiphae, and Catullus 68 treats Laodamia at length)[33], but we have seen that earlier associations of the word and genre "elegy" include poetry of love in a variety of genres. Building on observations of Norden's about Virgil's debt in 641–676 to erotic verse, Feldherr and Myers

---

29 Cairns 1989, 29–57, Hinds 2000, 230f., Saylor 1986, Harrison 2007, 208–214.

30 Hinds 2000, 223: "The role of the female in actual epics never becomes canonized within stereotyped descriptions of the genre, but a case can be made that *surprise* at the role of the female in actual epics *does* become so canonized: woman never becomes theorized into epic as an essential element of the genre, but woman does achieve a kind of essentialized theoretical status as an ambusher of the purity of epic. How the regular-as-clockwork involvement of the female in the actual plots of epic can be obsessively characterized as adulterating the genre, without ever really coming to be characterized as defining it, is a question that exposes the well-known but little understood tension between Roman generic theory and Roman generic practice". Cf. too Keith 2000, esp. (but not only) 8–35.

31 Cf. Horsfall 1991, 103–116 on "segnali per strada" and now Horsfall 2016, 95–110 on "signposts" in the *Aeneid* that point to other genres or bodies of poetry, among them the references to *annales* at 1.373, Venus' tragic *cothurnus* at 1.337 and *scaenis agitatus Orestes* at 4.469–473.

32 Horsfall 2013 ad locc. lists many modern suggestions for each figure, with extensive bibliography, as well as all we know of debts to various sources.

33 Alexandra Daly has suggested to me that Virgil may be reacting to and correcting the (largely) rosy picture of lovers (*cuicumque rapax Mors uenit amanti*) in Elysium in Tibullus 1.3.57–66.

have noted the many features of 6.441–476 pointing to love poetry, and the tension between elegy and epic that they evoke. We may mention here the *durus amor* and "cruel wasting" (*crudeli tabe*) of 442, the *secreti calles* and myrtle (sacred to Venus) wood of 443 f., the *curae* that survive death in 445, Dido's wandering (*errabat*, 451) and her wound (*uulnere*, 450) that is both a literal sign of how she died and an evocation of the word *saucia* of 4.1 and other wound imagery in 4, Aeneas' tears (455, 476 and perhaps 478) and his speaking to Dido *dulce ... amore*, and his telling her not to flee (*quem fugis?* 466). In 458 Aeneas swears an oath, as lovers often do, then in the most well-known line in the passage Virgil has him say *inuitus, regina, tuo de litore cessi*, "unwillingly, queen, I parted from your shore" (460), adapting a line spoken in the elegiac Catullus 66, itself adapted from the elegiac model in Callimachus.[34] As the passage closes Dido returns to her husband Sychaeus, who reciprocates her love in a way found in Latin poetry only in the longings of the epigrams of Catullus: *respondet curis aequatque Sychaeus amorem*, "Sychaeus responds to her cares and gives her love for love" (474). Aeneas weeps and feels pity for her as she leaves: *nec minus Aeneas casu percussus iniquo / prosequitur lacrimis longe et miseratur euntem*, "yet none the less, stricken by her unjust doom, Aeneas follows her with tears afar and pities her as she goes" (475 f.). Later in Book 6 Virgil puts another allusion to Catullan elegy, although Catullus 101 and not erotic elegy, in the mouth of Aeneas' father Anchises right before he tells Aeneas of how much he feared that his time at Carthage would "harm" him (692–694):

> quas ego te terras et quanta per aequora uectum
> accipio! quantis iactatum, nate, periclis!
> quam metui ne quid Libyae tibi regna nocerent!
>
> Over what lands, and through what wide seas have you journeyed
> to my welcome! What dangers have beset you, my son!
> How I feared the realm of Libya might work you harm!

This allusion to and reworking of the first line, *multas per gentes et multa per aequora uectus*, "Having journeyed through many peoples and through many seas", of Catullus' lament for his dead brother in Poem 101[35] caps the allusions

34 Catull. 66.39, Callim. fr. 110 Pf. See Feldherr 1999, 107–111, and for recent work see Nappa 2007, 387 f., Pelliccia 2011, Knox 2015.

35 Catullus' line of course comes already loaded with its own allusions to epic, in recasting the πολλὰ ... πολλῶν... πολλά of *Od.* 1.1–3, as Virgil will do in *Aen* 1.3–5; at 6.692–694, where *iactatum* echoes *Aen.* 1.3's *iactatus*, Virgil makes clear that he has seen what Catullus did. Cf. Conte 1986, 32–39, Harrison 2007, 221 f., Horsfall 2013, 470.

to elegy, love poetry, and lamentation that begin with 441 *Lugentes Campi; sic illos nomine dicunt.* Whether Aeneas and his epic mission have come through his experience in Africa without being "harmed" is a question different readers will answer in different ways, but the answer should involve thinking about genre, gender, and etymology. [36]

36 Cf. again Feldherr 1999, Myers 2013, Horsfall 2013, 470 f., with references. Questions about the function of the *Lugentes Campi* episode may be compared to those about the function of the speech of lament by Turnus' sister the rape-victim Juturna in 12.869–886; see the discussion by Perkell 1997 of whether "Juturna's lament is to be construed as marginalized and impotent" (264) or "Her lament temporarily halts the martial, forward-driving, male action of the poem and focuses the reader's attention on what I would claim is the immoral quality of Jupiter, even as he exemplifies Roman victory" (271).

Julia Hejduk

Saepe stilum uertas: Moral and Metrical Missteps in Horace's *Satires*

When teaching Latin poetry, I often tell my students that scanning is like riding a bicycle: keep at it, and one glorious day it will just work. But in Horace *Satires* 1.10, about the writing style of Lucilius and others (including Horace), we hit a pothole on lines 72f., *Saepe stilum uertas iterum quae digna legi sint / scripturus* ("You should often invert the stylus [that is, scrape the wax away with the blunt end, like an eraser] if you're going to write something that's worth re-reading"). Following the rule that the syllable before two consonants (other than stop + liquid) is always long would generate a "long-short-long" pattern in -ē stĭl-ūmv, an impossibility in the hexameter. We remarked that Horace himself should have used the eraser on this line, which apparently violates its own instructions, like saying "You gots to have good grammar"—and then we remembered that we had stumbled before over an E that should have been lengthened and was not. Intrigued, I decided to investigate just how often Horace had a syllable with a short vowel not lengthened before the ST beginning the following word, a phenomenon I call SEST (for "Short E -ST"), or before SP, SC, and SQ.[1] The content of the passages in which this occurs led me to conclude that a SEST would, in fact, have been perceived as a minor metrical solecism by Horace's readers and that *saepe stilum uertas* is the punch-line of a subtle metrical joke, a choice illustration of Horace's interweaving of the moral and the aesthetic throughout the *Satires*.[2]

My first surprising discovery was that I had stepped on a hornets' nest. Consider this sample from William Ramsay's *A Manual of Latin Prosody* (1859), a glimpse into a bygone era when metrical matters could stir passions:

> The quantity of a vowel naturally short, when it occurs at the end of a word, and the next word begins with S, followed by one or more consonants, has been a subject of keen controversy among metrical scholars; and different writers, after fully discussing the question, have arrived at opposite conclusions.[3]

1 For convenience, I use SEST for any short vowel before an S + stop consonant. Commentators tell us merely that Horace does this sometimes; see Palmer 1883, 238.

2 See Morgan 2011, 334–345 on Horace's exploitation of the dissonance between form and content, and in particular the paradox that "aesthetic principles and satire are fundamentally incompatible" (354).

3 Ramsay 1859, 271.

https://doi.org/10.1515/9783110545708-008

Ramsay begins by quoting some Latin doggerel from the treatise "On Syllables" by third-century grammarian Terentianus Maurus:

> quae sibi tres tantum poterit subiungere mutas,
> si quando SCutum SPumas vel STamina dico.
> haec sola efficiet, nudo ut remanente trochaeo
> spondeum geminae possint firmare sonorae.
> exemplis, an praua sequar uel recta, probato.
> quisquE SCire cupit vel quisquE SCRibere curat,
> antE STare decet cum dico et separo uerbum,
> antE STesichorum uatem natura creavit,
> ultima uocalis remanens finisque trochaei
> excipitur geminis, quis proximus exoritur pes;
> quae quamquam capite alterius uerbi teneantur,
> sufficiant retro uires et tempus oportet,
> consona quod debet geminata referre priori.
> (Terentianus Maurus, *De Syllabis* 1058–70)

> (The letter "S"), which will be able to subjoin to itself only three mutes,
> if I ever say *scutum*, *spumas*, or *stamina*.
> This alone will bring about, if the trochee remains bare,
> that two consonants can firm up a spondee.
> I shall prove by examples whether I'm following a crooked or straight path.
> Whoever desires to know, or whoever cares to write,
> *ante stare* is fitting, when I pronounce and separate the word ("ante");
> *ante Stesichorum uatem natura creavit*;
> the final vowel remaining, and the end of the trochee,
> is taken up by the doubled (consonants) with which the next foot begins,
> which, although they are stuck at the beginning of the second word,
> should supply backward that strength and time
> which a doubled consonant ought to give back to the previous
> (syllable in its own word).

Following this lead, Ramsay tells us, Richard Dawes derived the following "canon":

> *The Latin poets, after the time of Lucretius, lengthened a naturally short vowel at the end of a word, when the following word begins with* SC, SP, SQ, ST. *But this is not observed by the Satirists, in whose compositions, which are* sermoni propriora, *such minute accuracy could not be expected.*[4]

Ramsay, however, will have none of it. After painstakingly examining every occurrence of a short vowel before these consonant clusters in a variety of poets,

4 Dawes 1781, 4 f., paraphrased by Ramsay 1859, 272.

and accounting for apparent exceptions (foreign words like *smaragdos* or proper names like Scamander that cannot appear in hexameters otherwise), he puts forth an alternative canon:

> *The Roman poets of the Augustan age, and their successors, in serious compositions, carefully avoided placing a word ending with a short vowel before a word beginning with* sc, sp, sq, st, *and this collocation ought never to be introduced into modern Latin poetry.*[5]

Satire, of course, is not a "serious composition", and therefore need not obey the rules of decorum that must be observed in the "modern Latin poetry" produced by nineteenth century gentleman-scholars.[6]

Whatever the merits of Ramsay's interpretation and the prescriptive conclusion he draws from it, some interesting facts emerge from his analysis. One is that Augustan poets do avoid SESTs entirely or almost entirely.[7] Another is that Horace, in his *Satires*, has six short vowels before ST and two before SC. A third is that Horace in his *other* compositions has *no* short vowels, lengthened or not, before the above-named consonant clusters. How should we interpret this skewed distribution?

There appear to be three main possibilities. Option A is Dawes' view that in the deliberately colloquial genre of Satire, "such minute accuracy could not be expected": that is, that Horace is still doing something metrically incorrect, but we should forgive him because Satire does not require the same precision as other genres. Option B is more satisfying: that far from showing inattention to the demands of "minute accuracy", Horace's SESTs are intended to contribute to the *Satires'* conversational tone and flavor, like a novelist putting "ain't" in the mouth of a character. But option C, which includes and amplifies the other two, is the most satisfying: that Horace's "flaws" are intended to be perceived as such and to teach the reader a quintessentially Horatian lesson about flaws, namely,

---

5 Ramsay 1859, 280.

6 Personal footnote: I, too, require my advanced Latin students to produce four lines of metrically correct verse, and one eager to write about squirrels was deeply disappointed to find that Latin *sciūrus* cannot fit into a hexameter. (Have you ever seen a squirrel in the *Georgics?*) She had to write about cows instead.

7 Propertius appears to be the only one who allows SESTs with some frequency; Platnauer 1951, 62f. cites Prop. 3.11.53 (*bracchiă spectaui*—though *bracchia* could possibly be scanned as a spondee), 3.11.67 (*nunc ubĭ Scipiadae*), 3.19.21 (*uenumdată Scylla figura*), 4.1.41 (*iam benĕ spondebant*), and 4.4.48 (*tu capĕ spinosi*), to which could possibly be added 4.5.17 (*consuluitquĕ striges*, though the omission of *–que* and the lengthening of *strīges* are possible here: see Heyworth 2007a, 453). Virgil has only one instance, *Aen.* 11.309 (*ponitĕ. spes sibi quisque*); as Fordyce 1961, 320 notes, this is after a strong pause.

that one should combine the acumen to discern such blemishes with the wisdom to forgive them.

Two Horatian SESTs, from the diatribe on ridiculous sexual behavior in S. 1.2, form a complementary pair in phrases describing extreme types of women that the wise man had best avoid. The first hails from a passage asserting one of Horace's most important themes, that of finding the golden mean—a precept at which most men fail spectacularly when it comes to sex (1.2.28–30):

> nil medium est. sunt qui nolint tetigisse nisi illas
> quarum subsuta talos tegat instita ueste;
> contra alius nullam nisi olenti in fornicE STantem.

> There's no middle. There are some who'd refuse to touch any women
> but those with a flounce sewn into the hem that covers their ankles;
> others, on the other hand, only one standing in a stinking brothel.

Horace's point is reinforced by the metrical harshness of *fornice stantem:* the stinking brothel has become a SEST-pool, with a sexual *uitium* illustrated by a metrical *uitium.* The poem's second SEST, describing the opposite class of woman, employs the voice of a *mutto* momentarily endowed with speech. The man referred to is Villius, who was roundly beaten and otherwise humiliated for having an affair with the aristocratic Sulla's daughter (1.2.68–72):

> huic si muttonis uerbis mala tanta uidenti
> diceret haec animus "quid uis tibi? numquid ego a te
> magno prognatum deposco consule cunnum
> uelatumquE STola, mea cum conferbuit ira?"
> quid responderet? "magno patre nata puella est".

> To this man, as he gazes upon such evils, if his spirit
> should say in the words of his *mutto*, "What's wrong with you? I ask you,
> do I ever demand from you a *cunnus* descended from a great consul
> and veiled in a matron's robe, when my angry passion's boiling up?"
> What would he answer? "The girl is born from a great father".

This passage is full of shockers, metrical and otherwise: the harsh elision between the fifth and sixth foot in 70, *ego a te*, would have been at least as jarring to refined Roman ears as the obscene words I have left untranslated.[8] The reader or listener, already startled by the obscenity and the elision, would thus find the SEST in *uelatumque stola* right in character for the irascible speaker of these lines. The poem's two SESTs, then, *fornice stantem* and *uelatumque stola*—

8 See Nilsson 1952, 34 f.; Eskuche 1890, 386.

"standing in a brothel" and "veiled in a matron's robe"—happen to encapsulate in two pithy phrases the two contrasted extremes that the wise man in search of the *aurea mediocritas* of womanhood had best avoid. The first uses a distasteful metrical feature to describe a distasteful thing; the second helps to drag the *stola* through the mud, so to speak, both through the primary obscenity veiled by the matronly garment and through the primary obscenity that speaks the line. Despite the questionable persona of the speaker, it appears to be a spokesman for the satirist's true message: avoid extremes and don't be too persnickety. Moderation consists not in ignoring the disadvantages of certain types of female, disadvantages that the slight *frisson* of the SEST points up; rather, the wise man should set his sights on a type who herself represents a sort of "middle way".

The book's third SEST expands this message of moderation and tolerance, for it comes from the sermon in 1.3 on choosing to regard our friends' defects as endearing traits. Horace begins by scolding those who, blind to their own faults, discern with eagle-eyed exactitude those of others (1.3.25–28):

> cum tua peruideas oculis mala lippus inunctis,
> cur in amicorum uitiis tam cernis acutum
> quam aut aquila aut serpens Epidaurius? at tibi contra
> euenit, inquirant uitia ut tua rursus et illi.

> Whereas you look on your own evils blearily, with smeared eyes,
> why do you have such sharp-eyed vision for your friends' vices
> as an eagle or the Epidaurian serpent? But it happens
> that they, in turn, are scrutinizing *your* vices the same way.

This passage touches on one of the pervasive ironies of the *Satires*. On the one hand, the satirist's job is to see and express things clearly, to pinpoint the manifold faults of humanity and pounce upon them like an eagle upon its prey. The reference to the *Epidaurian* serpent reinforces the rectitude of this clear-sightedness: "Epidaurian" makes the serpent the avatar of Aesculapius, god of medicine (with a shrine at Epidaurus), implying that discernment precedes healing. On the other hand, several scholars have persuasively argued that images of poor eyesight, blindness, and voluntary smearing of the eyes point to what appears to be the opposite message: especially in the volatile political climate of the years between Philippi and Actium, it sometimes makes sense for the poet's vision not to be too acute.[9] On the journey to Brundisium, for instance, Horace famously smears his runny eyes with black salve just at the point where Maecenas and Cocceius are poised for some important diplomacy (1.5.27–31):

---

9 Oliensis 1998, 27f.; Reckford 1999, 525; Gowers 2002.

huc uenturus erat Maecenas optimus atque
Cocceius, missi magnis de rebus uterque
legati, auersos soliti conponere amicos.
hic oculis ego nigra meis collyria lippus
inlinere.

Excellent Maecenas was about to come here, and Cocceius,
both sent as ambassadors concerning great things,
skilled at reconciling friends who had grown apart.
Here, for my watery eye problem, I smeared some black salve
on my eyes.

The path of the wise satirist, like that of the Callimachean poet, includes a calculated avoidance of viewing "great things" (*magnae res*). This tension between seeing and not seeing, or choosing not to see, is thus a key element in the satirist's self-presentation.

After this prelude, Horace illustrates his point about overlooking vices with an entertaining twist on the *topos* of lovers' euphemisms. Whereas Lucretius had described this phenomenon with scathing sarcasm in his diatribe on romantic love (4.1153–1170), noting that the besotted lover will call his gangly girlfriend "gazelle" and so on, Horace affirms that in fact we *should* view our friends through the rose-tinted glasses of lovers or parents (1.3.38–48):

illuc praeuertamur, amatorem quod amicae
turpia decipiunt caecum uitia, aut etiam ipsa haec
delectant, ueluti Balbinum polypus Hagnae.
uellem in amicitia sic erraremus, et isti
errori nomen uirtus posuisset honestum.
ac pater ut gnati sic nos debemus amici
si quod sit uitium non fastidirE: STRabonem
appellat paetum pater, et pullum, male paruus
sicui filius est, ut abortiuus fuit olim
Sisyphus; hunc uarum distortis cruribus, illum
balbutit scaurum prauis fultum male talis.

Let's pay attention to this: how the disgraceful flaws
of his girlfriend escape the blind lover, or those very things
even delight him, as Hagna's nose-wen did Balbinus.
I could wish we'd make the same mistake in friendship
and virtue could have given an honorable name to that "error".
And as a father about his son's, so we should not
be fastidious about some flaw of our friend's: "squinty"
is what a father calls his cross-eyed son, and "chick",
if he's got one that's terribly short, as the preemie
Sisyphus once was; this one with deformed legs is "knock-kneed";
for that one badly supported on crooked ankles, his father coos, "rickety".

Far from being a culpable *error*, Horace argues, this inclination to forgive, and even to find beauties in apparent faults, should be considered a virtue. It is precisely where he tells us not to be fastidious about a friend's *uitium* that his own metrical *uitium* occurs, the SEST in *fastidire strabonem*. Moreover, amid all these metaphors of sight—the eagle, the serpent, the bleary-eyed friend, the blind lover —the sample euphemism Horace has chosen seems particularly apt: like the darling son, the poet and his disciples should be considered charmingly "squinty", not disgracefully cross-eyed. For their willingness to see things in soft focus derives from conscious choice and laudable affection, not from defective ability.

Supporting the idea that this fault—or virtue—of squintiness has thematic resonance are some potentially metapoetic implications in the *uitia* Horace subsequently highlights. The adverb *male* can be used in two opposite senses: its ostensible meaning here is as an intensive (*OLD* s.v. 10a), "awfully", but it can also have the sense of "imperfectly, poorly" (*OLD* s.v. 4), so that the phrase *male paruus* could mean either "awfully short" or "poorly short". The feminine of *paruus* can refer to a short syllable (*OLD* s.v. 1), and in fact, a "poorly short" syllable—that is, a syllable that is short but should by right be long—happens to be what Horace has just produced. The next set of vices involve deformities of the legs and the feet; given the ubiquitous association in Latin poetry between human feet and metrical feet, the designation "badly supported on crooked ankles" (*prauis fultum male talis*), especially with the awkward non-coincidence of ictus and accent in the fifth foot (*fúlTUM mále*), could again be tied to the metrical awkwardness of the poem's feet. A passage from the *Epistles* criticizing that hack playwright Plautus offers an interesting comparandum (2.1.173–176):

> quantus sit Dossenus edacibus in parasitis,
> quam non adstricto percurrat pulpita socco;
> gestit enim nummum in loculos demittere, post hoc
> securus cadat an recto stet fabula talo.
>
> What a big clown he is in his gluttonous parasites,
> with what a floppy slipper he pelts across the stage;
> for he's itching to get the coins in his cash box; after that
> he doesn't care whether his play falls or stands on sturdy ankle.

Foot puns and metonymies abound here: the *soccus*, a slipper worn by comic actors, of course stands for comedy itself; Horace imagines Plautus running across the stage with this shoe untied; but in the final metaphor, it is the play itself that either falls down or stands on its feet. While this passage again emphasizes the identification of an author with his work, it also illustrates Horace's ingenuity in combining genre-specific footwear with a foot metaphor for artistic success or failure. Such wordplay supports the idea that Horace's choice of various foot deformities in the *Satires* euphemism passage, along with the "awfully/poorly short" child, could be a playful, erudite nod to the metrically challenged foot he has just produced. Physical, moral, and artistic failings—all designated by that same loaded word, *uitia*—have a tendency to melt into one another for Horace; such are the risks a poet takes when he becomes his poem.

The precedent established by these first three SESTs helps to illuminate the self-mocking humor in the clause *saepe stilum uertas* (1.10.72) with which this essay began. Horace is defending his model Lucilius, again equating the man with his poetry (1.10.67–73):

> sed ille,
> si foret hoc nostrum fato delapsus in aeuum,
> detereret sibi multa, recideret omne quod ultra
> perfectum traheretur, et in uersu faciendo
> saepe caput scaberet uiuos et roderet unguis.
> saepE STilum uertas, iterum quae digna legi sint
> scripturus...

> But he,
> if by Fate he had been dropped into this age of ours,
> would be filing himself down a lot, cutting back everything
> dragged in beyond perfection, and in making verse
> would be often scratching his head and nibbling his nails to the quick.
> You should often invert the stylus, if you're to write things worthy
> to be re-read...

The advice to re-write what one hopes to make worthy of re-reading calls attention to itself as illustrating its own precept: we have in fact just "re-read" Horace's criticism of Lucilius' hasty composition from *Sat.* 1.4.[10] But why, if Horace is criticizing the roughness of Lucilius' verse, does he place a metrical flaw right in the middle of his injunction to polish? I would suggest that he is showing how, in this genre exploring the rough edges of human nature, the satirist should not be too smooth. Earlier in the poem, he praises the rough-and-tumble of the ancient Greek comedians while criticizing the effeminate preciosity of the neoterics.[11] Here he implicitly conveys that part of Satire's particular perfection is not to be too perfect—just as the unique quirks and imperfections of our friends should make us love them more, not less. With the SEST embedded in *saepe stilum*, Horace displays his own fallibility, his ability to poke fun at himself, and the avoidance of extremes so central to his poetry and his philosophy.

10 Gowers 2012, 333.
11 See Crowther 1978; Schlegel 2010.

The four remaining SESTs fit the pattern of thematically significant metrical violations, and also happen to appear in the context of insanity—not an uncommon context in the *Satires*, but still at least mildly suggestive. The first is from the journey to Brundisium, in which Horace and his companions encounter a small-town praetor too big for his toga (1.5.34–36):

Fundos Aufidio Lusco praetore libenter
linquimus, insani ridentes praemiA SCRibae,
praetextam et latum clauum prunaeque uatillum.

Fundi, with Aufidius Luscus the Praetor, we happily
left behind, laughing at the crazy clerk's insignia,
his toga with border and broad stripe and dish of coals.

What makes this minor official ludicrous, *insanus* even, is that he considers himself a major official, a small man trying to pretend that he is a big one. The metrical dissonance of *praemia scribae* reflects the dissonance between the man's inflated opinion of himself and the reality of his puny office; it is especially appropriate that this "scribe" should be implicated in a solecism involving writing (*scribere*), even if the writer in this case is Horace (who himself once held the position of quaestorian scribe, according to Suetonius' *Life*). The other SEST, from a sermon by the rustic sage Ofellus on temperate living (2.2), appears in a passage targeting people who lust after a big mullet because that fish is naturally small, and a small bass because that fish is naturally big (2.2.33–37):

laudas, insane, trilibrem
mullum in singula quem minuas pulmenta necesse est.
ducit te species, uideo; quo pertinet ergo
proceros odisse lupos? quiA SCilicet illis
maiorem natura modum dedit, his breue pondus.

You crazy one, you praise
a three-pound mullet you'll have to chop up in pieces for sauce.
Its looks attract you, I see; so how does it fit in
to spurn a big long bass? No doubt, because to those
nature has given greater measure, to these small weight.

As Stephen Harrison observes, Ofellus "is carefully chosen to resemble Horace himself" (2013, 157); the reader is encouraged to agree with his application of the epithet *insanus* to one with a disordered understanding of the proper sizes of things. Moreover, this passage is rife with vocabulary applicable to prosody, given that *breuis* can be used for a short syllable (*OLD* s.v. *breuis* 10), *modus* for a metrical beat (*OLD* s.v. *modus* 7a), and *natura* for a syllable long or short "by nature" (e.g., Quint. *Inst.* 1.5.29, *etsi natura breuis, tamen positione longa est*, "even if [the middle syllable of *uolucres*] is short by nature, yet it is long by position"). The SC of *scilicet* tampers with the short (*breuis*) syllabic measure (*modus*) given by nature (*natura*) to the A of *quia*—or would, if normal metrical principles were being observed—just as the crazy gourmet disrespects the "natural" sizes of the fish. Both of these SESTs appear after I's that could conceivably be taken as consonantal, turning *praemja* into a spondee and *quja* into a long monosyllable; in that case, the resulting metrical awkwardness and unnatural lengthening would suit the theme of inappropriate sizing even more dramatically.

Horace's two remaining SESTs confirm the phenomenon's association with insanity. Both appear in 2.3, the diatribe of the ridiculous Stoic convert Damasippus, who contrasts the wisdom of the Stoic philosopher with the foolishness of all other mortals. In the first, Damasippus quotes his Stoic mentor Stertinius (2.3.43–45):

quem malA STultitia et quemcumque inscitia ueri
caecum agit, insanum Chrysippi porticus et grex
autumat.

Whomsoever wicked stupidity and ignorance of truth
drives in blindness, him Chrysippus' colonnade
and herd calls crazy.

By now, it should not be surprising that the phrase for "wicked stupidity", *mala stultitia*, contains a metrical gaffe. The other SEST comes immediately after the extremely lengthy speech of Stertinius that Damasippus has just quoted (2.3.296–299):

haec mihI STertinius, sapientum octauus, amico
arma dedit, posthac ne compellarer inultus.
dixerit insanum qui me totidem audiet atque
respicere ignoto discet pendentia tergo.

Such arms did Stertinius, the eighth of the Sages, supply
for me his friend, so I wouldn't be challenged unavenged anymore.
He who has called me 'crazy' will hear it right back, and will
learn to look around at what's hanging on the back he can't see.

The irony is that this fanatic is himself the craziest and least self-aware of all. As Kirk Freudenberg has shown, the speech of Damasippus violates all kinds of decorum, both in its enormous length and in its other copious metrical anomalies: as he observes, "mad men are best painted in mad verse" (1996,

205). Specifically, Damasippus scorns and violates the Callimachean principles guiding Horace's poetic composition.[12] So it is appropriate for this nutty and artistically tone-deaf Stoic, especially when impugning the stupidity of others, to do so with a metrical irregularity that might bring to Horace's learned audience a knowing smile.

For a poet like Horace whose works disclose an abiding concern with both morality and *ars poetica*, a metrical flaw could well have moral implications. Though on some level this implicit equation of poet and poem seems odd, on another it makes intuitive sense. When we say, "I love reading Horace", or even "I love Horace", our shorthand reflects a deep reality, an intimacy beautifully exemplified in the passionate scholarship of this volume's honoree. Think of Horace's famous reference to shuffling Ennius' bombastic words and finding the limbs of a dismembered poet (*Sat.* 1.4.62), or Ovid's triumphant and accurate proclamation at the end of the *Metamorphoses*, "*I* shall live!" If a poem is the poet's second self, then the stakes are high; the emotionally charged intellectual duel of Dawes and Ramsay over metrical minutiae would have been perfectly understandable to the likes of Horace and Ovid. Are our own emotional priorities so much better aligned? While Horace's prosodic peccadilloes in his *Satires* may not provide the best model for writers of "serious" Latin verse, the discernment, humor, and charity they beg from his readers are perhaps worthy of emulation, never more so than in perilously divisive times.

12 Cf. Sharland 2009, 116f.

Hayden Pelliccia

The reception of Horace *Odes* 2.4 in Horace *Odes* 2.5

Nondum subacta ferre iugum ualet
ceruice, nondum munia comparis
    aequare nec tauri ruentis
        in Venerem tolerare pondus.
circa uirentis est animus tuae
campos iuuencae, nunc fluuiis gravem
    solantis aestum, nunc in udo
        ludere cum uitulis salicto
praegestientis. tolle cupidinem
immitis uuae: iam tibi liuidos
    distinguet autumnus racemos
        purpureo uarius colore.
iam te sequetur; currit enim ferox
aetas et illi quos tibi dempserit
    adponet annos; iam proterua
        fronte petet Lalage maritum,
dilecta quantum non Pholoe fugax,
non Chloris albo sic umero nitens
    ut pura nocturno renidet
        luna mari Cnidiusue Gyges,
quem si puellarum insereres choro,
mire sagacis falleret hospites
    discrimen obscurum solutis
        crinibus ambiguoque uultu.

She's not broken in yet and her neck hasn't the strength
to bear the yoke. She can't share duties
    with a partner yet or bear the weight
        of a bull plunging into love.
That young heifer of yours still has her mind
on grassy meadows, finding relief
    from oppressive heat in rivers, or longing
        to begin playing with yearlings
in willow marshes. Banish your desire
for the unripe grape. Autumn in all his variety
    will soon mark out the blue clusters for you,
        tinging them with purple.
She'll soon be following you. Time runs
on untamed and will credit her with the years
    it takes from you. Lalage will soon be butting
        her mate with lusty forehead
and be loved more than the elusive Pholoe,

https://doi.org/10.1515/9783110545708-009

more than Chloris, whose white shoulder gleams
like the pure moon glinting
on the night sea, more than Gyges.
Put him in a dance with girls and the subtle difference
would wonderfully deceive your most perceptive guests—
that flowing hair
and that ambiguous face.

Carm. 2.5 (transl. West, modified)

Nisbet and Hubbard (hereafter N-H) identify as "the primary problem of this poem" the lack of a clearly identified addressee, and settle on the poet himself as the least troublesome possibility. They ultimately spend more time on another problem, however:

> Our poem takes from Anacreon [417 *PMG*] the idea of talking about a girl in a series of sustained animal metaphors, but whereas the *double entendre* in the original is characteristically elegant and discreet, Horace seems to rush into love-poetry like a bull in a china-shop. The Romans were no doubt often brutal in their sexual habits, and Horace had a talent for sustained impropriety (*epist.* 1.20.1 ff.), but his crudity here needs some explanation; after all, he is purporting to show his restraint towards the girl.

To meet this problem the commentators suggest that Horace is not in fact showing restraint: at the beginning of the poem he adopts the mode of iambos in order to abuse a female who is unavailable to him; then, with the "dying fall" of the last two stanzas, the poet makes a "change from a major to a minor key": "we have proceeded from the iambic to the elegiac mood, in the manner of the *Epodes*". Thus, "[i]n spite of its brutal opening the poem turns out to have subtlety as well as ingenuity".[1] Other commentators accept that any reading must begin by addressing the problem of the apparent "brutality" of the beginning,[2] even if the solution is to deny it. West, for example, notes that the ode "is often condemned for its tastelessness or brutality, with particular reference to the weight of the plunging bull",[3] and works his way clear by abjuring any sexual subtext for the metaphors of the opening lines.[4]

1 N-H 78–80.

2 E.g., Günther 2013, 343 f., "ostentatiously crude", "crude"; Sutherland 2002, 98 "a vivid but disturbing image".

3 West 1998, 34.

4 West 1998, 36: "the details of the metaphor should be enjoyed for themselves, not milked for their sexual application" ("milked": cf. N-H's "bull in a china-shop"); he then says that it is only with *praegestientis* that "at last the sexual allusion surfaces"—puzzlingly, in light of *tauri ruentis in Venerem*, which perhaps in its pungent frankness does not count as an allusion.

My suggestion in this paper is that the brutality of the plunging bull mounting the too-young heifer is just what it seems and as such is intended to startle us out of the complacent "urbanity" with which we are likely to have read, with the poet's connivance, the previous poem in the book, which also takes as its subject love or sex with a problematic love- or sex-object:[5]

Ne sit ancillae tibi amor pudori,
Xanthia Phoceu; prius insolentem
serua Briseis niueo colore
  mouit Achillem;
mouit Aiacem Telamone natum
forma captiuae dominum Tecmessae;
arsit Atrides medio in triumpho
  uirgine rapta,
barbarae postquam cecidere turmae
Thessalo uictore et ademptus Hector
tradidit fessis leuiora tolli
  Pergama Grais.
nescias an te generum beati
Phyllidis flauae decorent parentes;
regium certe genus et penatis
  maeret iniquos.
Crede non illam tibi de scelesta
plebe dilectam, neque sic fidelem,
sic lucro auersam potuisse nasci
  matre pudenda.
Bracchia et uultum teretesque suras
integer laudo: fuge suspicari
cuius octauum trepidauit aetas
  claudere lustrum.

Do not be ashamed,[6] Phocian Xanthias,
of your love for a slave-girl. Ere now the slave Briseïs
with her white skin moved the heart
  of proud Achilles;

5 Sutherland 2002, 91–101 treats the two poems sequentially under the heading "Erotic training in *C.* 2.4–2.5", with a very different take on 2.4 from mine. Ancona 1994, 39 aptly notes that "[t]he placement of *Odes* 2.5 immediately after [the last stanza of 2.4] continues the theme of the problematic relationship between aging and sexuality".

6 Kiessling and Heinze (hereafter K-H), N-H, and Harrison (hereafter H) ad loc. say *ne … sit* is a purpose clause rather than a prohibition; I incline towards the latter, with Shackleton Bailey 1985 (semi-colon after *Phoceu*) and Syndikus (hereafter S) 2001, 358 n. 8, but Thomas 2011, 198 f., now the best discussion, inclines to the former. The difference between "In case you are ashamed, (consider that) Briseïs stirred Achilles" and "Don't be ashamed: B stirred A" is elu-

the beauty of the captive Tecmessa moved her master,
Ajax, son of Telamon; the son of Atreus in his hour
of triumph burned with love
for the maid who was ravished
after the barbarian squadrons had fallen
to the Thessalian victor, and the removal
of Hector made it a lighter task for weary Greeks
to raze Troy to the ground.
For all you know your flaxen-haired Phyllis
has wealthy parents, a credit to any son-in-law.
Her family, no doubt of it, is royal and she mourns
the gods who have turned against it.
Do not imagine that you could have picked such a one
out of the gutter, or that one so faithful,
so unmercenary, could have a mother
to be ashamed of.
I praise her arms, her face, her shapely calves—
but am immune. Do not for a moment
suspect a man when Time has raced
to close his fourth decade.

(transl. West, modified)

"[Horace] writes a cheerful love poem, adopting his familiar posture as the Professor of Love, *Praeceptor Amoris*, ... In the first half ... the teasing consists mainly of epic parody ... There is more fun with epic in the application of heroic exempla to this unheroic situation".[7] "The Ode is of course satirical throughout, and the style mock-heroic".[8] "Horaz macht sich offentsichtlich lustig".[9] "... il tono scherzoso di tutta l'ode".[10] "[A]vuncular banter"; "upper-class Roman banter"; Horace "professes to take seriously his young friend's infatuation";[11] "lediglich Neckerei".[12]

That is a representative sample of interpretative comments on 2.4.[13] The recurrent note is "banter": the avuncular Horace teases (N-H 66, West 1998, 36 *bis*,

sive but seems slight, and Brink 1969, 6, n. 1 declined to include the passage in his account of the idiom because it does not have the *forte* of *Ars P.* 406.

7 West 1998, 30.

8 Page 1920, 36.

9 S 359.

10 Pasquali 1920, 495.

11 N-H 67f.

12 K-H on line 13.

13 Selected with a view to pithiness. We could add lengthier versions such as Davis 1991, 22, "the pedagogic speaker of the 'light' love-lyric has built his humorous argument on the ruins of epic enterprise, having undermined military achievement and, conversely, glorified erotic

Günther 2013, 342) a young friend from the slave-owning class about his current not-to-be-taken-too-seriously infatuation with an *ancilla*. Fun is had "in the application of heroic exempla to this unheroic situation", then again with a tongue-in-cheek argument that so sterling a character as the girl's must derive from noble stock, and "a final twist" (N-H 68) by which Uncle Horace is himself brought into the joke.

I believe "banter from Uncle Horace" is how Horace himself set the poem up to be read. That is the direction in which its internal indications point: as the commentators observe, the mock-epic analogies of 1–12 yield to the coercive intimacies of stanzas four and five, where the irony cuts closer to the bone, but any potential pain is then palliated by the deft, Hephaestus-like (*Il.* 1.584–600) diversion of attention to Horace's own comic elderly self: the sight of a comely young *ancilla* is a pleasure that can be enjoyed by slave-owners of all ages.

So, summarily, 2.4 by its internal indications. External to 2.4 is 2.5, which abruptly thrusts before us a much less genial image of non-consensual though "natural" sex. The couplings of horses, deer, bovines, etc. tend to be violent and rape-like, and the hind legs of a young female often enough truly cannot "bear the weight" of the adult male, with ultimately deadly results if humans do not intervene to prevent them (possible only with the domesticated animals; for a young doe a broken hind leg is a death sentence).[14]

I think this shift in register is meant to make us uncomfortable about our reading of 2.4, though all the scholarship I have found on 2.4 takes the situation as Horace presents it, i.e., as normal. N-H, for example, give the historical context:

> Xanthias has admitted to loving a slave-girl. In real life such attachments were regarded with equanimity, and attested even of eminent persons. There is no incompatibility between the ode and contemporary ideology: Augustus himself was concerned with sexual morality only so far as it seemed to affect the national interest ... When Horace advises a

submission"; cf. Cairns 1977, 131–4 ("a strong admixture of irony and sarcasm ... One particularly humorous touch is ... Another touch of humour lies in ..."), Gagliardi 1993, 94; Ludwig 1957, 339 f. is an inventory of German expressions for "have fun with": "Zum Scherz schmückt ihn Horaz mit mythischen Exempeln ... Als Schalk spielt er ... Er macht sich den Spaß ..." Sutherland 2002, 91–6 reads the poem as overtly mocking Xanthias (part of the claimed joke is that he is too impercipient to recognize this).

14 In this article I concentrate on 2.4 to the neglect of 2.5, on which see, in addition to the basic commentaries, e.g., Fantham 1979, Jocelyn 1980, Treggiari 1985 (all three concerned chiefly with Lalage's age and social position), Sutherland 1997 and 2002, 96–101 and the references there. It is interesting that Aristaenetus 2.7, recounting the seduction of a free youth by an infatuated and virgin slave-girl, also uses the unripe grape imagery (2.7.21, 40–42) so conspicuously used in the third stanza of *Odes* 2.5.

social climber not to seduce his patron's slaves, he is only concerned because the great man may want them for himself (*Epist.* 1.18.72ff.).[15]

As an account of societal standards the historical statements here are likely to be correct, but they do not speak to the situation of the ode, which is that described in the first sentence (though "has admitted", presumably inspired by *Odes* 1.27.10–24, is in service of the "bantering" interpretation). If his situation corresponded to the one treated in the rest of the quotation, then why would Xanthias' *amor* cause him *pudor?* The problem posed by the ode is not that Xanthias is suborning a slave for physical relief, but that he has developed feelings for a person: "*amor* is what is at issue, not, as in *Sat.* 1.2, *uoluptas*".[16]

Do the exempla offered by the speaker in 2–12 encourage our minds to the point N-H argue to, i.e., that "such attachments were regarded with equanimity"? Quite clearly not. That a quarrel over concubines nearly destroyed the Achaean army at Troy is not a controversial statement. One of the subtleties of the *Iliad*, however, lies in the complex nature of Achilles' attachment to Briseïs (*Il.* 9.338–343):[17]

τί δὲ λαὸν ἀνήγαγεν ἐνθάδ' ἀγείρας
Ἀτρεΐδης; ἦ οὐχ Ἑλένης ἕνεκ' ἠϋκόμοιο;
ἦ μοῦνοι φιλέουσ' ἀλόχους μερόπων ἀνθρώπων
Ἀτρεΐδαι; ἐπεὶ ὅς τις ἀνὴρ ἀγαθὸς καὶ ἐχέφρων
τὴν αὐτοῦ φιλέει καὶ κήδεται, ὡς καὶ ἐγὼ τὴν
ἐκ θυμοῦ φίλεον δουρικτητήν περ ἐοῦσαν.

Why was it the son of Atreus assembled and led here these people? Was it not for the sake of lovely-haired Helen? Are the sons of Atreus alone among mortal men the ones who love their wives? Since any who is a good man, and careful, loves her who is his own and cares for her, even as I now loved this one from my heart, though it was my spear that won her.

This passage is often written off as a sophistical debating point, though some interpreters have taken it seriously, as do I.[18] Equally indefensible, in my view, is the allied dismissal of Briseïs' report of Patroclus' promises to her (19.295–300):

οὐδὲ μὲν οὐδέ μ' ἔασκες, ὅτ' ἄνδρ' ἐμὸν ὠκὺς Ἀχιλλεὺς
ἔκτεινεν, πέρσεν δὲ πόλιν θείοιο Μύνητος,

15 N-H 67.

16 K-H 176.

17 All translations of Homer are Lattimore's.

18 E.g., Whitman 1958, 186f.; cf. Mitsis 2010, 54–56. I have argued the case briefly in Pelliccia 2017.

κλαίειν, ἀλλά μ' ἔφασκες Ἀχιλλῆος θείοιο
κουριδίην ἄλοχον θήσειν, ἄξειν τ' ἐνὶ νηυσὶν
ἐς Φθίην, δαίσειν δὲ γάμον μετὰ Μυρμιδόνεσσι.
τώ σ' ἄμοτον κλαίω τεθνηότα μείλιχον αἰεί.

You would not let me, when swift Achilleus had cut down my husband, and sacked the city of god-like Mynes, you would not let me sorrow, but said you would make me godlike Achilleus' wedded lawful wife, that you would take me back in the ships to Phthia, and formalize my marriage among the Myrmidons. Therefore I weep your death without ceasing. You were always kind.

If the planned course of action Briseïs imputes to Patroclus here were blatantly nonsensical, why would she include it in her lament—why would Homer include it in her lament? It would be ruinous. But in fact this is the climax of the poem's characterization of Patroclus— μείλιχος αἰεί—and is meant to be taken seriously as such. That Patroclus' "sweetness" on occasion tempted him into making totally implausible promises to captive concubines would not enhance the desired portrait: he is being credited with a capacity, made evident elsewhere in the poem, to treat humans as humans, with compassion and dignity. But it is not by coincidence that Briseïs' account here agrees with what Achilles himself says in Book 9,[19] nor irrelevant that the two were regarded as paradigmatic lovers by Roman elegists.[20]

Of the other two exempla in *Odes* 2.4–12, Cassandra's life-history is exceptionally complicated—virgin princess, rape victim, followed by capture, concubinage, and slaughter—so I will discuss only the last sequence as treated in Homer (containing much of Aeschylus' *in nuce*). Agamemnon's account of his feelings towards Chryseïs is recognized to stand in some close relation to his actual behavior with Cassandra subsequently. At first glance, what he envisions seems to correspond to N-H's conception of how "such attachments" between master and slave worked (*Il.* 1.29–31):

τὴν δ' ἐγὼ οὐ λύσω· πρίν μιν καὶ γῆρας ἔπεισιν
ἡμετέρῳ ἐνὶ οἴκῳ ἐν Ἄργεϊ τηλόθι πάτρης
ἱστὸν ἐποιχομένην καὶ ἐμὸν λέχος ἀντιόωσαν·

19 It is sometimes argued that 9.395–400 conflict with 19.295–300, but the former is spoken (in the context of rejecting a daughter of Agamemnon as a wife) after Achilles has emotionally detached himself from Briseïs (9.336 f.). Achilles' contrafactual wish that Artemis had killed Briseïs on the day he captured her (19.59–60) is conditioned by the death of Patroclus; to call it "rhetorical" would be an injustice: as it cancels out the love he claimed to feel for her in Book 9, so it also cancels out any justification for his withdrawal from the army: that is the state of mind he is in; see Edwards' introductory discussion of 19.56–73 (1991, 241).
20 Rudd 1980.

The girl I will not give back; sooner will old age come upon her in my own house, in Argos, far from her own land, going up and down by the loom and being in my bed as my companion.

The possibility of domestic upheaval—in the royal family—is broached in his more emotional account a little later in the same book (1.111–115):

ἐγὼ κούρης Χρυσηΐδος ἀγλά' ἄποινα
οὐκ ἔθελον δέξασθαι, ἐπεὶ πολὺ βούλομαι αὐτὴν
οἴκοι ἔχειν· καὶ γάρ ῥα Κλυταιμνήστρης προβέβουλα
κουριδίης ἀλόχου, ἐπεὶ οὔ ἑθέν ἐστι χερείων,
οὐ δέμας οὐδὲ φυήν, οὔτ' ἂρ φρένας οὔτέ τι ἔργα.

I for the sake of the girl Chryseïs would not take the shining ransom; and indeed I wish greatly to have her in my own house; since I like her better than Clytemnestra my own wife, for in truth she is in no way inferior, neither in build nor wit, not in accomplishment.

This begins to sound as if something more disruptive than sexual diversion and loom-work is being contemplated. According to the *Odyssey*, Agamemnon did indeed take Cassandra home (11.421–3), whereupon Clytemnestra, showing "equanimity" of a sort, inflicted on his slave-mistress the same fate she accorded her master:

οἰκτροτάτην δ' ἤκουσα ὄπα Πριάμοιο θυγατρὸς
Κασσάνδρης, τὴν κτεῖνε Κλυταιμνήστρη δολόμητις
ἀμφ' ἐμοί·

I heard the most pitiful voice of Priam's daughter, Cassandra, whom cunning Clytemnestra killed beside me.

As in the case of Phoenix' father's παλλακίς (9.449–451), the threat to the wife is a threat to the social order and thus to the "national interest".[21]

The suffering caused by the confusions of status that result from such relationships is a major theme of Sophocles' *Ajax*, where we learn the effects not

---

21 The position of Phoenix' father Amyntor is unknown, but that he was of sufficient standing for the succession to be a matter of urgent interest to his extended family is implied by 9.462–477. Another depiction of saintly concubine vs. vengeful wife known to Horace will have been Euripides' *Andromache*; the character's fluctuations in status interested Virgil to the point that he added a new one (*Aen.* 3.294–345). There seems to have been debate among the Romans about what sort of mark even transitory enslavement could leave on a previously free person: see Seneca the Elder, *Controv.* 1.2.10 on a *virgo* captured by pirates, sold into prostitution, and finally recovered: can she become a priestess? Does what happened during this misfortune permanently count against her? A similar question is raised in John Ford's *The Searchers*.

only from the perspective of the concubine, Tecmessa, Horace's third mythical exemplum, but, by way of a kind of ventriloquism, from that of her bastard progeny: though her son, the κωφὸν πρόσωπον Eurysaces, does not himself speak, his in effect social-status double and half-uncle, Teucer, does, after Agamemnon boorishly mocks his illegitimacy (1288–1307), a memorably vigorous passage.[22] Writing in the period after the enactment of Pericles' citizenship law (by which children of only one citizen parent were disenfranchised, i.e., rendered illegitimate),[23] Sophocles seemed fascinated by the ambiguities engendered by such arrangements;[24] Tecmessa represents her own status as curiously labile (487–505, addressed to Ajax):

ἐγὼ δ' ἐλευθέρου μὲν ἐξέφυν πατρός,
εἴπερ τινὸς σθένοντος ἐν πλούτῳ Φρυγῶν·
νῦν δ' εἰμὶ δούλη. θεοῖς γὰρ ὧδ' ἔδοξέ που
καὶ σῇ μάλιστα χειρί. τοιγαροῦν, ἐπεὶ
τὸ σὸν λέχος ξυνῆλθον, εὖ φρονῶ τὰ σά,
καί σ' ἀντιάζω πρός τ' ἐφεστίου Διὸς
εὐνῆς τε τῆς σῆς, ᾗ συνηλλάχθης ἐμοί,
μή μ' ἀξιώσῃς βάξιν ἀλγεινὴν λαβεῖν
τῶν σῶν ὑπ' ἐχθρῶν, χειρίαν ἐφείς τινι.
ᾗ γὰρ θάνῃς σὺ καὶ τελευτήσας ἀφῇς,
ταύτῃ νόμιζε κἀμὲ τῇ τόθ' ἡμέρᾳ
βίᾳ ξυναρπασθεῖσαν Ἀργείων ὕπο
ξὺν παιδὶ τῷ σῷ δουλίαν ἕξειν τροφήν.
καί τις πικρὸν πρόσφθεγμα δεσποτῶν ἐρεῖ
λόγοις ἰάπτων, "ἴδετε τὴν ὁμευνέτιν
Αἴαντος, ὃς μέγιστον ἴσχυσε στρατοῦ,
οἵας λατρείας ἀνθ' ὅσου ζήλου τρέφει".
τοιαῦτ' ἐρεῖ τις· κἀμὲ μὲν δαίμων ἐλᾷ,
σοὶ δ' αἰσχρὰ τἄπη ταῦτα καὶ τῷ σῷ γένει.

I was the daughter of a free-born father mighty in wealth, if any Phrygian was. Now I am a slave, for somehow the gods so ordained, and even more so did your strong hand. Therefore, ever since I have come into your bed, I have wished you well, and I do beg you, by the Zeus of our hearth, by your marriage-bed in which you coupled with me, do not condemn

22 N-H on 2.4.5 point out that with the reference to Telamon "[t]he well-informed reader is also reminded without a waste of words that Telamon himself loved the captive Hesione". The product of that union is the bastard Teucer.

23 451. The date of the *Ajax* is unknown; Finglass 2011, 1–11 surveys the (exiguous) evidence, and (10 f.) "tentatively put[s] *Ajax* with *Antigone* in the 440s. A date in the early to mid 430s or very late 450s cannot be ruled out".

24 The question is raised again by the status of Iole in the *Trachiniai*, on which see MacKinnon 1971, to whom Davies 1991 on 1216 ff. defers, but whom I find too inclined to assess the non-Athenian literary evidence by the standards of 5th c. Athenian law.

> me to the cruel talk of your enemies, do not leave me to the hand of a stranger! On whatever day you die and widow me by your death, on that same day, be sure, I shall also be seized forcibly by the Greeks and, with your son, shall obtain a slave's portion. Then one of my masters will name me bitterly, shooting me with taunts: "See the concubine of Ajax, who was the mightiest man in the army. See what menial tasks she tends to, in place of such an enviable existence!" Such things will men say, and so will destiny afflict me while the shame of these words will stain you and your family. (Transl. Jebb, modified)

νῦν εἰμὶ δούλη—but if you die "I shall be seized forcibly by the Greeks and, with your son, shall obtain a slave's portion". Tecmessa faces a downward spiral of reiterated enslavement. As the ὁμευνέτις of Ajax she enjoys an enviable status, for a slave; at his death, however, she (and his son) will be reduced—to slavery. This incoherence is not due to oversight on the part of either Tecmessa or her creator: it accurately reflects an ambivalent reality that Athenians, many of whose upper class members (e.g., eventually, Pericles himself) had children by marriages with non-Athenian ξένοι, were now compelled to acquiesce to.

Such, then, are the heroic precedents the speaker of *Odes* 2.4 offers Xanthias for his own relationship with the *ancilla* Phyllis.[25] Such, in other words, that if Xanthias—or Horace's reader—has even a casual familiarity with the major classics of Greek epic and tragedy, he will know they are anything but encouraging. How then does the "bantering" interpretation of the poem survive them?

The answer must be that we read the poem back to front—as we do many poems of this poet whose inclination is for ending in a place far removed from where he began. After *ne sit ancillae tibi amor pudori* 2.4 unfolds in three stages: (1) the heroic exempla (2–12); (2) the New Comedy fantasy of the beautiful and loving slave with concealed upper-class or royal ancestry (13–20); and (3) the buffoonery of bottom-pinching family friend Horace (21–24). The bantering reading of the poem starts from (3) and works backward, imposing jollity as it goes: is it *in fact* very nice or very amusing to joke that an actual as opposed to literary-fictional slave's supposedly unmercenary character is evidence of a royal bloodline? But if that isn't actually funny, then what are we to do with the exempla of (1), which, comprising only recently enslaved aristocratic spear-captives of known parentage, have no relevance to a Roman *ancilla* to begin with?[26] (2), by providing the premise missing from (1), i.e., that Phyllis is like the exemplars a captive princess, enables the link between (3) and (1).

---

25 For a brief and fascinating account of the realities of the Greek historical situation, so far as they are known, see Golden 2011, esp. 146–151.

26 "The slaves loved by the Greek heroes were the daughters of wealthy and important parents" (Cairns 1977, 134). But in reality *eros* could lead an Athenian citizen to buy a slave's freedom, as Hypereides 5 shows (see especially § 24).

Horace forces us into a dilemma: either acknowledge the witless cruelty of (2), or disarm it by reading it with the harmless levity provided by (3), passing it along backwards, together with the missing premise, to (1). He learned this move—using ambivalent myth to force a dilemma—from his master Alcaeus (fr. 42):[27]

ὠς λόγος κάκων ἀ[
Περράμῳ καὶ παῖσ[ι
ἐκ σέθεν πίκρον, π[
 Ἴλιον ἴραν.
οὐ τεαύταν Αἰακίδαι̣[ς
πάντας ἐς γάμον μακ̣[αρας καλέσσαις
ἄγετ' ἐκ Νή[ρ]ηος ἔλων [μελάθρων
 πάρθενον ἄβραν
ἐς δόμον Χέρρωνος· ἔλ[υσε δ'
ζῶμα παρθένω· φιλο[
Πήλεος καὶ Νηρεΐδων ἀρίστ[ας.
 ἐς δ' ἐνίαυτον
παῖδα γέννατ' αἰμιθέων [,
ὄλβιον ξάνθαν ἐλάτη[ρα πώλων,
οἰ δ' ἀπώλοντ' ἀμφ' Ἐ[λένᾳ
 καὶ πόλις αὔτων.

As the story goes, because of evil deeds bitter grief came once to Priam and his sons from you, Helen, and Zeus destroyed holy Ilium with fire. Not such was the delicate maiden whom the noble son of Aeacus, inviting all the blessed gods to the wedding, married, taking her from the halls of Nereus to the home of Chiron; he loosened the pure maiden's girdle, and the love of Peleus and the best of Nereus' daughters flourished; and within the year she bore a son, the finest of demigods, blessed driver of chestnut horses. But they perished for Helen's sake—the Phrygians and their city.

In order to read this σύγκρισις γυναικῶν straight—in order, we might say, to give it an Augustan reception—we must suppress any puzzlement it occasions about the suitability of Thetis as a paragon of uxoriousness, or about the logic of chastising one woman for causing the destruction of Troy while congratulating the other for giving birth to its agent. But many readers have been successful in this suppression;[28] my own readers will I am sure make their own decisions

27 The translation is Campbell's in the Loeb (1982), from a heavily restored text; the text above is Voigt's (1971), with subscript iotas where she has adscript, and the supplements from Hunt printed by her.

28 See, e.g., Page 1955, 281 ("No more patriotic theme could inspire the poet, and delight his audience, than the praise of Thetis and her gallant son"), followed in the main by Degani-Burzacchini 1977, 194f., but finding the alleged patriotism "del tutto arbitraria"); Davies 1986 pro-

about it. I propose that Horace read the poem ironically, and selected his exempla for 2.4 on such a model as its non-suppressive reading provides. In the case of the topics and characters featured in Alcaeus 42 he will have found a precedent in the treatment accorded them in the *Song of the Parcae* of Catullus 64.

In *Odes* 2.4, however, the issue is not the nature of the spin we give certain Greek myths, but the Roman institution of slavery. Horace's familiarity with the literature of slavery we have cited above is not in doubt; but what of his experience of the institution itself? Playing the *libertino patre natus* card is risky, but I find its absence from the scholarly discussion of 2.4 puzzling: was "with equanimity" the only mode available to a Roman for looking at the situation posited?[29] It seems plausible to think that Horace might have been one upper class Roman who was willing to occasionally look at things from a slave's point of view.[30]

As I understand it, the current received view on these questions is something like this:

---

vides suppression with a theoretical justification derived from Fraenkel's "principle ... that the poet does not want us to take into account any feature of a tradition which he does not mention" (1950 II, 97: an apt partner to Fraenkel's rule that Attic tragedy never featured any stage action not explicitly signalled in the text). Davies' conclusion is (261 f.) that "if we are attuned to the methods by which the paradigmatic technique operates [i.e., in accordance with Fraenkel's dictum], we will not dwell on the later married life of Peleus and Thetis, or on Achilles' career at Troy (neither of which the poet mentions). Instead we will observe that Alcaeus tells us how the best of Nereus' daughters bore the greatest of heroes while Helen brought death upon the Trojans and their city. And with that contrast ringing in our ears the poem ends (as the papyrus makes clear)". We might say, ringing in our carefully waxed ears. What naivety to associate Peleus and Thetis' son with Troy!—dissenting views in Gomme 1957, 257–, followed by Campbell 1967, 292.

29 Williams 1995 argued that Horace's father suffered at worst only temporary enslavement. His argument is rebutted by Mouritsen 2011, 266 f., explaining the vitriolic denunciations of *Epode* 4 by way of a radical discontinuity in status and attitude between freedman and freedman's son. When discussing *Sat.* 1.6, however—the poem from which Williams started—Mouritsen admits a good deal more ambiguity and nuance: having earlier asserted that servitude is entirely defined by the slave's personal experience (the scars on his back, etc.), so that, e.g., a Horace who never experienced it is different in essential kind from his father who did, Mouritsen says the positive depiction of the father in the satire "enters the argument only to reassure the reader that he gave his son a proper upbringing and education. The affectionate portrait served to dispel any suspicion of 'servile' corruption, for while 'servility' could not be inherited, the lesser morals of the former slave might be imparted through nurture. This prejudice was the main cloud hanging over the reputation of the son ..." (Mouritsen 2011, 270). So the bullies of *Sat.* 1.6 taunted Horace for being servile by nurture but not nature?

30 *Epode* 4 poses a problem for this suggestion; see Mouritsen 2011, 265–268 for a recent though not in my opinion entirely convincing discussion (see previous note).

(1) rape is depicted in Roman comedy (and its Greek models) as a crime chiefly insofar as it violates the rights of the *paterfamilias* or other person in legal charge of the victim, and not very much at all from the perspective of the victim;[31]

(2) the psychological experience of slaves was of little or no interest to Romans, at least of the slave-owning class.[32]

My argument suggests that with the sequence of poems 2.4 and 2.5 Horace faithfully reflects this reality by provoking his audience to consider its human implications.[33] Some insulation from the painfulness of such an undertaking is provided by the thorough-going literariness of the treatment. It is a commonplace that the addressee of a poem sometimes stands for the speaker himself—that the device enables a form of self-address (so, e.g., N-H on the unidentified addressee of 2.5, as mentioned above); the presumably fictional addressee of 2.4, the lover of a slave, is himself given a slave name, Xanthias. It is not, however, a name for historical slaves: it is a classic *literary* slave name, unattested in the reasonably abundant onomasticon (almost 1,000 entries) of the real thing.[34] The speaker, Horace (as guaranteed by the sphragis of the last stanza), is the self-described *libertino patre natus* (*Sat.* 1.6.6, 45 f.). Who is the bull-like addressee of 2.5, ogling the barely pubescent Lalage in safe but, for the *Odes*, anomalous ano-

31 See, e.g., Pierce 1997, Barsby 1999, 185 f., and Goldberg 1999.

32 See, e.g., Bradley 2015, and especially 2001, a review of Fitzgerald 2000 that seems from the perspective of my very limited knowledge entirely apt, even though Fitzgerald's overall claim in his book is one that coincides with my own about *Odes* 2.4 and 5.—Musonius Rufus 12.31–48 Lutz has to do with the wrong done by the owners and the shame brought on them and not with anything suffered by the slaves; on the other hand, the anonymous mime, of possibly 2nd c. CE date, on the verso of *POxy* 413 (text at Page 1941:350–361, Cunningham 1987:47–51), depicting a monstrous mistress condemning to death (among others) a male slave who has refused, out of devotion to his slave lover, to service her, quite clearly portrayed the latter couple with some sympathy, perhaps more so than was granted Gastron in Herodas 5 (proposed by Page 353 to have been the anonymous mime's model), whose sufferings certainly illustrate the dangers posed to the slave in such relationships (for further literary examples—all free female + enslaved male, so subject to a special disapprobation—see Headlam-Knox 1922:xlv–vi; the situation in Aristaenetus 2.7, cited earlier—and again showing some limited sympathy for the slave—is the reverse). The *Lives of Aesop*, which I take to be of Roman date, and, mutatis mutandis, Apul. *Met.* cannot be dismissed as evidence that interest was sometimes taken in looking at things from the slave's point of view.

33 Cf. Bradley 2001, 475 n. 3: "It is not the possibility of affective intimacy between slave and master *at the occasional* but *at the general level* that I question" (emphasis added).

34 Vlassopoulos 2010, 123 f.; cf. Biles / Olson 2015 on Ar. *Vesp* 1. Murgatroyd 1980 perceives the role literariness plays with the name Xanthias here, though he was misinformed about its distribution.

nymity? “We have met the enemy and he is us”. As 2.5 tells us, Lalage will grow to nubile maturity; no ineluctable natural process, however, will advance Phyllis of 2.4 to freedom.

Barbara Weiden Boyd

Beatus ille qui procul ... otiis?: Ovid's Rustication Cure (*Remedia amoris* 169–98)

Ovid begins the *Remedia amoris* by establishing his credentials as *praeceptor*, and then offers what purports to be real advice to the lovers who now wish to extricate themselves from their affairs. In his arch assumption of the identity of a medical doctor, prepared to dispense *medicina amoris* to his clients, Ovid looks back at the entire arc of elegy's history in Rome to its probable codification by Gallus, the poet whose identification of love as the one disease that not even skilled physicians can effectively treat resonates definitively in the poetry of his successors (although not, unfortunately, in the extant remains of his poetry, of which only ten verses survive).[1] In other words, Ovid positions himself to demythologize, both literally and figuratively, the very foundations of elegiac love; I shall suggest in what follows, however, that even as he purports to release his readers from the thrall of love, Ovid uses the rhetoric of *otium* to challenge the medical mastery he asserts.[2] Careful examination of Ovid's critique of *otium* thus goes to the heart of what has recently been described as the "failure" of the *Remedia*;[3] Ovid's promises of recovery themselves betray symptoms of the incurable human tendency to relapse into love.

The first set of remedies he proposes all have to do with keeping busy. After briefly recommending that his pupil take up a political or military career—the former ironically prefiguring the legal career Ovid tells us he rejected (*Tr.* 4.10.17–40),[4] and the latter extravagantly (and impractically) illustrated by allusions not only to the Parthians but to the Trojan War—he moves on to the suggestion that his pupil leave town. This suggestion is presented as a logical

1 On the close association between Gallus and *medicina amoris*, see Tränkle 1960, 22f.; Ross 1975, 65–68 and 91; Boyd 1983; Knox 1986, 14–17; and O'Hara 1993.

2 Relevant to the topic but outside the parameters of this short paper are the attitudes to *otium* expressed in the histories, philosophical treatises, and other prose texts of the period; for a survey of the evidence, André 1966 remains the most comprehensive compendium of Roman views of *otium*.

3 Fulkerson 2004, following Conte 1989.

4 This autobiographical sketch closes with the image of the Muses persuading Ovid to pursue the *otium* he naturally preferred (*petere Aoniae suadebant tuta sorores / otia, iudicio semper amata meo*, 39f.).

https://doi.org/10.1515/9783110545708-010

one, or at least, so it seems; the reader of erotic elegy generally, however, and of the earlier *Ars amatoria* in particular, should find the idea somewhat alien, if not entirely breathtaking. After all, *rusticitas* is hardly a virtue in the Ovidian playbook; both the *Amores* and the *Ars amatoria* are played out against an almost exclusively urban background, with only the occasional foray into the country, subsequently abandoned as quickly as possible.[5] The only truly positive depictions of country life in Ovid's erotic poetry heretofore have been metaphorical: human involvement in the natural world, as represented by agriculture and husbandry, provides a tried-and-true basis for exempla intended to prove a point Ovid is making—but the point is generally about human nature and behavior, rather than about country life itself. Indeed, Ovid's frequent employment of agricultural exempla has been interpreted as evidence of parody of Virgil's *Georgics* (or at least, a parody of the subject matter, if not of Virgil's poem itself), since the images these exempla evoke all too often appear to trivialize or dehumanize both their subjects and their objects.[6]

Then again, the other elegists—especially Tibullus—find a rich vein of material for the development of an elegiac alternative in country life, where life and love can coexist under the aegis of divine Pax;[7] even the urbane Propertius flirts briefly with elegiac rustication, especially in his second book, although he ultimately rejects the model in his quest to emulate Callimachus.[8] In the lyric mode, meanwhile, Horace offers what appear to be heartfelt idyllic depictions of the country,[9] although the genuineness of the poet's praise of the country in the second *Epode* is definitively undermined by the eventual revelation of the identity of the speaker, the moneylender Alfius.[10] Ovid is clearly far less interested in "poetic rustication" than any of these predecessors; his sudden embrace in the *Remedia* of the rural life, with all of its physical demands throughout the year,

5 The natural charms of Ovid's birthplace among the Paeligni, Sulmo, are singled out for special attention in *Am.* 2.16; cf. also *Am.* 3.15.3–14. The suburban landscape of *Am.* 3.13, at a Faliscan cult-center of Juno, is given a place in the *Amores* by virtue of its being the birthplace of Ovid's wife; its inclusion in this collection makes this poem an outlier that anticipates the cult narratives of the *Fasti*.

6 Leach 1964 is the basic discussion; see also its more refined development by Fantham 1993.

7 See Lee-Stecum 2013, 71–79 for an overview of the importance of *rura* in Tibullus' love elegy; on Tibullan Pax, see Boyd 1984.

8 Keith 2008, 69–73 offers a succinct analysis of the points of contact shared by Tibullan and Propertian rustic elegy.

9 I here avoid the question of Horace's poetic persona, but caution suggests that I put quotation marks around "heartfelt".

10 On the many questions surrounding the relationship between the *Georgics* and *Epode* 2, see Mankin 1995, 63 f.; Watson 2003, 75–77.

is therefore not simply surprising, not simply to be seen as an attempt to expand the boundaries of his material. Rather, it suggests a confrontation with these predecessors, in a way that seeks to revisit the logic of their benign landscapes. In virtually all of the earlier elegiac and Horatian descriptions of the country, after all, the hard labor of farming is moderated by the occasional opportunities for *otium* that it provides. Tibullus defines his ideal country life as a form of *vita iners* (1.1.5), in which he can avoid storms while dining by a warm fire, his mistress in his embrace (1.1.45 f.); Propertius expresses a belief that a rustic sojourn will keep Cynthia far from any source of corruption (*nullus erit castis iuuenis corruptor in agris*, 2.19.3; cf. *corrumpere*, 2.19.9), and that as she learns some basic agricultural skills foreign influences will be kept at a safe distance (*omnia ab externo sint modo tuta uiro*, 2.19.16).[11] Among the many poems in which Horace praises the simplicity of the rustic life, of particular relevance is *Odes* 2.16, in which Horace reverses the association of *otium* with luxury previously suggested by Catullus in his creative adaptation of a Sapphic ode (poem 51):[12] whereas Catullus represents *otium* as an index of cultural decay, Horace responds by redefining *otium* as a prized possession available only to the humble rustic who works a small plot of land (cf. 37–40, *mihi parua rura et / spiritum Graiae tenuem Camenae / Parca non mendax dedit et malignum / spernere uolgus*).[13]

Against this background, Ovid's rustic escape is a very different affair: as the final couplet of the passage to which I now turn makes clear, Amor will be so discouraged by inattention on the farm that he will depart, and take his wounding arrows with him. Activity is to be the watchword here—and what extra-urban activity could be better than farming, with its relentless schedule (and impeccable literary pedigree)? On the other hand, what could be less provocative, less likely to stir the flames of desire? The incongruity of Ovid's foray into the country lies in the first place in its generic "impurity",[14] as it imports into elegy—or vio-

---

11 Fedeli 2005, 552–562.

12 On the vexed interpretation of Catullus' concluding stanza, see the ingenious suggestion of Knox 1984.

13 Cf. Fraenkel 1957, 211–214; he notes Horace's brilliant combination of "the σωφροσύνη of the private individual with the σοφία of a poet" (214). Fraenkel (followed by Nisbet and Hubbard 1978, 257, on *Od.* 2.16.5) understands Horace's imitation of Catullus as a direct rejection of the earlier poet, a perfect example of *oppositio in imitando.*

14 "Impurity" is a loaded word, and intentionally so; with it I hope to provoke an image similar to that of the *contaminatio* so often previously associated—to its detriment—with Roman comedy (although it was not in the first instance used to describe the willful transgression of generic norms). I use the idea of "impurity" here in response to recent attempts to mediate generic interaction with more neutral terminology such as "generic polyphony" (Hardie 1998, 57) or "generic enrichment" (Harrison 2007, 1 f. *et passim*), even as I acknowledge the real value of such

lates elegy's usual boundaries with—an explicit and assiduous emulation of themes and ideas not common to elegy, in which *otium* is so highly valued. In Ovid's rustic world, on the other hand, *otium* is explicitly banned (cf. *Rem. am.* 135–40); but can erotic elegy really exist in a world without *otium?* A consideration of the dense intertextuality of this passage shows that the advice Ovid gives explicitly demonstrates the conflicts that lie at the heart of the farm's *secura quies*, and indeed of all of erotic elegy. My focus here will be on Ovid's Virgilian intertextuality; I believe that it will become nonetheless evident in what follows that Ovid uses specific references to Virgil as a form of "window reference",[15] i.e., that Ovid uses Virgilian allusion as a way to encapsulate and to interrogate an entire literary tradition on the topic of *otium*, especially a tradition to which love's power is so central: the therapeutic credentials of *otium* face a daunting challenge when proposed as an antidote to love, a form of *medicina amoris*.

Ovid recommends rustication as a cure, a foolproof means of escape; but the more he describes this remedy, the more it appears to contain an inherent contradiction (*Rem. am.* 169–198):

rura quoque oblectant animos studiumque colendi;
  quaelibet huic curae cedere cura potest.
colla iube domitos oneri supponere tauros,
  sauciet ut duram uomer aduncus humum;
obrue uersata Cerialia semina terra,
  quae tibi cum multo fenore reddat ager.
aspice curuatos pomorum pondere ramos,
  ut sua quod peperit uix ferat arbor onus;
aspice labentes iucundo murmure riuos;
  aspice tondentes fertile gramen oues.
ecce, petunt rupes praeruptaque saxa capellae:
  iam referent haedis ubera plena suis.
pastor inaequali modulatur harundine carmen,
  nec desunt comites, sedula turba, canes.
parte sonant alia siluae mugitibus altae
  et queritur uitulum mater abesse suum.
quid, cum compositos fugiunt examina fumos,
  ut releuent dempti uimina curua faui?
poma dat autumnus; formosast messibus aestas;

formulations. It will become clear in what follows that, at least with Ovid, I consider such intergeneric activity to be aggressive in its appropriation of its intertexts, and to insist actively that the reader think about its effects. At least in the instance under consideration here, terms such as "enrichment" and "polyphony" are unhelpfully anodyne.

15 Thomas 1986, 188; see also *idem* 1995 more generally on rustic influences in the *Georgics*.

uer praebet flores; igne leuatur hiems.
temporibus certis maturam rusticus uuam
deligit, et nudo sub pede musta fluunt;
temporibus certis desectas alligat herbas
et tonsam raro pectine uerrit humum.
ipse potes riguis plantam deponere in hortis;
ipse potes riuos ducere lenis aquae.
uenerit insitio, fac ramum ramus adoptet
stetque peregrinis arbor operta comis.
cum semel haec animum coepit mulcere uoluptas,
debilibus pinnis irritus exit Amor.

Country places and the pursuit of cultivation also please the spirit; any care whatsoever can give way to this concern. Order the tame oxen to put their necks beneath the yoke, so that the curved plow may bruise the firm earth; bury Ceres' seeds in the overturned soil, which the field can render back to you with great interest. Look at the branches curved with the weight of fruits, so that each tree can hardly carry the burden which it itself has produced; look at the streams gliding by with a gentle murmur, look at the sheep shearing the lush grass. Lo, goats are seeking the cliffs and broken rocks: soon they will bring home full teats for their kids. A shepherd tunes his song on the uneven pipe, nor are his companion dogs, a hard-working crowd, absent. In another spot, the lofty forests resound with mooing, and a mother laments that her calf is gone. And when the swarms flee the compound fire, what of how the hives made of curved wicker are lightened by the removal of honeycomb? Autumn offers fruit; summer is fair with harvests; spring brings forth flowers; winter is lightened by fire. At fixed times the country-dweller picks the mature fruit, and the juice runs beneath his bare foot; at fixed times he binds up the cut hay and sweeps the shorn earth with a fine-toothed rake. You yourself can set a seedling in irrigated gardens; you yourself can draw off streams of gentle water. When the time for grafting has come, see to it that one branch adopts another and that a tree stands dressed in foreign tresses. Once this pleasure has begun to soothe the spirit, Amor departs unfulfilled, with his wings weakened.

Ovid's appeal to the healthful virtues of country life partakes of a long didactic tradition. Farming is, after all, the substance of the first great didactic poem in the tradition, Hesiod's *Works and Days*. In his portrayal of the natural world and animal behavior, Ovid also acknowledges Lucretius, an important model for much of later didactic idiom; while Lucretius' topic is not farming per se, agricultural and natural metaphors abound in his verse. Other didactic influences are in the background as well, as we can see from the context from which this excerpt is taken: in the immediately following lines, Ovid complements his recommendation of agricultural pursuits with another equally distracting field of activity, hunting and fishing (199–210). Both types of activities are themselves the subjects of a number of other didactic works from roughly the same period: the anonymous *Halieutica* ascribed to Ovid himself by Pliny and in some manuscripts,[16] and the *Cynegetica* of Ovid's contemporary Grattius.[17] Propertius, furthermore, explicitly links the two activities in the poem which I mentioned earlier: while Cynthia learns to farm, says Propertius, he himself will take up hunting (though he will limit himself to small and not terribly fearsome creatures: 2.19.17–26). Ovid, however, deploys agricultural pursuits for a new purpose here: he recommends farming and hunting not because of their inherent interest or value, nor as the pastimes of two lovers far from the madding crowd, nor even as part of any existential metaphor, but because they are very effective distractions from love. Each area of activity entails both skill and hard work; Ovid urges them on his pupil because the latter of these in particular will ensure a good night's sleep ("at night, sleep occupies the tired fellow, not love for a girlfriend; and sleep relaxes his limbs with welcome rest", *nocte fatigatum somnus, non cura puellae, / excipit et pingui membra quiete leuat, Rem. am.* 205 f.).[18]

The physical labor involved in farming is familiar to any reader of the *Georgics*, and at first Ovid appears to be following in Virgil's footsteps. After announcing his subject (*rura ... studiumque colendi*, 169), Ovid details the effectiveness of farming as a distraction from urban life. The sequence of agricultural activities recommended by Ovid falls into two subsections, with the second (187–196) revisiting from a slightly different perspective some of the instructions already given in the first (171–186). The first subsection echoes the *Georgics*, recommending a sequence of activities that recall a prominent theme or themes in each of Virgil's four books: yoking oxen, plowing, planting seed, and reaping (171–174 ~ *Georgics* Book 1); cultivating fruit-trees (175 f. ~ *Georgics* Book 2); tending sheep, goats, and cattle (177–184 ≈ *Georgics* Book 3); and apiculture (185 f. ~ *Georgics* Book 4). The second subsection introduces the importance of time and season in farming (187–192), and of hands-on engagement in agricultural chores (193–196). Ovid thus complements the evocation of Virgil's didactic poem with an allusion to Virgil's model Hesiod, whose *Works and Days* is organized into

---

16 Plin. *HN* 32.11. Richmond 1962 proposes that Ovid is not the author; his view is reflected in the current consensus.

17 Sometimes called Grattius Faliscus, and perhaps to be identified with the Gratius mentioned by Ovid at *Pont.* 4.16.34; see Enk 1918.

18 While I limit my remarks in this paper to the passage on farming, I note the structural parallel that links the two distractions: The two sections of the passage are clearly defined by similar opening phrases (*studium colendi*, 169; *uenandi studium*, 199), and concluding couplets (197 f. and 211 f.) reminding the reader that the prescribed remedies will take time, but perseverance will ultimately prevail. While I cannot do the hunting section justice here, many of my comments could, *mutatis mutandis*, be extended to the second half of this passage as well: after all, hunting is the activity *par excellence* that Virgil associates with Gallus in love (*Ecl.* 10.55–61).

sections on essential tasks, i.e., the works of the poem's title (*Op.* 381–617), and the appropriate days of the month for each, i.e., the days (*Op.* 765–828).

Closer scrutiny of Ovid's "Little Georgics", however, soon yields evidence of their limited didactic value. I do not mean to suggest that we should read Virgil's poem as a reliable handbook to agriculture, although his recent commentators have abundantly demonstrated his care with technical detail; but it is just this sort of technical detail that, by and large, is missing in Ovid.[19] The work of plowing is addressed in one couplet from start to finish (171 f.), as is that not only of planting but of reaping (173 f.). The management of bees and their hives merits one couplet (185 f.), as do the harvesting of grapes and the production of wine (189 f.). Likewise, raking the fields (191 f.), irrigation (193 f.), and grafting (195 f.) all receive a single couplet; and in each one, Ovid not only describes the activity but also proceeds to its result. In other words, the overall impression Ovid gives to his pupils considering the rustication cure is that farming is simply a series of foolproof steps to be followed according to a set schedule (cf. *temporibus certis*, 189 and 191).[20] None of the challenges that face the actual farmer receives so much as a word of notice here; none of the skills that must be developed over time is mentioned. In fact, Ovid's "Little Georgics" is more like a series of subject headings than actual instruction, and its didactic value is virtually nonexistent; since it is also lacking any obvious metaphorical significance, we may well wonder what the point is at all.

---

19 Thomas 1988, vol. 1, 4: "[A] poem which is to be truly didactic in content as well as form (such as the *De Rerum Natura*) implies the existence of an audience which is to be instructed, and in spite of the long-held view that the function of the *Georgics* was to restore an interest in Italian agriculture, the fact is that no Roman farmer would have read the poem for practical instruction when Varro's *Res Rusticae* was available; had he done so, moreover, his success would have been limited, for Virgil is extremely selective with his precepts". In a footnote on this observation (n. 12), Thomas adds: "Ovid ... was to expose the generic fiction [i.e., of the sort found in *Georgics*] with the *Ars Amatoria*, which had little intention, but all the formal appearances, of teaching its audience". From any practical assessment, the *Remedia amoris* falls into the same category of utility, in Thomas' terms, as its predecessor, the *Ars*.

Even if we allow, as have many scholars writing in the wake of Thomas' commentary, that the poem is in fact "instructive" in an allegorical or metaphorical sense, the validity of Thomas' assertion stands, as a careful reading of the poem itself cannot help but reveal. See Nappa 2005, who reads Augustus as the ideal reader/pupil for the poem; and cf. Kronenberg 2009 on agricultural allegory more generally.

20 Cf. *tempore certo* at *G.* 4.100. Curiously, even as Ovid draws attention to the "proper times" for different tasks, he gives the seasons in reverse order—from autumn to summer to spring to winter: *poma dat autumnus; formosa est messibus aestas; | uer praebet flores; igne leuatur hiems*, 187 f.. This is, after all, poetry, not really instruction at all.

Further examination of the structure of the passage only complicates the problem. Let us look at the approximate center of this passage, beginning with the couplet in which Ovid imagines his pupil by the banks of a river, tending his contented flock (177 f.). The next couplet (179 f.) describes goats frolicking in the rocky hills and returning at the end of the day to their thirsty young, and the third couplet (181 f.) introduces a shepherd, playing the pan-pipe while relaxing among his dogs (presumably herding dogs, although there is not even specificity about this, aside from the expression *sedula turba* to suggest that they serve a function beyond accompanying their master). This landscape even contains a reminder of the echoing sounds that are so central to the pastoral world in the lament of the heifer for her lost calf (*sonant ... siluae mugitibus altae / et queritur uitulum mater abesse suum*, 183 f.): here Ovid cleverly echoes a moving description of a bereft cow from Lucretius (*DRN* 2.352–366), subsequently transformed by Virgil into a bucolic vignette (*Ecl.* 8.85–89)—but whereas Virgil's transformation of the Lucretian image entails a change from maternal to erotic love,[21] such an emotion would be seriously inappropriate here, so Ovid restores the less dangerous (at least, from an amatory perspective) Lucretian livestock to the landscape.[22]

We have gradually, almost imperceptibly, moved from the world of the *Georgics* into that of the *Eclogues*, a place inhabited by sheep, goats, and their herders, who pass the days in tuneful relaxation. *Almost* imperceptibly—but Ovid wants his readers to register the shift. Line 181 is a careful reworking of two lines in the *Eclogues* that we can describe without hyperbole as unmistakable signatures of Virgilian bucolic;[23] *modulatur*, the variant verb used by Ovid in place of a form of *meditor*, appears in two of the remaining *Eclogues:*[24]

Rem. am. 181, *<u>pastor</u> inaequali <u>modulatur</u> <u>harundine</u> <u>carmen</u>*
Ecl. 1.2, *siluestrem tenui Musam <u>meditaris</u> <u>auena</u>*
Ecl. 6.8, *agrestem tenui <u>meditabor</u> <u>harundine</u> Musam*

21 Breed 2006, 39; see also his discussion of echoes in Chapter 4.
22 On the daring character of Virgil's eroticization of the scene, see Ross 1987, 159 f.; on Ovid's play with this scene elsewhere in his poetry, see Boyd 1997, 83–89.
23 On the significance of the repetition, see Clausen 1994, xxv; Coleman 1977 ad locc. notes that in both instances Virgil seems to echo Lucretius—4.589 and 5.1398, respectively. The latter of these, celebrating the *securitas* of early human existence (cf. Coleman ad loc.), lends additional color to the Ovidian line.
24 Elsewhere poets evoke the language of these verses when they want to give their work a definitively bucolic flavor: see, e.g., Tib. 2.1.53 f.; Ovid again, at *Tr.* 4.1.12; and cf. Prop. 2.34.67–76 for a broader review of the *Eclogues* that incorporates some of these details.

Ecl. 5.14, *carmina descripsi et modulans alterna notaui*
Ecl. 10.51, *carmina pastoris Siculi modulabor auena*

The specificity of Ovid's bucolic allusion here, should additional evidence be sought, is also reflected in the clause attributed by Donatus (*Vita Vergiliana* 169 f.) to the opening of the *Aeneid: ille ego qui quondam gracili modulatus auena / carmen.*[25] Regardless of the accuracy of Donatus' attribution, his claim indicates clearly how closely the image of the shepherd and his pipes is associated with the *Eclogues*. The Virgilian character of the Ovidian passage is reinforced in the next line (182), which in the phrase *comites, sedula turba, canes* features the precious stylistic device known as "inserted apposition"; the first secure Latin example of this device appears in the *Eclogues*.[26] And let us not overlook the *capellae* of 179—creatures that are all but synonymous with the world of the *Eclogues*.[27] Ovid has in fact guided his pupils far away from the farm, and to a very different mental, and metapoetic, locale—from the "Little *Georgics*" to the "Little *Eclogues*".

To bring out the metapoetic dimension of this passage, Ovid complements the potential conflict or oxymoron in the juxtaposition of "Georgic" and "Eclogue" features with the use of a narrative trope that is a favorite component of highly stylized verse: ecphrasis. Of course, ecphrasis has a long history, one that far precedes the self-conscious manipulation of the concept by Virgil, Ovid, and others, and is traceable to Homer's *Iliad*, where the description of the crafting of the shield of Achilles by Hephaestus (Book 18) is already an elaborate and richly resonant scene of central significance for the interpretation of the poem and its characters.[28] Ecphrasis is conventionally understood to be a de-

25 Cf. also Thomas 1988 ad loc. on the concluding lines of the *Georgics* (4.563–566), in which Virgil indicates the close association between pastoral and *otium*.

26 Skutsch 1956 calls this pattern "schema Cornelianum", in the belief that it originates with Gallus; whether Virgil learned this from Gallus or not, it thereafter becomes an unmistakable token of Virgil's style at its most self-conscious. Solodow 1986, who introduces the term "inserted apposition", counts eight examples of the pattern in the *Eclogues* (137–140). Ovid is fond of the effect (presumably for metrical as well as stylistic reasons), with 50 precise examples (as well as other examples of word-order that do not precisely imitate the pattern but contain some of its features). Ovid's wording here may also include a reminiscence of Prop. 3.3.31, *uolucres, mea turba, columbae*, itself modeled on *Ecl.* 1.57, *raucae, tua cura, palumbes*. If we agree with Skutsch that Gallus is the ultimate model, Ovid's use of it here may be yet one more suggestion of its Gallan provenance.

27 Geymonat 2004.

28 The bibliography on ecphrasis, especially in Virgil, is immense. For a clear and comprehensive introduction to the trope in its ancient deployment, see Webb 2009; on the shield of Aeneas

tailed, often elaborate description of a work of art (like Achilles' shield, or the shield of Aeneas modeled on it, in *Aeneid* Book 8), monument (the doors on the temple of Apollo at Cumae, in *Aeneid* Book 6), or landscape (the cave of the nymphs, in *Aeneid* Book 1), that is set into the frame of another narrative. Ecphrasis is usually recognizable from its descriptive focus, often made explicit through the use of verbal markers that point to the location of one detail in relation to others ("and over here", "in that spot", etc.)[29] and through an exhortation to the reader to "see" what is being described.[30] If we look again at the Ovidian bucolic scene as a whole, framed as it is by a sketch of the farming life loosely based on the *Georgics*, we might say that the one scene is effectively embedded within the other; Ovid even gestures to the ecphrastic character of the design with his repeated command that his pupil "see" what he is describing (*aspice* 175, 177, and 178; *ecce* 179), and with the phrase *parte ... alia* (183) with which the bucolic cameo closes. Of course, these markers of ecphrasis are also associated with didactic, especially the repeated imperative *aspice*;[31] Ovid's brilliance here is expressed in his ability to combine the formal signatures that characterize two different narrative forms, and so to bring out the contradictions inherent in the combination.

The end result is both quite pleasing and perplexing: the ostensible purpose for this advice, and for Ovid's imitation of Virgil, is to endorse the good clean value of work on the farm as a surefire distraction from love; yet in addition to the limited—at best—practical value of Ovid's agricultural instruction, the details that appear at the very center of his advice seem to undermine the whole project.[32] In particular, we should consider the nature of the song that Ovid's *pastor* creates; Ovid does not need to spell it out for us to be confident that it is a love-song, like the songs with which so many of the *Eclogues* concern themselves; and our knowledge of those songs also tells us that, like Corydon in *Eclogue* 2 and Gallus in *Eclogue* 10, the lover who seeks to escape his passion in this way is doomed to fail. Thus, at the very center of his constructive advice about

---

and its relationship to earlier ecphrases, see especially Casali 2006, whose approach to the self-reflexivity possible with ecphrasis very much complements my treatment here.

29 Examples from one particularly detailed example, the shield of Aeneas (*Aeneid* 8) include *nec procul hinc* (635), *post* (639), *haud procul inde* (642), *in summo* (652), *atque hic* (655), *hic* (663), *hinc procul* (666), *haec inter* (671), *in medio* (675), *hinc* (678), *parte alia* (682), *hinc* (685), *in mediis* (696), *medio in certamine* (700), *desuper* (705), *contra* (711), and *hic* (724 and 725).

30 Again, from the shield of Aeneas: *aspiceres* (650), *cernere erat* and *uideres* (676), *credas* (691), and *uidebatur* (707); several expressions denoting viewing also frame the ecphrasis proper: *oculos per singula uoluit* (618), *miratur* (619), and *miratur* and *imagine gaudet* (730).

31 On *aspice* as a marker of didactic instruction, see Kenney 1958, 203.

32 Thomas 1983 is of central importance on the significance of centrality in ecphrasis.

the virtues of the *uita actiua* in the form of a rustication cure, Ovid locates a scene that undermines its fundamental premises. In so doing, he not only exposes the grey area that lies between *Eclogues* and *Georgics*, the ambiguous territory where two different imaginary landscapes meet and come into conflict, but also comments on his own erotodidactic undertaking in terms that replicate that conflict by juxtaposing *otium* and *medicina amoris*. In the midst of a poem that offers as its motto the phrase *cedit amor rebus* (*Rem. am.* 144), the contradictory assertion of the last words of Virgil's Gallus, "*et nos cedamus Amori*" (*Ecl.* 10.69), insists on being heard.[33] Although Ovid's *praeceptor* claims the ability to provide effective *medicina amoris* to his pupils, his claim is undone by its own intertextuality.[34]

33 See also the universalizing rephrasing of Gallus' sentiment at *G.* 3.242–244, *amor omnibus idem.*

34 See Ross 1975, 81–106 for the probability that Gallus explored in his elegies points of contact with pastoral.

Alexander Sens

Envy and Closure in the Greek Anthology

In the concluding lines of Callimachus' *Hymn to Apollo*, Apollo kicks Envy (Φθόνος) for whispering that the poet's work is insufficient, and goes on to assert his preference for quality and refinement over quantity (*h.* 2.105–113). Structurally, as critics have observed, Apollo's rejection of Envy is a version of epilogic "break-off" formulae in which the poet seeks to control the reception of his work by bringing his theme to an end without engendering the resentment of the internal or external audience.[1] In the final lines of the Callimachean hymn, Apollo's rejection of Envy's insinuations amounts to a proleptic claim about the way the poem should, and will, be received by the reader: in dramatizing Apollo's satisfaction with the treatment he has been afforded in the preceding narrative, the passage also advances a defense against any member of the audience who would be hostile to the hymn on the ground that, through its brevity, it failed adequately to recount the god's accomplishments and excellence.[2] All of this reflects the complicated economy of praise poetry, in which the singer and honorand stand in reciprocal and mutually reinforcing relationship to one another, to the effect that the closural rejection of Envy embodies what the poet hopes will be not only the favorable response of the god to the praise he is afforded, but also that of the audience to the composition itself.

In this paper, I wish to explore how another genre of Hellenistic poetry, epigram, adapts this epilogic concern with *invidia*. Though the convention according to which a poet concludes a poem, or a section of it, by reflecting on the threat posed by the potential resentment of the audience has a rich background,[3] it acquires a special significance in literary epigram, because, in the context of a form whose principal original functions included commemorating deaths, references to envy resonate against the traditional characterization of death as hostile and invidious. Both inscribed and fictive funerary epigrams from the Hellenistic age treat the death of the honorand as the envious response of a god who has resented and thus brought an end to his or her accomplishments. A fourth-cen-

1 For closure in choral lyric, see Rutherford 1997.

2 Bundy 1972; Köhnken 1981 notes that while Pindaric and Bacchylidean versions regularly comment on the possibility that prolixity might engender envy, here Phthonos finds fault with the poet's brevity. For Pindaric break-off formulae in Callimachus, see Fuhrer 1988. For envy in Pindar, cf. Most 2003.

3 Cf., e.g. Pind. *Ol.* 8.53–55, *Nem.* 4.33–43 with Kyriakou 1996; Bacchyl. 13.199–203; Timotheus fr. 791.202–240.

https://doi.org/10.1515/9783110545708-011

tury epitaph from Thebes, for example, praises the honorand's preeminent virtue before attributing his death to "Fortune envious of the good" (*CEG* 635.4 ὤλε[σ-σεν] φθονερὰ τ[οῖς ἀ]γαθοῖσι Τύχ[η). In a Hellenistic epitaph from Egypt (*IMEGR* 64.6), death takes the form of personified Envy (Βασκανίη), while in an undated poem from Stratoniceia, Callinicus is said to be the victim of an invidious Hades, who has resented his accumulated achievements in the arts and athletics (*SGO* I 02/06/18 ὁ πάντα Μούσαις Καλλίνικος ἁρμόσας / ὁ καὶ παλαίστρᾳ ποικίλᾳ κεκασμένος / ἐνταῦθα κεῖται ... Βάσκανος γὰρ Ἀίδας / ἐσθλοῖσι τάκων ὄμματ' ἂν τόσαν χάριν); in a late Hellenistic poem from the Black Sea Chersonesus, Xanthus, a man "wise in the Muses, blameless to all the citizens, honored among the youths, a star of beauty", is said to have been killed by an invidious Ares as he fought for his fatherland (*GVI* 767 = *IosPE* I^2 482 Ξάνθον ... / τὸν σοφὸν ἐν Μούσαις, τὸν ἀμεμφέα πᾶσι πολείταις / τείμιον ἠιθέων, ἀστέρα καλλοσύνης /βάσκανος ὃν κατέπεφνεν Ἄρης πάτρῃ προμαχεῦντα).[4]

In literary epigrams from the Hellenistic and Imperial periods, poets sometimes engage with this conventional funerary idea in contexts having to do, directly or indirectly, with literature. A well-known and obvious example is Callimachus *Anth. Pal.* 7.525 (21 Pf.), which purports to be an epitaph for his father but directs much of its focus to the poet's own victory over envious resentment, βασκανίη:[5]

ὅστις ἐμὸν παρὰ σῆμα φέρεις πόδα, Καλλιμάχου με
  ἴσθι Κυρηναίου παῖδά τε καὶ γενέτην.
εἰδείης δ' ἄμφω κεν· ὁ μέν ποτε πατρίδος ὅπλων
  ἦρξεν, ὁ δ' ἤεισεν κρέσσονα βασκανίης.
οὐ νέμεσις· Μοῦσαι γὰρ ὅσους ἴδον ὄμματι παῖδας
  μὴ λοξῷ, πολιοὺς οὐκ ἀπέθεντο φίλους.

5–6 athet. Pfeiffer 5 οὐ νέμεσις PPl : ἄχρι βίου ex 6 Faraone 6 μὴ λοξῶι Σ Hes., cf. *Aet.* fr. 1.38 : ἄχρι βίου PPl

You who bear your foot past my tomb, know that I am child and father of Cyrenaean Callimachus. You would know both: the one led the army of his fatherland and the other sang greater than envy. There's no need for resentment: those whom the Muses look on when they are children without averting their eye, they do not reject as friends when they're old.

As critics have well observed, the epigram's thematic and verbal links to *Anth. Pal.* 7.415 (35 Pf.), Callimachus' fictive epitaph for himself, invite readers to

4 Cf. Fraser 1972, 869 n. 466.

5 The word, properly used of fascination by the evil eye, is closely connected to Phthonos, and Hellenistic poets use it as roughly equivalent to it in contexts having to do with the reception of literary work; cf. Fraser 1972, 1.758.

treat the poems as a complementary pair in which one provides information missing in the other and in which the poet's own poetic excellence marks the culmination of this family's accomplishments.[6] Interpretation of the epigram is complicated by the problematic status of the final couplet, which as it has been transmitted is almost identical to the conclusion of the *Aetia* prologue, but whether one amends the final couplet, excises it, or attempts to explain it in more or less the form it has been transmitted,[7] the poet's own claim (itself placed in the fictive voice of his dead father) to have conquered *baskania* reflects a broader engagement with the conventional threat that envy, whether directed at the poet him- or herself or at his honorand, poses to literary labor. That Callimachus the poet is to be imagined as already deceased is clear from the poem's connections to *Anth. Pal.* 7.415 (35 Pf.), where he is explicitly so treated. The speaking voice thus pretends to look back posthumously on the poet's entire oeuvre, and this retrospective perspective allows him to comment from a position of confidence that the destructive risk that envy poses to the reception of a poet's oeuvre has been avoided. The generic context lends special resonance: inasmuch as resentment in inscribed epitaphs is often treated as bringing about the end of mortal activity, Callimachus' transcendence of it implies the continued survival of his poetic voice even after his death.

Similarly, in an early fictive epitaph for Plato (*Anth. Pal.* 7.60),[8] the speaker's insistence that the philosopher's extraordinary achievements did not engender envy invites being read against the conventional treatment of envy in inscribed epitaphs:

σωφροσύνῃ προφέρων θνητῶν ἤθει τε δικαίῳ
    ἐνθάδε κεῖται ἀνὴρ θεῖος Ἀριστοκλέης·
εἰ δε τις ἐκ πάντων σοφίης μέγαν ἔσχεν ἔπαινον,
    οὗτος ἔχει πλεῖστον καὶ φθόνον οὐ φέρεται.

4 οὗτος P : τοῦτον D.L. 3.43 πλεῖστον D.L. : πουλὺν PPl καὶ φθόνον οὐ φέρεται PPl : καὶ φθόνος οὐχ ἕπεται D.L

6 For discussion, cf. Gutzwiller 1998, 212f; Scodel 2003, 258–262; Kirstein 2002, 117–121. Contra, Cameron 1995, 78f.

7 For an overview of the extensive bibliography on the question, see Harder 2012, 83f.

8 The poem is assigned to Simias in P, but given without ascription by Pl and Diogenes Laertius, who claims that it was inscribed on the philosopher's tombstone. It must in any case be the product of the Hellenistic period, since, as Notopoulos 1939 demonstrates, the view that Aristocles was the philosopher's original name first arose then; for further discussion, Notopoulos 1942; Tarán 1984, 75. For the probability that the poem is by Sim(m)ias of Rhodes rather than the Theban of the same name mentioned in the *Phaedo*, see Gow–Page 1965, 2.515.

> Surpassing other mortals in self-control and just character, Aristocles, divine man, lies here. If any person at all acquired great praise for his wisdom, this one has the greatest amount and doesn't garner envy for it.

Whatever the precise text of the end of the poem—πλεῖστον at any rate produces a sharper point in context than does πουλύν[9]—the basic idea is clear: Plato's virtue and wisdom, and the praise they generate, do not arouse resentment and envy. The poem thus has a background in the conventional idea that the dead person being commemorated perished because his or her qualities and accomplishments excited the resentment of a divine force. At the same time, however, the final clause of the poem also makes a claim similar to that at the end of the *Hymn to Apollo.* After lauding Plato's ethical qualities in the first couplet, the speaker in the second notes that despite receiving tremendous praise for his wisdom, the philosopher is not the subject of envy. At a basic level, the assertion is self-reflexive, since the poem itself is a vehicle for praise, and the larger point is that its treatment of Plato does not—and by implication, should not—arouse a hostile response from the reader. In this sense, the end of the poem depends on the reciprocal relationship between the poet and honorand, in which the threat that envy poses to the latter also jeopardizes the former's ability to accomplish the work of praising him (cf. e.g. Pind. *Ol.* 8.54f.).[10] The poem, in other words, not only resonates against the traditional role played by envy in funerary epigrams, but also exploits that role to comment on and shape its own reception: just as Plato's talents transcend envy, so too should a poem that honors them. Like the end of Callimachus' *Hymn to Apollo*, where the god's rejection of Envy makes an argument about the way the poem should be viewed by the reader, so here the final assertion that even the most bountiful praise of Plato's wisdom does not generate envy will be applied to the description of the philosopher that has immediately preceded: the poem, that is, should be well received by the reader, who will join in feeling φθόνος towards neither honorand nor laudator. The final clause, then, amounts to a self-referential *sphragis* in which the poet seeks to ward off a hostile reaction to his own project.

---

9 Cf. Gow–Page 1965, 2.515.

10 That relationship is, in the epigram, reinforced by the reality that the philosopher's achievements include his wisdom, σοφία, since that word is equally applicable to the achievement of poets (cf. Pind. *Ol.* 1.116, *Pyth.* 4.248, *Isth.* 7.18, *Pae.* 7b.20, Sol. fr. 13.51, Ar. *Ran.* 1519, Callim. fr. 1.18, *Anth. Pal.* 12.150.4). For philosophers in Hellenistic epigram, see White 1994, 146f.

A more complicated dynamic may be seen in *Anth. Pal.* 7.13,[11] an epigram attributed to Leonidas or Meleager. The poem treats the death of the poet Erinna as the product of the envy of Hades, who occupies the role played by Phthonos in Callimachus' hymn:

παρθενικὰν νεάοιδον ἐν ὑμνοπόλοισι μέλισσαν
  Ἤρινναν Μουσέων ἄνθεα δρεπτομέναν
Ἅιδας εἰς ὑμέναιον ἀνάρπασεν. ἦ ῥα τόδ' ἔμφρων
  εἶπ' ἐτύμως ἁ παῖς· "Βάσκανός ἐσσ', Ἀίδα".

Hades abducted for marriage the virgin Erinna, a new-singing bee among poets, as she was culling the flowers of the Muses. Indeed, the prudent girl said this rightly: "You are invidious, Hades".

The opening of the epigram, which belongs to a series of mock funerary poems for the poet, rewrites the opening of the *Homeric Hymn to Demeter*, where Hades abducts Persephone for marriage as she is picking flowers (1–5):

Δήμητρ' ἠΰκομον σεμνὴν θεὰν ἄρχομ' ἀείδειν
αὐτὴν ἠδὲ θύγατρα τανίσφυρον ἣν Ἀϊδωνεὺς
ἥρπαξεν ...
παίζουσαν κούρῃσι σὺν Ὠκεανοῦ βαθυκόλποις,
ἄνθεά τ' αἰνυμένην ...

I begin to sing of holy, fair-haired Demeter herself and her slender-ankled daughter whom Hades snatched ... as she was playing with the deep-bosomed daughters of Ocean and picking flowers...

The verbal and syntactical correspondences are unmistakable: Ἀϊδωνεὺς ... ἥρπαξεν is echoed by Ἅιδας ... ἀνάρπασεν, ἄνθεα δρεπτομέναν by ἄνθεα δρεπτομέναν. In reworking the hymn, the epigram evokes the idea, commonplace in funerary context, that young women who have died before marriage are brides of Hades (cf. 3 εἰς ὑμέναιον).

Erinna's principal, and perhaps sole, composition was a poem of some three hundred verses called the *Distaff*. In it, the singer lamented the death of her friend Baucis, who died before her marriage. A crucial feature of Leonidas' epigram, then, is that it assimilates the poet's premature death before marriage to that of the girl honored in her own poem. Indeed, Leonidas' epigram seems to treat Erinna herself in terms used of Baucis in the *Distaff*. In the final verse,

---

11 The question of authorship cannot be unambiguously resolved, but I here treat the poem as Leonidean. That the representation of Erinna as a bee gathering flowers resembles the opening of Meleager's *Garland* (cf. *Anth. Pal.* 4.1.1–4) could cut in either direction.

the narrator remarks on the truthfulness of Erinna's own words, 'You are invidious, Hades' (Βάσκανός ἐσσ', Ἀίδα). The same expression appears in an epigram attributed to Erinna in which the speaker is the tomb of Baucis ([Erinna] *Anth. Pal.* 7.712):

> νύμφας Βαυκίδος εἰμί· πολυκλαύταν δὲ παρέρπων
> στάλαν τῷ κατὰ γᾶς τοῦτο λέγοις Ἀίδᾳ·
> "Βάσκανός ἐσσ', Ἀίδα". τὰ δέ τοι καλὰ σάμαθ' ὁρῶντι
> ὠμοτάταν Βαυκοῦς ἀγγελέοντι τύχαν,
> ὡς τὰν παῖδ', ὑμέναιος ἐφ' αἷς ἀείδετο πεύκαις,
> τᾶσδ' ἐπὶ καδεστὰς ἔφλεγε πυρκαϊᾶς·[12]
> καὶ σὺ μέν, ὦ Ὑμέναιε, γάμων μολπαῖον ἀοιδὰν
> ἐς θρήνων γοερὸν φθέγμα μεθαρμόσαο.

> I am (the tomb) of the bride Baucis. Passing by my much-lamented stele, please say to Hades beneath the earth, 'You are envious Hades.' This beautiful tomb will announce to you who look on it Baucis' very cruel fate: how her in-law burnt on this pyre the child with the very torches to the accompaniment of which her marriage hymn was being sung, and you, oh Hymenaeus, retuned the sung song of marriage into a wailing cry of lamentation.

The authenticity of the epigrams attributed to Erinna is open to serious doubt; those poems are nowhere mentioned in the testimonia, which cite only the *Distaff*, and the ascription of *Anth. Pal.* 7.712 to her may simply be an erroneous guess based on the contents of the poem.[13] Although one cannot completely exclude the possibility that Leonidas was drawing from an epigram ascribed to Erinna rather than the *Distaff* itself, it seems on its face rather more likely that both Leonidas and the author of *Anth. Pal.* 7.712 were drawing on the *Distaff*. Whatever the case, Leonidas' epigram, in underscoring the truthfulness of her words, marks the poet's appropriation of language used by 'Erinna' in connection with the death of Baucis, thus assimilating the two women.[14]

---

12 The text of 5 f. is problematic, but as these verses do not materially affect my argument, I give them as printed in Gow–Page 1965; for discussion, see Neri 2003, 436 f.

13 Discussion in Neri 2003, 85–88.

14 The same phenomenon seems to be found in Asclepiades *Anth. Pal.* 7.11 (28 Gow–Page, Guichard, Sens), in which the speaking voice explains the small size of Erinna's corpus, which it treats as the sweet product of labor, γλυκὺς ... πόνος (1), by reference to her death in her nineteenth year (2 παρθενικᾶς ἐννεακαιδεκέτευς). The surviving papyrus fragment of the *Distaff* contains the ordinal 'nineteenth' (*SH* 401.39 ἐννεα̣[και]δέκατος) in a context that, when read against Asclepiades' poem, suggests it refers to the girls' age at the time of Baucis' death, and the poem as a whole may thus be read as conflating Erinna's biography with that of the subject of the *Distaff* (Sens 2003, 2011). The overlaying of the poet on her honorand suggests a broader analogy between Baucis' spinning and Erinna's poetic labor, which the epigram treats in terms that

Given the role that *baskania* plays in inscribed funerary epigrams (above, pp. 101 f.), some of the point of the phrase as used of Baucis must surely lie in Hades' envy of her good character and the esteem in which she was held for it, at least among her age-mates. But in light of the place that Baucis' work at the loom must have occupied in the poem, it would seem a reasonable speculation that her labor in that area was part of the larger picture, and that in the *Distaff* (as in Asclepiades 28, where Erinna's own work, πόνος, is interrupted by Hades' premature arrival), some of the point was that her early death had curtailed production. Leonidas' epigram, for its part, makes Hades' jealousy a direct response to Erinna's poetic labor. Unlike Persephone, who in the *Hymn to Demeter* plays girlishly with her friends in the literal meadow, Erinna's companions are not nymphs but poets (ἐν ὑμνοπόλοισι) and the flowers she picks are metaphorical flowers of the Muses. She is, moreover, explicitly cast as a bee, an image that evokes numerous passages in which the activity of poets is likened to that of bees among flowers,[15] including not only the characterization of her poetry as a "sweet work-product" by Asclepiades (above, n. 14) but also to its designation as honeycomb in an anonymous epigram (*Anth. Pal.* 9.190.1 f. Λέσβιον Ἠρίννης τόδε κηρίον· εἰ δέ τι μικρόν, / ἀλλ' ὅλον ἐκ Μουσέων κιρνάμενον μέλιτι).[16]

The language, indeed, suggests the quality of Erinna's work. As Camillo Neri has observed, the neologism νεάοιδος is multivalent, simultaneously suggesting both Erinna's youth and the novelty of her poetry, a traditional desideratum from the earliest period (e. g. *Od.* 1.35 f., Pind. *Ol.* 9.47–49 ἔγειρ' ἐπέων σφιν οἶμον λιγύν, / αἴνει δὲ παλαιὸν μὲν οἶνον, ἄνθεα δ' ὕμνων / νεωτέρων, Callim. *Aet.* fr. 1.25–28 with Harder ad loc.). In this context, the emphatic (ἦ ῥα) insistence on the veracity of Erinna's words (εἶπ' ἐτύμως) operates both at the literal level—Erinna's early death proves the accuracy of her own words—and also at a symbolic one: 'truth' is, in Hellenistic poetry, often a metaphor for literary quality (e. g. Theoc. 7.44, Posidipp. 63.7 AB),[17] and the phrase thus also amounts to an endorsement of her poetic voice, which, it is implied, is being quoted verbatim.

---

were, for a Hellenistic poet, highly marked (cf. Hunter 1996, 15): her work, sweet and small but also the product of intense effort, shares the poetic mode championed in the *Aetia* prologue, whatever the precise significance of that passage (Cairns 2016, 153 less persuasively claims that δυνατώτερος in *Anth. Pal.* 7.11.3 stakes out an anti-Callimachean position). That both Leonidas and Asclepiades, in different ways, treat Erinna in terms she used of her honorand may suggest that they are picking up a feature already found in the Distaff itself.

15 Cf. Nünlist 1998, 60–63.

16 For the epigram, see Neri 2003, 194–196.

17 Sens 2005, 209–212.

In the context of this epigram, then, the traditional topos of Hades' envy is overlaid on and conflated with the equally conventional threat that the envious reaction of the audience poses to a poet's project. The god's traditional resentment of her achievement thus takes on a specifically literary quality, like the hostility of Envy in Callimachus' *Hymn to Apollo* or the Telchines, the ὀλοὸν γένος Βασκανίης against whom that poet defends himself in the *Aetia* prologue (fr. 1.17 Pf.). Understood against this backdrop, the direct quotation of Erinna's own work simultaneously engages with and subverts the well-established topos of the invidiousness of death. Though death has brought Erinna's life and work to an end, the final quotation, in preserving the voice of the poet verbatim, suggests the conventional idea that the poet's voice will continue even after her own death, an idea made explicit in another, anonymous epigram for Erinna, adesp. *Anth. Pal.* 7.12: σὸς δ' ἐπέων, Ἤριννα, καλὸς πόνος οὔ σε γεγωνεῖ / φθίσθαι, ἔχειν δὲ χοροὺς ἄμμιγα Πιερίσιν ("Your beautiful poetic labor cries out that you have not perished, but hold your choruses with the Pierian Muses").

At the same time, inasmuch as the poem assimilates Erinna to her honorand Baucis, the poem makes its own speaking voice analogous to that of Erinna herself. As it quotes Erinna, the poem embodies her voice, so that the final quotation is spoken simultaneously by the poem and by its honorand. The epigram itself, then, is treated as a doublet of Erinna's own poetry, and as living proof of its survival. In other words, in its placement at the very end of the poem, the quotation of Erinna's own work mirrors traditional poem-concluding apologia that address the possibility that the work will be invidiously received, but also kicks against them by suggesting the continued durability of her verse, despite Hades' intervention. Moreover, inasmuch as the poem treats Erinna in terms similar to those she had used of her own honorand, it also links the speaker's voice with hers, and makes a simultaneous, if implicit, claim about its own continued survival, even in the face of potential resentment on the part of the audience. That audience includes the internal addressee Hades but may also be read as encompassing the reader, who is implicitly cautioned against feeling resentment of the literary accomplishment not only of Erinna but also the epigram in which she is honored.

A pair of later epigrams from the *Garland* of Philip conclude by explicitly cautioning against and critiquing the envy that threatens their work. These poems are not funerary, and in them the threat posed by envy takes a different form, but they nonetheless participate in a set of closural strategies similar to those found in earlier Hellenistic epigrams. The first of these epigrams, Evenus *Anth. Pal.* 9.251, is addressed to a cockroach, who is treated as an enemy of the Muses and urged to flee far from them:

ἐχθίστη Μούσαις σελιδηφάγε, λωβήτειρα
    φωλάς, ἀεὶ σοφίης κλέμματα φερβομένη,
τίπτε, κελαινόχρως, ἱεραῖς ψήφοισι λοχάζῃ,
    σίλφη, τὴν φθονερὴν εἰκόνα πλαττομένη;
φεῦγ' ἀπὸ Μουσάων, ἴθι τηλόσε, μηδ' ὅσον ὄψει
    βασκάνῳ ἄψηφον δόξαν ἐπεισαγάγῃς.

6 βασκάνῳ ἄψηφον Page : βάσκανον ἐν ψήφῳ P ἐπεισαγάγῃς Saumaise: –ῃι P

Column-eater most hateful to the Muses, destructive hole-hider, always feeding on what you've stolen from wisdom, why, black-skinned one, do you hid in my sacred accounts, cockroach, forming therein an invidious image? Flee from the Muses, go far, and don't so much as with an invidious glance bring me the reputation of someone of no account.

Interpretation of the epigram is complicated by uncertainty about the meaning of ψήφοισι and by what appears to be the corrupt paradosis of the final verse, where the transmitted expression ἐν ψήφῳ does not make good sense. Gow and Page (1968, 2.290) suggest that the book in question might have been called Ψῆφοι and that its contents reflected that title. Whatever the reality that lies behind the poem, however, the epigram, in not only associating the work with the Muses but also treating it as the product of *sophia*, represents it as literature rather than merely technical writing. As such, the poem demands to be situated against a broader set of epigrams in which invidious readers are represented as destructive insects. Two of these poems explicitly associate this hostile audience with grammarians linked to Callimachus (Antiphanes *Anth. Pal.* 11.322 and Philip *Anth. Pal.* 11. 321):

γραμματικῶν περίεργα γένη, ῥιζώρυχα μούσης
    ἀλλοτρίης, ἀτυχεῖς σῆτες ἀκανθοβάται,
τῶν μεγάλων κηλῖδες, ἐπ' Ἠρίννῃ δὲ κομῶντες,
    πικροὶ καὶ ξηροὶ Καλλιμάχου πρόκυνες,
ποιητῶν λῶβαι, παισὶ σκότος ἀρχομένοισιν,
    ἔρροιτ', εὐφώνων λαθροδάκναι κόριες.

Officious races of grammarians, diggers of the roots of another's muse, unfortunate moths who tread on thorns, taints of the great, so proud of Erinna, bitter, dry running-dogs of Callimachus, harm to poets, darkness to children starting out, be gone, bedbugs who secretly bite the well-spoken.[18]

γραμματικοὶ Μώμου Στυγίου τέκνα, σῆτες ἀκανθῶν,
    Τελχῖνες βίβλων, Ζηνοδότου σκύλακες,
Καλλιμάχου στρατιῶται, ὃν ὡς ὅπλον ἐκτανύσαντες,
    οὐδ' αὐτοῦ κείνου γλῶσσαν ἀποστρέφετε,

18 The translations adapt those of Cairns 2016.

συνδέσμων λυγρῶν θηρήτορες, οἷς τὸ 'μίν' ἢ 'σφίν'
εὔαδε καὶ ζητεῖν, εἰ κύνας εἶχε Κύκλωψ,
τρίβοισθ' εἰς αἰῶνα κατατρύζοντες ἀλιτροί
ἄλλων· ἐς δ' ἡμᾶς ἰὸν ἀποσβέσατε.

Grammarians, children of Stygian Blame, book-worms who eat thorns, Telchines of books, dogs of Zenodotus, soldiers of Callimachus, whom you extend as your weapon though you don't spare even him with your tongue, hunters of grievous conjunctions, to whom it is pleasing to investigate '*min*' and '*sphin*' and whether the Cyclops had dogs, may you forever be worn down in carping at others, sinners. But extinguish your poison against us.

As scholars have noticed, both of these poems redeploy Callimachean imagery to attack a set of values that they tendentiously associate with that poet.[19] Whereas Callimachus connects his poetry to the chirping of the cicada, these epigrams treat grammarians as worms and bedbugs, destructive insects that produce nothing of value of their own but are only derivative of and injurious to the work of others. Although Evenus' dates are unknown—indeed, the poems ascribed to that author in the *Anthology* may be by different authors[20]—the thematic and verbal connections between these poems and Evenus' address to the book-destroying roach are clear. Whereas Antiphanes and Philip treat hostile critics as metaphorical insects, here, the poet addresses a literal bug. Like Antiphanes' grammarians who dig the roots of another's Muse (*Anth. Pal.* 11.322.1 f.), the roach feeds on wisdom stolen from others: the phrase σοφίης κλέμματα φερβομένη refers at the literal level to the bug's consumption of the book, and the papyrus it consumes is thus represented as stolen material, but the language simultaneously treats the roach as a metaphorical thieving artist: the phrase τὴν φθονερὴν εἰκόνα πλαττομένη seems to mean that in eating holes out of the papyrus, the roach creates his own forms that invidiously rival the symbols or words written on the material, but the diction also casts the insect as a plastic artist producing a work that at the literal level competes with and destroys the author's text.

In this context, the speaker's final command for the roach to flee from the Muses and not cast an invidious glance at his work resonates against Callimachus' command for the Telchines to go to hell (fr. 1.17 Pf. ἔλλετε), as well as against similar warnings directed by Antiphanes at critical grammarians (*Anth. Pal.* 11.322.6 ἔρροιτ') and effeminate, Callimachean poets (*Anth. Pal.* 11.20.1 φεύγετε). Though the corrupt state of the paradosis complicates matters, the basic point is clearly that the insect should not, out of spite and resentment, destroy the speaker's work and thus damage its reception and his reputation. In this

19 See especially Cairns 2016, 161–172.
20 See Gow–Page 1968, 2.289.

sense, the final injunction serves a function similar to that of the end of the *Hymn to Apollo*—which is to say that it operates within the tradition according to which the poet seeks to shape and control the reception of his work in its final lines. If Page's plausible ἄψηφον for transmitted ἐν ψήφῳ is correct, the final verse plays upon the characterization of the book as ψήφοισι (3). In its context, then, the adjective means 'of no account,' but also suggests that if the roach destroys the constituent features (ψῆφοι) of the work, the speaker will have a reputation of "not having ψῆφοι".

Whatever the precise significance of ψήφοισι, the epigram is fundamentally self-referential. Although Gow and Page speculate about the nature of the work that the speaker has in mind, the papyrus columns that the poem warns the invidious roach against destroying are at a basic level those that constitute the book in which the epigram appears. Understood in this way, the poem constitutes a *sphragis* that represents itself as the product of artistry (3 σοφίῃ) and the Muses (and that warns its audience against filching and destroying its contents; with κλέμματα, cf. Thgn. 19.20 f. λήσει δ' οὔποτε κλεπτόμενα / οὐδέ τις ἀλλάξει κάκιον τοὐσθλοῦ παρέοντος "they won't be stolen covertly, and no one will exchange something worse for the good in them"). In this sense, the final injunction against the invidious evil eye belongs to the same tradition as Apollo's rejection of Envy at the end of the *Hymn to Apollo*. Insofar as it implicitly warns away those who would invidiously destroy it, the epigram makes a proleptic attempt to shape and control its own reception for eternity.

Antiphanes *Anth. Pal.* 9.256 engages with the *topos* in a different way. Here, the speaker of the poem is a half-dead apple tree whose single fruit is destroyed by an invidious caterpillar:

> ἥμισύ μευ ζώειν ἐδόκουν ἔτι, κεῖνο δ' ἔφυσεν
> ἓν μόνον αἰπυτάτου μῆλον ἐπ' ἀκρεμόνος·
> ἡ δὲ κύων δένδρων καρποφθόρος, ἡ πτιλόνωτος
> κάμπη καὶ τὸ μόνον βάσκανος ἐξέφαγεν.
> ὁ Φθόνος εἰς πολὺν ὄγκον ἀπέβλεπεν· ὃς δὲ τὰ μικρὰ
> πορθεῖ, καὶ τούτου χείρονα δεῖ με λέγειν.

5 ὄγκον Jacobs : ὄχλον P 6 τούτου Reiske : τούτους P χείρονα δεῖ με λέγειν Graefe (alia alii) : γηρὰν αει μ' ελεγεν P

Half of me seemed still to be alive, and that produced but a single fruit on its highest branch. But the bitch who destroys the fruit of trees, the downy-backed caterpillar, ate even that one out of spite. Envy looks to great substance, but the one who destroys small things I must call even worse than that.

Despite the uncertainty generated by the corruption that has damaged the final line of the epigram and that can only be healed conjecturally, the poem evidently engages in interesting ways with the sort of closural expressions of concern about *baskania* that we have witnessed in other poems.

The poem alludes to an erotic epigram by Callimachus in which the speaker notes the division of his soul into two parts, of which one still breathes, while the other has disappeared from a cause that the speaker initially professes not to understand (*Anth. Pal.* 12.73.1 f. = 41.1 f. Pf. ἥμισύ μευ ψυχῆς ἔτι τὸ πνέον, ἥμισυ δ' οὐκ οἶδ' / εἴτ' Ἔρος εἴτ' Ἀΐδης ἥρπασε, πλὴν ἀφανές "half of my soul is still breathing, but half—I don't know whether Eros or Hades snatched it—except that it's missing"). As I plan to discuss the interconnections between the two poems and their programmatic significance for Antiphanes more fully elsewhere, I note here only that, in affiliating the speaking voice with that of its Callimachean predecessor, the epigram, in which the speaker not only seems to be old[21] but is the producer of a small, singular (ἓν μόνον ... μῆλον), and difficult to access (αἰπυτάτου ... ἐπ' ἀκρεμόνος) fruit, both resonates against and confounds the oppositions of the Callimachean esthetic program, and particularly that of the *Aetia* prologue, in which the speaker defends himself for not having produced a single (ἕν) large-scale work and endorses the difficult byway over the well-traveled highway.[22] The tree's produce, in other words, has one of the qualities—unity—desired by the Telchines of the *Aetia* prologue, but remains fundamentally different from the sort of large-scale, accessible poetry that the Telchines endorse. Like Evenus' cockroach, the destructive caterpillar that ruins the speaker's small output is a markedly literary insect, a figure motivated by the sort of spite and envy against which the works we have been considering caution.

Despite the corrupt form in which they have survived, the final verses of the epigram seem to play at the formal level on the placement of such reflections on Envy and its effect on the poem at the conclusion of the work. Here, however, the basic terminology of the topos is challenged and subverted. Though the tree's small, inaccessible produce has in fact been destroyed by the invidious (βάσκανος) creature, the speaker questions the proper way to define its motivation. If the reconstructed form of the final couplet is on the right track, the speaker asserts that because Envy is properly and conventionally directed against success and so against great things rather than small ones (e.g. Pind. *Pyth.* 11.29 f., Soph.

21 The reason for the speaker's diminished state is left implicit, but it is reasonable to infer that he is half-dead of old age (as Höschele 2016, 115, assumes), in which case he resembles the allegedly senescent speaker of the *Aetia* prologue in yet another respect.

22 Whether one prints Jacobs' ὄγκον 'substance' or P's ὄχλον "crowd" in 5, the word resonates against the opposition between quantity and mass, on the one hand, and smallness and lightness, on the other, in the *Aetia* prologue.

Aj. 157), what has compelled the caterpillar to attack his work is something worse. The poem thus caps the opposition of great and small things that one finds in (inter alia) Callimachus' poetry—Antiphanes' apple tree has had to confront even worse than Callimachus did— but also turns it on its head. Indeed, in his epitaph for his father, Callimachus claims to have sung 'greater than envy' (*Anth. Pal.* 7.525.4 = 21.4 Pf., above, pp. 102 f.), while in the *Aetia* he imagines his critics invidiously criticizing him for the small size of his work. Antiphanes' epigram may pick up and subvert the use of the comparative κρέσσονα in the epitaph: the speaker's claim that what he has produced has been destroyed by something worse (χείρονα) than φθόνος or βασκανία, then, resonates not only against Callimachus' programmatic language and imagery, but also against traditional closural claims about the capacity of a work to survive the hostility of its external or internal audience. The final lines, so understood, operate in a manner similar to the end of Leonidas' poem for Erinna. At a basic level, the speaking tree laments the loss of its produce to a hostile force. At the conclusion of the poem, however, the speaker reasserts his control. With his final words, he underscores the continuity of his voice: despite the damage that the caterpillar has done, the tree—and by extension, the poet—continues to speak (λέγειν), and it is he who retains the power to define, even in opposition to the conventional language of poetic *sphragides*, the terms by which he describes what has happened to him. Antiphanes' epigram, despite being far removed at the level of content from the funerary poetry that informs the epigrams like Leonidas' tribute to Erinna and the mock epitaph for Plato, resonates against the original commemorative function of epigram as a genre: as in epitaphs that preserve the voice and memory of the deceased even long after his or her death, so the voice of Antiphanes' apple tree survives the assault of a destructive and invidious force, just as Erinna's poetry and Leonidas' epigram celebrating it ultimately transcend the death of its author.

All of the epigrams under consideration here come to an end with a reference to the threat that Envy poses to the production of literary art, whether that art is represented literally or figuratively. In this respect, their common structure seems likely to reflect not so much reminiscence of the *sphragis* of Callimachus' *Hymn to Apollo* or any other particular poem as an awareness of a broader closural tradition of which Callimachus' poetry constitutes merely one highly influential part. That same tradition, indeed, is operative in Latin poetry at the level of both individual poems and entire poetry books, which sometimes conclude by adverting to their own ability to survive the *invidia* or *livor* that threatens to interfere with their receptions, at least during the poet's lifetime, and thus to transcend the boundaries of the poet's own life (e. g. Hor. *Carm.* 2.20.4 f., Ov.

Am. 1.15.39 – 42, Stat. *Theb.* 810 – 819).[23] Such passages not only engage with Callimachus and other Hellenistic poetry, but also play on the relationship between the end of the poet's voice and the conclusion of his poetry book: as the author brings his work to an end by imagining a moment at which he will have been silenced by death, he represents his poetry—at the literal level now finished, in the sense that the reader has completed her reading of the book—transcending the boundaries of both book and life.[24] In this regard, these poems engage in a strategy similar to that found in Hellenistic epigrams, whose generic background as the form designed to preserve a person's posthumous memory (and, in many cases, voice) lends special force to the power of the poetic voice to transcend the invidious finality of death.

I began this paper—offered in insufficient tribute to a cherished teacher, mentor, and friend—by noting that in Hellenistic literary epigrams, the poet's attempt to ward off the resentful envy of his audience not only plays off a closural convention typical of Pindaric lyric, but also gains force from the topos of the invidiousness of death. The same overlaying of these topoi is perhaps also visible in a Latin poem that Richard Thomas has done much to explicate, Horace *Odes* 4.2, where the poet comments on the perils of emulating the style of Pindar himself. Verses 10 – 24 are an 'artful catalogue of Pindaric genres,' beginning with those that treat gods and concluding with the *threnoi*, which have at their core an engagement with issues of human mortality.[25] The entire passage concludes with a reference to *invidia*, but here the poet and his work is not the target of envy. Instead, poetry, with its capacity to overcome death, is the agent: *viris animumque moresque / aureos educit in astra nigroque / invidet* Orco 'and leads out to the stars his [sc. a dead youth's] strength, spirit, and character of gold, and begrudges them to black Orcus' (22 – 24, tr. Thomas). At an obvious level, Horace is playing on the usual representation of Death as invidious in sepulchral contexts: poetry, in the ode, has the power to reverse the usual relationship between Death and youths snatched too early, so that *invidia* can be treated as a positive force with the power to outstrip and undo the conventional enviousness of the god.[26] Beyond this, the concluding position of the reference to *invidia* within Horace's miniature Pindaric catalogue may reflect an awareness of the impor-

---

23 For the conventional idea that envy is diminished after death, see Nisbet and Hubbard 1978, 339 f., on Hor. *Carm.* 2.20.4.

24 Gutzwiller 1998, 211 f.

25 Thomas 2011, 107; cf. Freis 1983, 35.

26 Cf. Thomas 2011, 112; Putnam 1986, 54: '[o]nly a speaker who has himself surmounted the envy of others can dismiss for himself and the subjects with which he empathizes the envy of death.'

tance that such references to the danger posed by envy (and its connection to death and destruction) play at moments of closure and transition in the literary tradition, including both Pindar and the Hellenistic poets who engaged with him.

Brian W. Breed

Some Second Poems: Theocritus, Virgil, Tibullus

In ancient poetry books the beginnings, middles, and ends are the sites most often scrutinized for evidence of totalizing authorial intent: here, we assume, structure, design, and "architecture" are to be discovered. And yet, perceptions of textuality and intertextuality in a book might be very different at points in between and over the course of reading, where things are not, or not yet, locked into a pattern but emerging and undergoing revision. As an exercise in the latter sort of reading, my paper looks to some second poems—Theocritus 2, Virgil *Eclogue* 2, and Tibullus 1.2—for an account of textual form and meaning that emphasizes what is flexible, dynamic, and interpretable. By tracing connections among these poems, especially where they treat the theme of genre, I hope to reveal some of the different aspects a book's order might present, whether shaped by authorial design or by a subsequent editor. Moreover, different principles of organization are not simply inert facts determined at the moment of a book's creation. Readers must interpret the principles of organization observed by the poets in the selection and arrangement of poems in their books. Because variation among texts and modification of books by readers were normal, a view of textuality that encourages readers to question what goes where and why, like Alessandro Barchiesi's "fuzzier model" of book poetics (2005, 337), has the advantage of being consistent with ancient evidence for how readers interacted with books.[1]

A comparison between books of poems forms the framework for my paper, but the subject, second poems, also requires taking into account relationships within books. A second poem only exists as such by virtue of its position in a book, where it represents an answer to the question "what's next?". The relationship between second poems and introductory poems is distinctive. The programmatic or generically identifying content that is common in first poems leads readers to form expectations that a second poem can confirm or modify or sup-

---

1 See Hutchinson 2008, 1–41 on evidence from papyri and from testimonia about ancient books, for example, the differences in the sequencing of collected extracts in P. Tebt. 1 and 2 (Hutchinson 2008, 12) and, on the Roman side, Catull. 14's depiction of idiosyncratic textual assembly (2008, 31). From the perspective of textual criticism Tarrant 2016, 85–104 makes a strong case for seeing many manuscript "interpolations" as traces of an ancient context in which readers, such as the one who added the lines at the beginning of Hor. *Sat.* 1.10 (91), actively collaborated in fashioning the texts they used.

https://doi.org/10.1515/9783110545708-012

plement. This means that with regard to the components of generic identity—affiliations, consistency, setting, formal considerations, etc.—a second poem has an important role in the evolving "plot" of a poetry book. This was previously noticed by Eleanor Leach with regard to the second poems of the *Eclogues* and Tibullus 1, along with Horace's first book of *Satires*, "whose function as a second stage of introduction to each new book is to make us aware of an unresolved tension between old subjects and new points of view" (1978, 85).

In the present discussion, I emphasize the degree to which this dynamic extends also to the evocation of specific model texts and of what they put in second place. Virgil's second *Eclogue* has models in more than one Theocritean poem, especially poems 11 and 3, but it also relates in a number of particulars to Theocritus 2, a poem that does not fit easily within the frame of Theocritean bucolic that represents the predominant stream of inspiration for the *Eclogues*. In taking from Theocritus 2 Virgil shows a tendency to add to the pastoral character of what he adapts. "Pastoral" in this case, emerging as it does as the *Eclogues* unfold, means alignment with *Eclogue* 1, and the close connection between the two poems at the outset of Virgil's book contrasts with the formally and generically complex relationship of Theocritus 2 to Theocritus 1. Complexity is a feature of Theocritus' poems not only because of the generic diversity of his output, encompassing bucolics, mimes, hymns, encomnia, etc., but also due to the variety of forms in which Theocritus' poems circulated in antiquity, a subject to be addressed directly below. By homogenizing some of the diversity of the model, Virgil's intertextuality highlights a difference between the *Eclogues* book as a tightly-controlled product of authorial design and a Theocritean book, or books, impacted by different editorial choices. In his second poem Tibullus both extends the affiliation between elegy and the *Eclogues* that he introduced in poem 1 and reaches out past Virgil to Theocritus 2, especially for language to describe the practice of magic. References to *Eclogue* 8, which is where we find Virgil's most sustained imitation of Theocritus 2, suggest that Tibullus read the *Eclogues* with an eye on the relationship between Virgil's book and its Theocritean model. In all three examples, second poems are a place to observe the possibility that readers can play an active role in construing the organization of a book in ways that are not well captured by static and totalizing descriptions of authorial design.

While the *Eclogues* and Tibullus 1 are well known as authorially designed poetry books, there is a lot of uncertainty about the organization of the poems of Theocritus in books in antiquity.[2] In fact, the poem I am calling "Theocritus 2" comes second in only one of the three families of Theocritean manuscripts, the Vatican, which formed the basis for Stephanus' first printed edition and so for most modern editions after that (Gow 1950, 1.lxvi–lxix). In papyrus fragments there is no evidence for any ancient text of Theocritus with the poems in this order. The only papyrus witness to Theocritus 2 is the Antinoe papyrus, where the poem appears after poem 12 and before 18, in what is the second of the three sections of the codex. In manuscripts, poem 2 does not have a single stable position but tends to be more closely associated with poems 14–18, which include the other urban mimes, rather than with poems 1 and 3–13. Variation in where the poem appears is not unique to Theocritus 2. The order for all the poems varies a great deal, with one notable exception. In all manuscripts and papyrus where we can tell, Theocritus 1 comes first.[3] Gow's conclusion is that there was "no canonical order" for Theocritus' poems in antiquity and no definitive edition (1950, 1.lxii). At the same time, all is not random. Language, metrical technique, and dialect are important principles for associating poems into the groupings that are generally stable despite the differing order of individual poems from one ancient book to another.[4] But the Vatican order, and its placement of Theocritus 2 to follow Theocritus 1, does not conform to any other pattern. Gow describes it as the result of the "aberrant" (1950, 1.lxviii) choice of some ancient editor of a Theocritean book.

Variation in the order of poems in Theocritean books, as well as the inclusion of pseudonymous poems alongside authentic ones, suggests that either an authorially-designed collection never existed or was lost to subsequent manipulation.[5] The choices of editors, which might be formalistic and arbitrary,[6] were thus an important factor in how ancient readers experienced Theocritus' poems. Book-buyers and consumers themselves might act as editors, taking a hand in selecting poems and choosing the order for arranging them when purchasing a book of poems.[7] We do not know who paired 1 and 2 at the start of a

2 On the early history of the text of Theocritus' poems, see Gow 1950, 1.lix–lxii, Gutzwiller 1996, Sens 1997, 55–58.

3 Cf., e.g., Gutzwiller 1996, 128, attributing this to the poem's "extraordinary character" and "programmatic significance", though this could be as much the result as the cause of the poem's primacy.

4 See Hunter 1996, 28–45.

5 Note also the apparent omission of at least one authentic poem (Gow 1950, 1.lx); Hunter speaks of "significant textual variation...from an early date" (1999, 28).

6 Using alphabetization, for example, to arrange a book: Gutzwiller 1996, 126f.

7 Hutchinson 2008, 14f.

Theocritean collection, or why, though a reader might have noted their shared use of refrains and thus juxtaposed them.[8] The effect of this pairing is worth exploring, in part because, as I will discuss below, it seems to have had an impact on the books of Virgil and Tibullus.

In the second idyll, a woman called Simaetha both performs a magical incantation and gives a first-person narrative of her love affair with a youth called Delphis. The poem is an example of a common Theocritean form, a lover's monologue, like Theocritus 11 and 3. But the poem is also an outlier in the Theocritean collection, as a so-called "urban mime". The label, which is not an ancient one, while describing the setting and quasi-dramatic form of the poem, also signifies that it is not "bucolic" as the term is commonly understood, i.e., poems by or about herdsmen and matters of the countryside.[9] The position Theocritus 2 occupies in the standard modern order of Theocritus' poems emphasizes the difference. It follows Theocritus 1, which is structured around a double-barreled blast of emphatic generic self-definition. First comes a microcosm of Theocritean poetics in the form of a description of a bowl carved with scenes of non-heroic life, called a "wonder of the herdsman's world" (αἰπολικὸν θάημα, 56).[10] This then is followed by Thyrsis' song of lament for the legendary cowherd Daphnis, which is punctuated by refrains that name the performance as "bucolic song". Because bucolic is not a concept previously known and defined in Greek literature, the components of generic identity in Theocritus 1 only really become a program through confirmation and repetition later in the book; hence the importance of the reappearance of Daphnis (a character in Theoc. 6), the god Pan (7.103), and especially bucolic singing (5.44, 7.36).[11] In retrospect Theocritus 1 can be seen to define the contours of a new genre. Theocritus 2, however, avoids the conspicuous badges of bucolic identity, and the poem distinguishes itself from the preceding poem in other ways. Instead of a dialogue between male herdsmen in a noontime rural setting, Theocritus 2 is a monologue by a female in the city at night. Then again there is also common ground. Both poems use refrains. Erotic experience is an important source for thematic connections, and Homeric intertexts, a singularly important foundation for Theocritean verse, are prominent in both poems. Still, as a reading of a Theocritus' poems gets underway with these two poems the flipping of binary switches—dialogue / monologue; male / female; day / night; country / city— makes for an intriguing

8 So Gow 1950, 1.lxix; cf. Gutzwiller 1996, 124, 127

9 The urban mimes, which include Theoc. 14 and 15 along with 2, are given treatment as a coherent category within the poems of Theocritus by Burton 1995.

10 On the bowl as generic touchstone, see, e.g., Halperin 1983, 161–189.

11 Hunter 1999, 5–12, 60–68.

diversification. To the extent that such formal considerations put generic definitions in play, the reader is pressed to decide whether the poems belong in different categories or the generic definition provisionally based on idyll 1 needs to be revised to accommodate the second poem with an eye more on theme and intertextuality than on characters, settings, and the like. If nothing else, a reader who had only poems 1 and 2 to go by would have a very different idea of what a book of Theocritus' poems was about than one who could look back after having read all the way to the end.

As a reader of Theocritus, Virgil in the *Eclogues* frequently uses Theocritean intertextuality in ways that express a perspective on the arrangement of Theocritus' poems in a book. The opening lines of *Eclogue* 1, for example, allude to the beginning of Theocritus 1 specifically as the opening poem in a collection.[12] And when it comes to Theocritus 2, the intertextual fine print confirms a relationship between it and *Eclogue* 2. So, for example, the woman who prepares lunch for the reapers (*Ecl.* 2.10) shares the name "Thestylis" with the maid of Simaetha, the woman who performs an incantation to win back the affection of her lover in Theocritus 2. Such a reference might suggest the potential for deeper connections, and if we look, we find that Corydon's erotic predicament is comparable to Simaetha's. In lines 66–68 Corydon describes his passion in terms directly reminiscent of her (*me tamen urit amor, Ecl.* 2.68; Theoc. 2.38–40 ἀλλ' ἐπὶ τήνῳ πᾶσα καταίθομαι, 40). Corydon's love madness (*dementia*, 69) likewise has an analogue in the words of Simaetha (19, πᾷ τὰς φρένας ἐκπεπότασαι). The Theocritean line is repeated at Theoc. 11.72, and Virgil duly repeats his line that glosses it (*Ecl.* 6.47). Intertextuality here is operating not just at the level of poem to poem, but book to book, and within books, and on that score, *Eclogue* 2 exhibits similarities to more than one Theocritean poem. As mentioned above, Theocritus 11 and Theocritus 3 are especially rich targets for intertextual comparisons with *Eclogue* 2.[13] Virgil's overlapping and complementary references often reflect formal and thematic connections that already exist in the Theocritean collection, as here through the combination of references to lovers' monologues.

Variation, specifically variation in formal and generic terms, characterizes a Theocritean collection that begins with idyll 1 and 2. In the *Eclogues*, by contrast, relationships between the first and second poem more strongly suggest convergence towards a norm. Corydon is a herdsman (*pastor* 2.1), like Meliboeus (1.12–15) and Tityrus (1.7–10) in the preceding poem, where Theocritean intertex-

12 So, e.g., Clausen 1994, 29.
13 Du Quesnay 1979.

tuality is a primary component of a strong generic program.[14] The setting for *Eclogue* 2, like *Eclogue* 1, is the agricultural countryside (2.3–5), though it is not somewhere in the vicinity of Rome as it was in the introductory poem (1.19–25). Corydon seems to locate himself in Sicily (21), a gesture towards Theocritus (cf. esp. Theoc. 11.34), whose presence in the *Eclogues* continues from the first poem. Corydon is a singer and piper (*carmina*, 6) like Tityrus (cf. 1.2, 10). In fact, Corydon's song (*o formose puer*, 2.17) might give us the flavor of Tityrus' song for *formosam...Amaryllida* (1.5),[15] and, for what it's worth, Corydon has a history with Amaryllis (2.14 f., 51 f.). In the *Eclogues* names shared among poems raise the possibility of dramatic continuity and a stable cast of characters, but in this case repetition is perhaps less an indication that Corydon inhabits "the same world" as the characters of *Eclogue* 1 than a pointer towards the parameters of the book and its models as the site for unity.[16] The name Thestylis, which links *Eclogue* 2 and Theocritus 2, is representative. The *Eclogues*' roster of pastoral names largely derives from Theocritus, including, for example, Amaryllis, who is an absent/unseen beloved serenaded by a herdsman in Theocritus 3 and mourned as dead in Theocritus 4. In *Eclogue* 2 we also encounter a Daphnis (26 f.), the Theocritean touchstone. At the same time, there is also a connection to the Delphis for whom Simaetha longs in Theocritus 2. To perform her sympathetic magic in the poem's first line she calls for *daphnai*, "laurel leaves" and then burns them in order to make Delphis burn with desire (23–26), indicating that the name is effectively a substitute for "Daphnis". That is in fact the name Virgil uses in his adaptation of the poem in *Eclogue* 8 (68, etc.). One effect of the closely-woven texture of the *Eclogues* is to connect a character like Corydon to larger structures of the book. The name, for example, repeats at *Eclogue* 5.86 in a direct citation of *Eclogue* 2, and Corydon is then the name of a character competing in a singing contest in *Eclogue* 7. There is nothing comparable in Theocritus that associates Simaetha with the structures of a book, which is not to deny that her character and language represent important Theocritean themes.

While the momentum of the *Eclogues* draws Corydon into structures and patterns of consistency, in one way at least *Eclogue* 1 and *Eclogue* 2 also replicate differences of the sort that characterize Theocritus 1 and Theocritus 2 as the opening poems of a Theocritean collection. We see it in the variation in speech format: Corydon's monologue follows a collection-opening dialogue, and this variation is revisited later in the book. The Theocritean switch between genders

14 Breed 2006, 95–97.

15 Breed 2006, 113.

16 See now the nuanced discussion in Kania 2016, esp. 1–33.

is absent as *Eclogue* 2 follows *Eclogue* 1, but gets picked up in *Eclogue* 8. There Damon's song takes as a model Thyrsis' lament for Daphnis in idyll 1, to which the performer Alphesiboeus responds with a version of Theocritus' incantation from idyll 2 and, in the process, adopts the voice of a female singer.[17] *Eclogue* 8 is a carefully balanced dialogue constructed from two solo songs, both of which notably deploy refrains.[18] *Eclogue* 8 in itself thus replicates a Theocritean book in which idylls 1 and 2 were the opening poems. A conclusion that we might draw from the allusions to Theocritus 2 in *Eclogue* 2 and the pairing of Theocritus 1 and 2 as the combined models for *Eclogue* 8 is that Virgil was working with a Theocritean book that had idyll 2 in second place.

If Virgil was to some extent modeling his own book after a Theocritean book that juxtaposed idylls 1 and 2, whether he knew or cared that such a book also included non-Theocritean poems, as would be suggested by his imitations of Theocritus 8 and 9, or that it contained both "bucolic" and "non-bucolic" poems, as is indicated by the imitations of Theocritus 17 in addition to Theocritus 2, we don't know. In the universe of books available to him, Virgil was familiar with authorially composed books and collections edited by others, and with hybrids. The combination of roles of author and editor in Meleager's *Garland*, for example, represents a particularly influential model for Roman book poets.[19] It is possible that Virgil knew Theocritus in more than one format, for instance a book of the author's collected poems and another one, perhaps the one by Artemidorus commemorated with the epigram *Anth. Pal.* 9.205, that gave concrete expression to an idea of "bucolic poetry" by selective editing of Theocritus and some of his imitators.[20] Uncertainty about this remains, and the best course might not be to speculate about which book or books Virgil was following, but to note both that the *Eclogues'* imitations of Theocritus frequently evoke textual realities such as the position of Theocritus' poems in a book and that they reflect features of more than one type of book, whether multi-generic or constructed along the lines of a single generic idea, whether the work of a single author or of various authors.

For his part, Virgil, acting as author and as editor of his own poems, produces markers of architecture and design—unity, symmetry, responsiveness—in abundance, and against the backdrop of alternative models for book organization, these effects are anything but inevitable. And it is not merely a contrast between Theocritean fluidity and locked-in design in the *Eclogues*. Rather, author-

17 Breed 2006, 36–41.
18 On the construction of *Ecl.* 8, cf. Clausen 1994, 237–239.
19 Cf. Barchiesi 2005, 322f.
20 Gow 1950, 1.lx–lxi; cf. Gutzwiller 1996, 123–128, Vaughn 1981.

ial control in the *Eclogues* is something that is itself subject to negotiation with readers. The book format after all depends on a soft fiction that it is a collection of actually separable parts that have been chosen and arranged, not a single product that only ever had one form. Questions about what motivates the placement of one poem next to another, and contemplation of alternative ways of organizing things suggest that there is something to be gained from recentering our account of the book poetics of the *Eclogues* along the lines of Barchiesi's "fuzzier model" for poetry books "in which the idea of the controlling author as editor and architect is complicated by the activity of readers, imitators, scribes, and scholars" (2005, 341). Or we might at least expand our expectations to allow for authorial control that extends even to the anticipated entropy of textuality in the hands of the users of his book, so that variation and dynamism are already effectively part of the design. And these two alternatives might not be entirely distinct. Even if we did not have the Vatican manuscript family that juxtaposes idylls 1 and 2, the allusiveness of *Eclogue* 2 and especially *Eclogue* 8 could be said to generate a kind of virtual edition of Theocritus in which the two poems are paired. That is not to say that the *Eclogues* directly guided a reader or readers to give physical expression to editorial choices in the form of the text that put Theocritus 1 and 2 next to each other at the beginning. Speculation along precisely those lines has, however, been offered.[21]

The important place of the *Eclogues* in the history and development of Roman poetry books meant that Virgilian choices, and choices by readers of Virgil, had lasting consequences. Pastoral coloring in second poems, whether a thoroughgoing take on the countryside as imagined world like that of *Epode* 2 or a more isolated and decorative allusion like Prop. 1.2.25 (cf. *Ecl.* 7.41 f.), suggests that even in books with different generic affiliations from the *Eclogues* the second position was recognized as a place for acknowledging Virgil's book. Perhaps too much pastoral in an introductory poem would be distracting, especially in light of the model of book programmatics represented by Theocritus 1 and *Eclogue* 1. The possibility of generic distraction apparently did not trouble Tibullus, whose first book not only conforms to the ten-poem pattern of the *Eclogues* and *Satires* 1, but also exhibits a deeper indebtedness to the *Eclogues*. Reminiscences of the *Eclogues* are prominent in the first poem,[22] and in the second poem intertextuality with the *Eclogues* is both a factor in how the generic plot develops for Tibullus' book and a point from which to observe how the *Eclogues* relate to a Theocritean book or books.

21 Gutzwiller 1996, 127 n. 30.

22 See Putnam 2005, who highlights the importance of *Ecl.* 1 especially; cf. Boyd 1984 more generally on Virgilian language.

Magic, specifically female magic, is prominent in Tibullus 1.2, for which Tibullus draws on the incantation of Simaetha in Theocritus 2 and on Virgil's imitation of it in *Eclogue* 8, while also making reference to *Eclogue* 2. The Virgil to whom Tibullus is indebted at the outset of his first book is, in other words, not only the inspiration for Tibullus' rural imagination, but also a reader of Theocritus attuned to physical realities of textuality, such as a poem's position in a book, as a component of intertextual relationships.

After the Virgil-inflected rural reveries that are prominent in the first poem in Tibullus' book, Tibullus 1.2 pointedly adopts an urban form, the paraclausithyron. In darkness of night the poet pleads and laments at the closed door of his beloved.[23] Moving from country to city, and from day to night, Tibullus' book follows a path like a Theocritean book that has idyll 1 and 2 at its beginning. In the second poem when Tibullus invites Delia to escape her confinement within her home, he invokes a witch who has provided a spell to blind her husband to his wife's affairs (41–64), and Theocritus 2 is one of Tibullus' sources for the enumeration of the witch's powers (43–52). The magical heroines and models Tibullus cites for his witch, Medea and Hecate, for instance, have parallels in Theoc. 2.11–16. But the scope of the theme means the passage encompasses many other related texts beyond Theocritus 2. For example, prior to Tibullus references to necromancy in the practice of magic (45–48) are found in the epic tradition, most notably *Odyssey* 11. In *Eclogue* 8 the ability to conjure the dead is credited to the male magician Moeris: *saepe animas imis excire sepulcris* (98). This particular magical procedure is not addressed in Theocritus 2, but the description there of Hecate "coming over the graves of the dead and the dark blood" (13) would indicate the proper location and materials needed for summoning the dead. In some instances Tibullus' apparently Theocritean references may be filtered through *Eclogue* 8, as, for example, with the dogs (Tib. 1.2.52) who are a sign of the presence of Hecate and the effectiveness of the incantation (Theoc. 2.35, *Ecl.* 8.107). When Kirby Flower Smith calls details like this "conventional" (ad Tib. 1.2.42), he is using just another word for intertextual complexity. So Tibullus' witch can make rivers run backwards. This power is included among the effects of magic by Propertius (1.1.19–24), as well as Apollonius (*Argon.* 3.532), but in *Eclogue* 8 it is an effect of song (4), a reminder that magic as a poetic theme carries significance for poets' representation of their own capacities and limitations, which is important for Tibullus.[24] Tibullus' reference to "drawing

---

23 See Bright 1978, 133–149 for a reading of Tibullus 1.2 against the conventions of paraclausithyron.

24 See, e.g., Lee-Stecum 1998, 86–92 on witchcraft, taken to undermine trust in the poet's mastery and credibility.

down the moon" (Tib. 1.2.43) corresponds to *Ecl.* 8.69, but in triumviral poetry, and elsewhere, this is a common attribute of a witch (Prop. 1.1.19; Hor. *Epod.* 5.45 f., 17.77 f.). It does not have a direct precedent in Theocritus 2, though Simaetha does address herself to the moon and calls on her aid. The instruction from Tibullus to Delia to spit three times after performing the incantation (54) cites another convention of magical descriptions, but it does so by a specific combination of references to *Eclogue* 8 and Theocritus. Virgil and Theocritus both invoke magical tripling (*terna...terque...tribus*, *Ecl.* 8.73–78; ἐς τρὶς ἀποσπένδω καὶ τρίς, πότνια, φωνῶ, Theoc. 2.43), but there is no spitting in *Eclogue* 8. Tibullus could point to several instances in Theocritus, including Theoc. 6.39 f., as well as Theoc. 2.62, ἐπιφθύζοισα (a variant not printed by Gow, who prefers the papyrus' ἐπιτρύζοισα).[25] Richard Thomas might call this a "window reference" (Thomas 1999, 130–132), which in this case highlights Virgilian decorum in omitting earthier elements in Theocritus.

After he realizes that magic might be more effective at banishing love than at binding Delia to him (65 f.), Tibullus' thoughts shift and his references shift with them. In contrast to someone (her husband?) who would choose travel and soldiering over the companionship of his beloved (67–72), Tibullus expresses a desire for a simple life in the country with Delia. Re-entry here to the metapoetic space of Tibullus 1.1 coincides with a renewed focus on the *Eclogues* and on questions of genre, as Tibullus alludes to *Eclogue* 2. He does so at the intersection of elegy and pastoral. He spins a rural fantasy for Delia, which reverses one standard image of the paraclausithyron (e.g., Prop. 1.16.22, Callim. *Anth. Pal.* 5.23.1–2): he will sleep together with his beloved on hospitable ground, rather than alone on the cold stone of her threshold (71–74):

ipse boves mea si tecum modo Delia possim
    iungere et in solito pascere monte pecus
et te dum liceat teneris retinere lacertis
    mollis et inculta sit mihi somnus humo.

Delia, my darling, if I could just yoke oxen together with you and graze a flock on the familiar mountain and, while I'm able, embrace you by soft shoulders and have gentle sleep on untilled ground.

---

25 For spitting in the lap three times, cf. also *Ciris* 372–373, which quotes *Ecl.* 8.75 *numero deus impare gaudet*, and see Lyne 1978 ad loc., who notes the connection to Tib. 1.2 and thinks there may be a source in Cinna's *Zmyrna*, also now Kayachev 2016a, 139–141, for whom Homer, seen through references by Theocritus and Apollonius, is primary.

The lines are reminiscent of ideas prominent in Tibullus 1.1 (cf. esp. 1.29–36, 45–48) and of *Eclogue* 2, where Corydon invites Alexis to join him in the countryside (28–30; cf. also Theoc. 11.42–48). Tibullus and Corydon both desire to overcome separation from their beloveds, and they face comparable obstacles to reuniting with them, each kept by a "master": *delicias domini* (*Ecl.* 2.2); *ianua difficilis domini* (Tib. 1.2.7). Familiarity of setting and scenario is a deliberate strategy on Tibullus' part. His characterization of his rural retreat as customary practice, i.e., pasturing a flock on the usual mountain (*in solito pascere monte pecus*, 72), signals the manufacture of literary tradition through textuality. This process is on the one hand specific and internal to the book: Tibullus' devotion to pasturing is "usual" because it has been established previously in poem 1, where, in addition, the world of the farm and companionship there with Delia were already characterized as customary; note *solito...toro* (1.1.44). But the *Eclogues* and pastoral stand alongside poem one as the place where such things are "usual". Mountains are where Corydon sings (*montibus et silvis*, *Ecl.* 2.5) and where his lambs graze (*mille meae Siculis errant in montibus agnae*, 21). Corydon is himself tradition minded (*canto quae solitus...*, *Ecl.* 2.23). On this basis we might imagine Tibullan elegy to be an outgrowth of pastoral, the continuation of habits on display in the *Eclogues*, or we might prefer to identify Virgil as an elegiac predecessor lacking only elegiac meter, but the generic connections are not simply conjured by Tibullus for self-interested reasons. Pastoral verges on elegiac ideas and language in his source material,[26] whether or not Virgil is himself drawing on elegiac poetry by Gallus.[27] The image of the grazing flock in *Eclogue* 2 is given an erotic slant by Virgil later in his collection (*a virgo infelix tu nunc in montibus erras*, *Ecl.* 6.52) possibly on the basis of Calvus' *Io*, as described by Thomas (1999, 303–305). A Tibullan tendency to highlight what is already generically intermingled in the *Eclogues* is apparent also at the beginning of Tibullus 1.2.[28] In line 11, Tibullus' reference to his own love madness, *dementia*, as Maltby rightly notes ad loc., "echoes the amatory language of Virgil's *Eclogues*", but that is language already carrying elegiac

26 See Kenney 1983 for a classic discussion of *Eclogue* 2's "transposition of the elegiac situation into the pastoral mode" (51).

27 Possible Gallan influence on Virgilian pastoral as described by Ross 1975 is relevant, and Tibullus might be deploying what Thomas would term multiple references or conflation (Thomas 1999, 135–140).

28 We can compare Propertius' elegiac rewriting of pastoral as described by Thomas 1999, 263–266.

overtones.[29] More than that, love as *dementia* contributes to the creation of a relationship between the *Eclogues* as a book and a Theocritean book, as we have already seen. It is the focus of the book-oriented intertextuality at *Ecl.* 2.69 and 6.47 (in the same neoteric context as *in montibus erras* above), duplicating a Theocritean self-reference (Theoc. 2.19 and 11.72). For Tibullus *Eclogue* 2 is thus a significant site for the double construction of Virgil as a predecessor, as quasi-generic model, and as model of book poetics. Both aspects of Virgil's authority are expressed through his active reading of Theocritus.

Still, for all that the coordinated outcomes and overlapping significances of Tibullus' references to Virgil and to Theocritus have their basis in the particulars of textual form, departing from the order imposed on poems by authorial design in the setting of a book activates further meaning for Tibullus. The prominence of *Eclogue* 8 and Theocritus 2 among the intertexts of Tibullus 1.2 subtly suggests that the magical incantation should come second in the book on the basis of Virgil's Theocritean precedent. Tibullus shows himself to be the sort of reader of the *Eclogues* to acknowledge all the intricacies of authorial design and yet still say, "Well, I would've put X there instead of Y". However we parse Tibullus' varying roles—as author, or editor, or author as editor, or reader (as author and editor)[30] – with respect to the *Eclogues* in making sense of Virgilian allusions to Theocritus he recognizes the role of a poem's position in its book as potentially crucial to the contextual meaning of pointed allusions. But that is just to replicate the authorial role as Virgil had performed it with respect to Theocritean books.

In poetry books the order of poems is one more feature of the text to interpret. Reading as "plot" takes in so much, including the construction of generic identity.[31] And in the analysis of choice and selection related to generic identity, readers can be empowered to act like editors, whether they are physically intervening to create or to modify a text—like the unknown person who put idylls 1 and 2 together in his text of Theocritus—or merely annotating the text with mental notes of type that says "*my* order is defined by this criterion" or "this doesn't *go* here", which may be closer to Tibullus' stance as a reader of the *Eclogues* and Theocritus. In the case of the *Eclogues* and Tibullus 1, with a Theocritean book or books in the background, genre and intertextuality conspire to cast reading the book as a process that is evolving and flexible and that resists closure, at least

---

29 The reference is specifically to Corydon's self-reproach: *quae te dementia cepit* (*Ecl.* 2.69). The recurrence of erotic *dementia* in the *Georgics* again takes place on elegiac territory; cf. Thomas 1988 on *G.* 4.488, 494 f.

30 And he shows a Virgil-like regard for the model of Meleager, alluded to in the opening lines of Tibullus 1.2 (*Anth. Pal.* 12.49); see Maltby ad 1–4.

31 The discussion by Zetzel 1980 holds up well.

until it can't be resisted any more because the physical end of the book has come. Second poems are key to this effect. They represent the first test of consistency, however defined, for a book of poems. They are the first chance to put into practice the programmatics indicated by poem 1, but also the first opportunity to disrupt or recast expectations generated at the beginning. In the sample of texts that have been under discussion here, we are dealing with highly sophisticated readers who are also poets, for whom intertextuality as analysis of editorial choices is a self-reflexive spotlight on their own creative roles. Their means of expressing their analysis though, picking and choosing, reordering, introducing variation in relationship to a previous book, work in the same spaces where active intervention by ordinary readers is conceivable, even expected.[32]

32 To Richard Thomas I am especially grateful for two things he always generously shared: friendship and perspective. It is a pleasure also to thank the editors of the volume first for the invitation to contribute and second for their beneficial criticism.

Charles Martindale

The Horatianism of Marvell's "Horatian Ode"

We are all historicists now. But of course there are many variants of historicism—few today would share all of the views of Hegel, the great originator, the man who, to use his own phrase about Winckelmann, "initiate[d] a new organ for the human spirit".[1] In Classics, as elsewhere, there is a strong tendency to stress horizontal over vertical contexts; the only legitimate basis for interpretation becomes the context in which the text was originally produced (though what might be meant by this "original" context is perhaps rather less clear than is usually supposed, as we shall see). This sort of contextualism seems to me to make the mistake of the earnest designers of historical dramas on film and television who conscientiously labour to ensure that the furnishings of the buildings are all from the exact point of time in which the story is set. But the world is seldom like that. The room in which I wrote this essay contains comparatively few artifacts made in the last two decades; in it objects from different periods happily co-exist, the oldest of them from nearly two centuries ago. What we call the present is normally interpenetrated in just this way by multiple pasts. Furthermore, the view that the meaning of a poem is fully realized when text and context fit perfectly together in an originating moment of plenitude is a kind of idealism, though of course historicists do not see the matter in this way (almost always believing themselves to be materialists).

In one way it is odd that Latinists should make this particular mistake. For Latinists are very much concerned—some would say to the point of obsession—with intertextuality. And intertextuality constantly takes us away from contem-

I am delighted to write in honour of Richard Thomas, who has taught us so much about intertextuality, but whose interest in reception means that his work breathes a *largior aether* than many of his fellow intertextualists. This essay is a substantial reworking and expansion, designed to bring out some broader theoretical issues, of my brief discussion of Marvell's poem included in Cheney / Hardie 2015, 548–551. My interest in Marvell's Horatianism goes back more years than I care to remember to my sister's Oxford PhD thesis: Joanna Martindale, 'The Response to Horace in the 17th Century' (1977). I would like to thank David Hopkins, Tania Demetriou, and Elizabeth Prettejohn for helping me to improve this essay.

1 Hill 1980, 141. I am not suggesting of course that historical awareness began with Hegel; Pope's Homer notes, for example, arguably offer a closer engagement with the tangible specificities of historical difference/ similarity than Hegel's larger and more abstract claims.

https://doi.org/10.1515/9783110545708-013

porary context to the transtemporal and cross-cultural. It is obviously possible to argue that Virgil, say, was interested above anything else in the writings, both Greek and Latin, of his predecessors in the past, from Homer onwards, was more interested in that perhaps than in the events and writings of his own day. Servius' initial statement of the *intentio* of the *Aeneid*, whatever its shortcomings, at least neatly combines the transtemporal with contemporary context: Virgil sought not only to "praise Augustus through his ancestors" but also "to imitate Homer". A contextualist might respond that Virgil's reading of Homer is not the same as our reading, or of Homer's 'original' meaning, and thus still part of the contemporary context. There are two objections to this, one practical, the other theoretical. The practical objection is that we know little about how in detail Virgil read Homer other than what he made of him in his own writings (and, if we get some help from Servius, we should remember that he wrote many centuries later). The theoretical objection is that we are asked to believe that Virgil's encounter with past authors was wholly presentist, that Virgil in reading Homer experienced nothing of cultural or temporal displacement. This seems highly implausible, even if his experience was not the same as that of a reader trained in historical criticism as developed from the nineteenth century onwards.

There are, however, signs of a growing interest in what we may call the "transhistorical", the connections or *correspondances* (to use a word of Baudelaire's) between different periods and the products of those periods, including our own. The transhistorical, which retains a sense of the historical distinctness of different periods, is not to be confused with the universal (the view that in what most matters human beings are deep down the same).[2] This critical turn involves re-examining, with more sympathy for its positive uses, the notion of "anachronism", traditionally one of the most serious charges that historicizing critics can bring against interpretations of which they disapprove.[3] Alexander Nagel and Christopher S. Wood in their book *Anachronic Renaissance* coin the term "anachronic" to denote a desirable "bending of time" that an artwork in particular, "whose relation to time is plural", can generate:

> The artwork is made or designed by an individual or by a group of individuals at some moment, but it also points away from that moment, backward to a remote ancestral origin,

2 For some reason historicism is often claimed today as a virtuous, "progressive" position; but both historicism and universalism have no simple political/moral entailments—both can be either emancipatory or repressive.

3 On anachronism see de Grazia 2010; Martindale 2013; Porter 2017; Prettejohn 2017, 50–57; Rancière 1996.

> perhaps, or to a prior artifact.... At the same time it points forward to all its future recipients who will activate it as a meaningful event. The work of art is a message whose sender and destination are constantly shifting.[4]

Clearly anachronism so conceived fits naturally with the practices and methodologies of classical reception studies. It becomes not an error but an enabling condition of art and of its interpretation:

> The work of art when it is late, when it repeats, when it hesitates, when it remembers, but also when it projects a future or an ideal, is "anachronic". We introduce this term as an alternative to "anachronistic", a judgmental term that carries with it the historicist assumption that every event and every object has its proper location within objective and linear time. From a historicist point of view, an artifact that has been unmoored from its secure anchorage in linear time and has drifted into an alien historical context is an "anachronism".

Unsurprisingly this "anachronic" approach is especially prevalent in relation to the Renaissance, the period premised on the idea, real or imagined, of a great revival or renovation of classical antiquity, Vasari's *rinascita*, a rebirth. Classicists, as the heirs of the Renaissance humanists, accordingly need to pay careful attention to this set of concerns:

> "Art" is the name of the possibility of a conversation across time, a conversation more meaningful than the present's merely forensic reconstruction of the past. A materialist approach ... tends not even to notice that the artwork functioned as a token of power, in its time, precisely by complicating time, by re-activating distinguished forebears, by comparing events across time, by fabricating memories.

I want to look at these issues by examining the most famous Early Modern lyric in English inspired by Horace, Marvell's "An Horatian Ode upon Cromwell's Return from Ireland", a poem that has proved perplexing and elusive, its stance and meaning contested.[5] On the occasion of Cromwell's homecoming from his now notorious Irish victories, the Ode looks back to his rise to pre-eminence among his Parliamentary colleagues, the regicide, and creation of the Republic, and forwards to the expected campaign against the Scots. The professed point of reference is the lyric Horace, but the poem is packed more generally with Roman

---

4 Nagel / Wood 2010, 9; subsequent quotations in this paragraph are from pp. 13 and 18.
5 Significant discussions include Newton 1972, 125–133; Norbrook 1999; Syfret 1961 (on the interplay between Horace and Lucan); Wilson 1969; Worden 1987. See also the bibliography in Smith 2003, whose Longman *Annotated English Poets* edition and commentary assembles the relevant sources and analogues.

images, ideas, and terminology. In the last century the Ode became something of a critical battleground in disputes about poetic ambiguity and irony and about how poetry works, disputes in which the complex classical presences necessarily played their part. In 1947 Cleanth Brooks published his influential New Critical reading of the Ode, which alleged irony at Cromwell's expense; it received an avowedly "historicist" reply in 1952 from Douglas Bush, who accused Brooks of importing his own liberal beliefs into the poem and insisted that Marvell "wrote as an Englishman of 1650".[6]

Critics do not point out how unusual, indeed how odd, is the title of Marvell's ode: "An Horatian Ode upon Cromwell's Return from Ireland" (which ostensibly dates the poem's setting to June-July 1650). Early Modern poems often refer to contemporary events, for example Sir Richard Fanshawe's "An Ode upon Occasion of his Majesty's Proclamation in the Year 1630, Commanding the Gentry to Reside upon their Estates in the Country". (Fanshawe wrote some of the most accomplished translations of Horace of the period, and a number of his original poems, like this one, show obvious "Horatian" characteristics.) Likewise it is common to indicate that a poem is an imitation of a particular Horatian poem, as in the case of "Horace his ode to Venus, Lib. IV Ode 1, Imitated by Mr. Pope" (1737). Indeed imitations of Latin poems, Horace's not least, are two a penny throughout the seventeenth and eighteenth centuries. But to include the word "Horatian" in the title (or "Virgilian" or "Ovidian" for that matter) is, so far as I am aware, without precedent or parallel, and we ought to ask how we might respond to this unusual feature. One answer, to anticipate, is that the title puts as it were the whole poem in scare-quotes, creating a distancing, even a faint flavor of irony, and a degree of self-consciousness about what sort of a poem we are reading, and therefore about how it is to be interpreted. Certainly, like Servius' account of the *intentio* of the *Aeneid*, the title links contemporary context (a very precise moment in English history) to the transhistorical—to a poet dead for hundreds of years who wrote under very divergent conditions in a different, non-Christian culture.

6 This classic exchange is reprinted in Carey 1969, 179–210; the quotation is from p. 208. Even those of us who reject the historicist assumptions of Bush may find Brooks' analysis, seductive as it is, overly vulnerable. Its combination of complacent liberalism and moralism with a distaste for politics, which makes it difficult to talk interestingly about power, removes the poem's capacity to shock. Moreover the concept of ambiguity needs more scrutiny; it is true that the poem contains an array of puns, double or multiple meanings, and wordplays, but these can be read as a species of hard wit rather than as rich "Shakespearean" ambivalence. Brooks' debate with Bush is parallel to that between Rancière and Febvre (Rancière 1996).

In general interpreters assume that the title merely draws our attention to the fact that the poem contains echoes and imitation of Horatian lyric. In one way "imitation" may be a better word than "allusion" for the procedures involved, because that is the word used in the period and because awareness of Horatian intertextualities is not essential for interpretation in the way that many instances of allusion are often held to be. On the other hand the etymology of "allusion", from the Latin word for "play with", *alludere*, is highly appropriate, as Marvell encourages a free-play, an oscillation, a movement, that respects readerly freedom, between his text and Horace's Odes. Certainly, title aside, elements from Horace are not hard to locate. Nigel Smith offers a serviceable summary: "it is...in the condensed diction and cryptic syntax of the Ode...the sense of detachment and poise, and the simultaneous rendering of past, present and future, that similarities lie".[7] This will do well enough, though Ode 1.37, among the Horatian intertexts, is hardly marked by detachment, in its joy in victory and extreme abuse, in its opening stanzas, of Cleopatra as mad, immoral, and drunk. Furthermore "poise" may not be quite the *mot juste*, if it is taken to imply a measured and wholly controlled balancing of alternative possibilities; alternative possibilities are certainly present in Marvell's poem, but how far they are measured or controlled is itself a matter of debate. And there is certainly a puzzling mismatch between the calm surface movement of the verse, and the tensions that may, or may not, lurk within or beneath. These tensions sometimes depend on potential ambiguities at the level of the individual word or phrase, which may, or again may not, have more than a single meaning. Where this is the case, the result is not so much a matter of rich suggestiveness, in the manner of Shakespeare or Virgil, but of something closer to a pun, a doubleness or tripleness that might produce a hint of irony or even sarcasm (though any resulting "tone" remains highly elusive). So "advent'rous" in line 11 might mean "hazardous" or "enterprising"; and similar stories have been told about "forward" (1), "restless" (9), "inglorious" (10), "ruin" (34), and indeed many other words.[8]

Let us look in more detail at aspects of the Ode's use of Horace. For a start Marvell devises an English equivalent for an Horatian stanza. This verse-form (two tetrameters followed by two trimeters, both rhyming) had previously been used by Sir Richard Fanshawe for versions of Horace's Odes, and serves well enough to suggest a metre like Alcaics; Fanshawe's Horace had not yet been published but Marvell could have seen the poems in manuscript.[9] Marvell

---

7 Smith 2003, 268.

8 See the commentaries, including Smith 2003.

9 See Simeone 1952, 317 f.; Everett 1979, 74–77.

uses monosyllabic strong rhymes to give his stanzas weight and heft (though the snap of the rhyme introduces a neatness that is more Marvellian than Horatian):

> But those do hold or break,
> As men are strong or weak. (39 f.)

Marvell had earlier worked in detail with Ode 1.2, adapting it to celebrate the birth of Charles' daughter Anne in 1636/7 in *Ad Regem Carolum Parodia*, from which close encounter he will have learned much about the nuts and bolts of Horatian lyric.[10] It is impossible in English, a language less fully inflected than Latin, to reproduce Horace's dense "mosaic of words", each slotted perfectly into place, in which, in the often quoted words from Nietzsche, "every word, by sound, by position and by meaning, diffuses its force right, left, and over the whole, that *minimum* in the compass and number of signs, that *maximum* thus realised in their energy", which "[i]n certain languages ... cannot even be hoped for" (Milton is probably the English poet who on occasion gets closest to such a compacted way of writing).[11] The opening stanzas of "An Horatian Ode" recall lines from the Ode to Iccius (1.29) where Horace twits a friend for exchanging Socratic books for Spanish breastplates to go on a lucrative military expedition. Marvell captures the concreteness of Horace's style and his tendency to argue in images, not abstractly:

> 'Tis time to leave the books in dust,
> And oil the unusèd armour's rust;
> Removing from the wall
> The corselet of the hall. (5–8)

Instead of a general statement "it is time to exchange peace for war", we are given vivid pictures of associated activities.

The Ode adheres to a lyric subgenre (*prosphonetikon* in the terminology of the rhetoricians), in which the poet praises a general returning victorious from a campaign (Horatian examples include 3.14 and 4.4). And indeed Marvell has a number of Horace's Odes in view, not a single model (another poem that makes its contribution is 4.2). But he pays special attention to 1.37, the so-called "Cleopatra Ode" celebrating the battle of Actium and its aftermath (though Cleopatra is never named, simply termed, in sinister gendered opposition to the vic-

10 For this poem see Smith 2003, 5–9.

11 Quoted (from 'My Indebtedness to the Ancients', in *The Twilight of the Idols*) e.g. by Tomlinson 1993, 244.

torious Octavian, *regina*, "queen"). Horace likes to begin an Ode with a translation or motto taken from one of his Greek predecessors; similarly Marvell's "now" (2), acting as a signal, translates Horace's opening *nunc* ("now we must drink") and "'tis time" (5) his *tempus erat*. The hunting imagery was possibly suggested by Horace's simile of hawk and doves, though its deployment is more analytical. But, more importantly, the memorable lines (to use Marvell's own twice repeated adjective) describing Charles' execution (57–64) reproduce the turn in Horace's poem whereby abuse of Cleopatra gives place to a measure of admiration for her Stoical courage and transcendence of her gender in defeat:

> That thence the royal actor born
> The tragic scaffold might adorn,
> While round the armèd bands
> Did clap their bloody hands.
> He nothing common did, or mean,
> Upon that memorable scene;
> But with his keener eye
> The axe's edge did try.
> Nor called the gods with vulgar spite
> To vindicate his helpless right;
> But bowed his comely head
> Down, as upon a bed.

There is no undue pathos, but credit is given where credit is due, and the king behaved well. Charles shows dignity at his execution, and history becomes a stage where great deeds are done and fine words spoken. Charles' virtue is indicated by his calmly courageous testing of the axe and his refusal to complain. The penultimate line contains a striking enjambment, as it appears to stand on its own, but is then modified by the strong monosyllable "down", ending the passage on a sonorous note. "Helpless right" relates to Marvell's earlier exposition of historical process:

> Though justice against fate complain
> And plead the ancient rights in vain;
> But those do hold or break,
> As men are strong or weak. (37–40)

Justice and right(s) are the terminology of the old order; the poem does not disparage them, but shows how they have been superseded. Charles is seen as it were *sub specie historiae*, in accordance with the claim of the Roman historians that they wrote without partisanship, *sine ira et studio* in the words of Tacitus. Both poets correctly identify a historical turning point (in Rome from Republic to one-man rule, in England the reverse, at least if you discount any suggestions in the poem that Cromwell might be seeking to make himself king[12]) and oppose two principal figures involved in it. Thereby they also turn historical events into a kind of resonant story that might be called mythic (in the way that Dunkirk has become a myth for the British). Early modern panegyrics tended to undue extravagance, like Marvell's own "The First Anniversary of the Government under His Highness the Lord Protector":

> Cromwell alone with greater vigour runs,
> (Sun-like) the stages of succeeding suns;
> And still the day which he doth next restore
> Is the just wonder of the day before.
> Cromwell alone doth with new lustre spring,
> And shines the jewel of the yearly ring. (7–12)

Horace provided Marvell with a more controlled, measured, even prosaic classical mode (good examples are Odes 2.1 and 4.9, the odes for the prominent *nobiles* Pollio and Lollius). And in all this there is a measure of ideological revision. The Odes themselves, various in tone and subject matter, reveal a tension between a drive to sublimity and classical stature, and a preference, in the manner of Callimachus, for the small-scale, arty, and refined. Horace, very often associated, especially by Royalist poets such as Robert Herrick, with retirement and quietude on the Sabine farm, is reclaimed in the Ode for the poetry of political *action*. Horace's gendered contrast between Octavian and Cleopatra is reapplied to Republicanism and monarchy: active Cromwell with his erect sword contrasted with the comely Charles who lays his head down as on a bed.

The critics return again and again to the question of what Marvell's beliefs and attitudes were, about the English Revolution, and about Charles and Cromwell. The attempts to answer this question sometimes focus on the poem itself and sometimes on the overall development of Marvell's political views, in so far as we can establish these from other sources (in broad terms he progressed from a royalist beginning to become a supporter of Republicanism and Cromwell and then, after the Restoration, a proto-Whig). In neither case has this led to generally agreed results: historical and biographical data external to the Ode cannot resolve the issues about the poet's precise political allegiance. It is likewise puzzling why the poem should have been published first during the Restoration

---

12 In lines 31 f. ("As if his highest plot / To plant the bergamot") "plot" has a more sinister import for those critics who believe that Marvell is hinting at the fact that the bergamot was known as the royal pear (see the note in Smith 2003).

(1681), but then immediately cancelled from most copies.[13] Marvell has been seen as supporting Cromwell and the Republic, or Charles and monarchy, as vacillating between the two, or just sitting on the fence. Today the poem is most often read as an endorsement of apocalyptic Protestant imperialism, but doubtless the whirligig of time will soon again bring in his revenges. There is some evidence that it was circulated among Royalists, which suggests that an anti-Cromwellian reading was possible at the time (it was also echoed after the Restoration by Dryden). If the Ode is given a Republican reading, that creates the problem of why, only a few months later, in "Tom May's Death", Marvell, if indeed he is the author, ventriloquized Ben Jonson in satiric mockery of the Republican translator of Lucan, criticizing him for talking of liberty by "some Roman-cast similitude" (44):

> Transferring old Rome hither in your talk,
> As Bethlem's house did to Loreto walk.
> Foul architect thou hadst not eye to see
> How ill the measures of these states agree. (49–52)[14]

Had not Marvell himself done something precisely similar in the Ode? But perhaps the question of the author's own commitment is the wrong question to ask of an "Horatian" poem. The "Horatian Ode" is not a private poem, and there is no obvious sense of the presence of its author's personality, in this too like the "Cleopatra Ode" (Horace does not represent himself as drinking Caecuban wine, or have an ancestral wine-store, 5f.). It may thus be that we are given not Marvell's personal views, but a presentation of political events and the two main actors within a classical framework associated with Horace. Horace had witnessed and testified to a different revolution in which the Roman state was changed from a Republic to an autocracy created within a traditional Republican façade, a change which was broadly supported by the poet in his maturity (though later to be denounced by Lucan, another voice in Marvell's poem, as we shall see). In other words interpreters need to take into account precisely the

---

13 On the question of the removal of the Ode (and other poems on Cromwell) from the 1681 folio Hammond 2006, 21–24 suggests that this was done to avoid the embarrassment of associating a prominent figure from the opposition with Cromwell's government. Marvell's *Miscellaneous Poems* was advertised in February during the Exclusion Crisis; Hammond speculates that someone on the Whig side intervened to avoid giving ammunition to the court party by a reminder that this well-known champion of Protestant liberties had been a servant and panegyrist of Cromwell.

14 For a good discussion, including of the authorship question, see Smith 2003, 116–120. George de F. Lord was the main proponent of the view that the poem was not by Marvell.

anachronism necessarily involved in describing the English Revolution as though it were, so to say, an event in *Roman* history.

To try to bring greater precision to the debate Blair Worden, in a fascinating essay, limits the Ode's context to the few weeks following Cromwell's return from Ireland.[15] The result is a sort of *reductio ad absurdum* of this kind of contextual criticism, which raises important questions about method. How long does an original context last: a week; an hour; a month; a year? When Milton was contemplating his epic, he expressed the hope that "I might perhaps leave something so written to aftertimes as they should not willingly let it die", and "that what the greatest and choicest wits of Athens, Rome, or modern Italy, or those Hebrews of old did for their country, I in my proportion with this over and above of being a Christian might do for mine".[16] Milton knew that Virgil had been read for nearly two millennia, and presumably hoped his own productions might endure as long. Marvell was perhaps more modest in his aspirations, but must still have written his poem to last more than a few weeks. It is a further problem that poets often continue to rework their productions (this could well be true of the "Horatian Ode", which was first printed in 1681, as we have seen, but of which a variant manuscript version exists). What constitutes a context (original or otherwise) is in general far from clear. Contexts are not simply lying about, but have to be constructed, on some principle of relevance. "Contexts" just as much as "texts"—and indeed they are themselves composed of other texts—require interpretation, and this creates the theoretical risk of an infinite regress of signification. Intertextuality rests on the very reasonable claim that no text stands on its own. But when the intertextualist brings her text into play with another, she needs to justify her particular choice: why this particular intertext and not others? And she needs also to recognize that the intertext may well not serve to clarify or resolve a problem, but may rather introduce yet further complexity. Intertextuality may thus be seen as analogous to figuration, with the simultaneous recognition of sameness and difference that is characteristic of most tropes, and that grants readerly freedom to each interpreter, who determines this amount of difference, that amount of similarity. In short, intertextuality prompts the Kantian free-play of the mental faculties, a free-play necessarily involved by the dialectic of difference and similarity which readers will construe differently. Literary hermeneutics are anyway not best understood according to a simple binary opposition between "right" and "wrong" (on the model of a simple data-point that is either "true" or "false"). Critics mobilize par-

15 Worden 1987.
16 Wolfe 1953–1982, vol. 1, 810, 812, from *Reason of Church-Government*.

ticular features of a poem to tell a story that is perhaps better described as "powerful" or even as "beautiful" than as "true". As the poet W. H. Auden puts it, in *The Dyer's Hand*, "in poetry, all facts and all beliefs cease to be true or false and become interesting possibilities".[17]

By highlighting Horace, Marvell to an extent draws our attention away from other voices that speak within the Ode. The frameworks that are used to interpret poems are closely bound up with the results they generate; to use a different metaphor, switch the lens and you see something different. So if we titled the poem "A Machiavellian Ode", other facets would come to the fore. Cromwell would correspond to Machiavelli's *nuovo principe*, who displays *virtù* and *industria*, and seizes the occasion for decisive action. The Ode also claims that Cromwell with Machiavellian craft tricked Charles into fleeing to the Isle of Wight, thereby encompassing his death (something doubted by most modern historians):

> Where, twining subtle fears with hope,
> He wove a net of such a scope
> That Charles himself might chase
> To Caresbrook's narrow case. (49–52)

Even more plausible would be the title "A Lucanian Ode". Marvell echoes several passages from Lucan, which he knew in Latin but also in May's translation.[18] Marvell takes the simile comparing Cromwell (who clearly corresponds in some respects to Lucan's Caesar) to a lightning flash from the *Pharsalia* (as the poem was then titled), while the opening lines quoted above conflate Horace's Ode 1.29 with a passage from the end of Lucan's first book (239–243), rendered thus by May:

> With this sad noise the people's rest was broke,
> The young men rose, and from the temples took
> Their arms, now such as a long peace had marred,
> And their old bucklers now of leathers barred,
> Their blunted piles not of a long time used,
> And swords with the eatings of black rust abused...

(Since the young men are taking up arms to resist Caesar, this echo is used by some scholars to support a Royalist reading.) Lucan's poem is violently pro-Republican, with Caesar the subverter of the constitution as its evil genius. It is thus

17 Auden 1948, 19, from Prologue, "Reading".
18 Smith 2003, 268 f. collects the relevant passages.

possible to argue that the co-presence of Horace and Lucan might help to explain any political ambivalence the Ode may be held to exhibit.

The Horatian elements in the Ode are thus part of a wider *color Romanus*. Marvell adopts a style, and with it a way of being and feeling. For example, the story of the "bleeding head" (69) foretelling that Rome will be the capital (*caput*) of empire appears in Livy, Varro, and Pliny the Elder. While in general Marvell is usually today termed a "Metaphysical" poet, it is equally or more plausible to see him, like his friend Milton, as primarily a classicist.[19] That point (apart from the comparison with Milton whom he disliked) is central to T. S. Eliot's view set out in his short but highly influential essay on the poet, which includes the famous definition of "wit": "it involves, probably, a recognition, implicit in the expression of every experience, of other kinds of experience which are possible".[20] To Eliot Marvell's wit, in poetry which "displays a tough reasonableness beneath the slight lyric grace" and an "alliance of levity and seriousness (by which the seriousness is intensified)", belongs to a classical tradition, being "more Latin, more refined, than anything that succeeded it" (Eliot mentions Catullus, Horace, Propertius, and Ovid, as well as "the vast and penetrating influence of Ben Jonson"). Like Milton's, Marvell's world is certainly radically bilingual. We have two pairs of poems (*Ros*, "On a Drop of Dew"; *Hortus*, "The Garden") where scholars are not sure which is the "original", which the "translation", and where each pair tests the differences as well as the compatibilities between Latin and English. Marvell, like Milton, loves translingual puns. In "The Garden" (another poem strongly indebted to the lyric Horace, poet of the Sabine farm) Ovidian metamorphosis plays on the fact that, in Latin, *ut* clauses with the subjunctive can express purpose or result: "Apollo hunted Daphne so, / Only that she might laurel grow" (29 f.; *ut fieret laurus*). In the Ode Charles's courageous testing of the axe ("But with his keener eye / The axe's edge did try", 59 f.) exploits the double meaning of the noun *acies* in Latin, "keen eyesight" as well as "sharp edge of a weapon". *Pictus* is Latin for "painted" or "tattooed", but also "deceptive", "vain", a play activated in the lines on the Scots ("The Pict no shelter now shall find / Within his parti-coloured mind", 105 f.), where "parti-coloured" describes persons united in a cause while also alluding to the colours of the tartan and the deviousness of the partisan.

These puns and wordplays can themselves be seen as "Horatian". But Marvell's classicism is of a special kind, not quite the mainstream inheritance of

---

19 On Marvell's classicism in general see Davis 2011; Leishman 1966.

20 Eliot, 1951, 303. Subsequent quotations in this paragraph are from pp. 293, 296, 301. 'Andrew Marvell' was first published in the *Times Literary Supplement*, March 31, 1921.

classical "equipoise" in the manner of Ben Jonson, "a balance and proportion of tones", for which Eliot sought to claim him.[21] We might call it rather that form of mannerism, by which the classicism takes a partly unclassical turn to the bizarre. In comparison with Jonson (who is portrayed with a touch of irony as a rather old-fashioned figure in "Tom May's Death"), Marvell seems weirder and more cryptic, less centred and grounded. In common with earlier Early Modern poets Marvell imitated classical models, but he did so in ways that are paradoxical or involve an unusual twist or an idiosyncratic use of genre: gardens which both are and are not utopias; pastoral in which mowers replace shepherds and where there is a surprising element of violence ("For Death thou art a mower too": "Damon the Mower", 88); an increasingly febrile *carpe diem* poem "To His Coy Mistress" deriving from Catullus and Horace, in which there are strange and again violent pressures just offstage; and in the Ode a panegyric that has also been read as an attack. The protagonist of "Damon the Mower" sees himself reflected in a scythe, therefore subject to distortion:

> Nor am I so deformed to sight,
> If in my scythe I lookèd right:
> In which I see my picture done,
> As in a crescent moon the sun. (57–60)

In his classical models, Virgil and Theocritus, the reflection is in water; since reflection is a possible figure for imitating, associated in the Early Modern period with the myth of Narcissus, the passage may suggest a metapoetic reading acknowledging the mannerist twist.[22] The almost "pat" surface of Marvell's verse —he is perhaps the supreme English master of the short line—is at odds with the never-quite-fathomable or not-fully-articulated possibilities that lie, or may lie, beneath.[23] In all this he belongs with a second phase of Early Modern classicism, after the great initiating period of joyous exploration of the Classics circa 1580 – 1610, which takes various new directions: a greater proto-Augustan polish, refinement, and sweetness (as with Waller); greater witty ingenuity (as with Cowley in Metaphysical vein); or, in the case of Marvell, this mannered allusiveness, and elusiveness, which is so hard to pin down.

---

21 Eliot 1951, 302.

22 In the Renaissance the Ovidian myth of Narcissus was so familiar (it is everywhere in Shakespeare's *Sonnets*, for example) that any mention of image, reflection, mirror, or the like, can serve to call it to mind. So to suggest—anachronically!—that the Theocritean/Virgilian trope may evoke it here is no stretch.

23 This point, and this way of formulating it, I owe to an e-mail exchange with David Hopkins.

The Ode's melding of ancient and modern, and its deployment of divergent authorities, in particular Horace, judicious supporter of Caesar Augustus the first emperor, and the extravagantly Republican Lucan, creates a two-way traffic of signification, in which—as in translation—a complete fit is never possible and where consequently there are constant slippages. So first Charles and then Cromwell are figured as Caesar (23, 101). Cromwell's velocity and generalship align him with Julius Caesar the energetic mould-breaker in the *Pharsalia* who, however, is the villain of Lucan's poem for subverting, not sustaining the Republic. And, for Marvell, is Augustus the benign father of his people as in Horace, or the tyrant and destroyer of liberty as in Tacitus and Lucan (*cum domino pax ista venit*, "with a master comes that peace", *Pharsalia* 1.670)? The classical framework occludes some contemporary issues: we read of "angry heaven's flame", "fate", "the gods" (26, 37, 61), but not of the Christian God (pace some scholars, Cromwell can hardly be holding his erect sword by the blade to make a sign of the Cross at the poem's end), and this allows a world, almost unspeakable in Christian terms, in which power might be self-legitimating and God might care nothing for "ancient rights" (38), or even for virtue. (The sense that justice and right belong to an old order extends to the dignity of Charles at his execution, in lines that as it were inhabit their own capsule of decorum.) The poem seems to accept (without necessarily exactly approving) the reality of power as conferring its own legitimacy. Whether or not there is dubiety, the detached style, and unruffled calm, of the poem, what Eliot called Marvell's "bright, hard precision" scarcely suggest significant anxiety or perturbation.[24] The cool, almost toneless surface, in which there is no protest and little compassion, is a world away from other more engaged political lyrics. Compare, for example, Milton's great sonnet "On the late Massacre in Piedmont", where the poet deplores, in the angry accents of an Old Testament prophet, the slaughter of the Vaudois by Catholic troops:

> Avenge O Lord thy slaughtered saints, whose bones
>   Lie scattered on the Alpine mountains cold
>   Even them who kept thy truth so pure of old
>   When all our fathers worshipped stocks and stones,
> Forget not

Appropriately the last two words come as a hammer blow, forcing the reader to adjust her understanding of the syntax. Yeats is not fully committed to a cause

24 Eliot 1951, 299.

like Milton, but, despite his liberal anxieties about the Easter Rising in "Easter, 1916" he is fully engaged, at an emotional level:

> I write it out in a verse—
> MacDonagh and MacBride
> And Connolly and Pearse
> Now and in time to be,
> Whenever green is worn,
> Are changed, changed utterly:
> A terrible beauty is born.

Marvell's self-contained uninvolvement is by contrast a remarkable thing: and this about a civil struggle over which honourable and brave men on both sides were passionate, and fought and died. The poem reveals an extraordinarily acute and subtle mind and sensibility without any corresponding moral weight or overt feeling (of the kind we encounter with Ben Jonson or Milton), which creates a curious void in the decorum. From that point of view Marvell's great political lyric is hard not to admire, but may also be hard to love.[25]

The title of "The Horatian Ode" clearly encourages the reader to have Horace in view and in mind when reading Marvell's poem. In the end, however, she may decide that the Ode is as much, or more, unHoratian than Horatian (it is, for example, considerably more intellectual and analytical, and one might contrast, for example, the colour and verve and sheer excitement of the "Cleopatra Ode"). However, clearly without Horace, and the transhistorical dimension that necessarily accompanies his name, Marvell could never have conceived it. I do not claim in this short essay to have solved the problem of the poem's stance (if it has one), but I hope that two points of general application have emerged clearly from the discussion. First, however much he may be a contextualizer, the interpreter cannot afford to neglect the detailed surface texture of the work he is discussing. The New-Critical slogan for this critical principle is "the words on the page", and, while we know words are never just on the page, the prime job of the literary critic surely remains to address *this* particular combination of words in a poem or piece of prose. Poems or artistic prose in particular know things that contexts (that is, other texts from the period) may not know, or know explicitly, and that their authors might not have been able to put into other words. Secondly, and most importantly for this essay, while it is not necessarily wrong to try to situate poems within their original contexts

25 Eliot 1951, 294 by contrast prefers Marvell, in his view "a lukewarm partisan", to Milton for just this lack of commitment (of course he particularly dislikes Milton's politics).

(though what those are may not be a straightforward matter), it is so to claim that the *only* legitimate interpretation of a poem is of such a kind. Indeed I think we can go further: contextualization can be valuable, even vital, in some respects—we would not want words glossed in ways that were impossible at the time of writing (though this is not necessarily always certain)—but it is only valuable when integrated with an "anachronic" understanding. Other temporalities, including our own, and those of multiple pasts, are operative, and legitimately so, when we engage in the challenging and never-to-be-completed task of the interpretation of great literature, in contention with others, for the refreshment of the human spirit.

Thomas Palaima

Masters of War: Virgil, Horace, Owen, Pound, Trumbo, Dylan and the Art of Reference

> "[C]riticism which frees itself from attention to detail, particularly when the subject of study is Virgil, is in my view very likely to go astray, for the writer starts thinking of the (Augustan) reception of Virgil rather than of Virgil". (Thomas 2001, xvi)

Part of the art and pleasure of intertextuality lies in recognizing when the author of the work being read or heard is pointing toward other writers, reciters, or singers with single words—commonplace or exotic, with phrases, and even with word-placement, within prose or verse or song lyrics. These then awaken in informed readers or hearers the associations in the target passage (or model) at which the author is pointing. These can then infuse the author's work with fuller and richer meanings.

This is not a mechanical process. It need not even be a conscious process on the part of the writer/speaker or the reader/listener. This is all the truer when a complex of ideas, feelings, beliefs, and emotional and intellectual responses is attached to a well-known and much-used articulation. Here, as one *exemplum*, I will be discussing Horace's *dulce et decorum est pro patria mori* (*Carm.* 3.2.13), particularly because it is well-worn and time-worn and now part

---

This paper was written hearing the echoes of Richard's voice talking with me about *inter alia* Augustan poetics and Bob Dylan at University of St. Andrew's, Harvard, Boston University, University of Missouri St. Louis and while taking in Bob at Austin's Back Yard music venue. My special thanks to Christopher Brown for his comments on my thoughts and his own astute insights into the tradition of Greek and Latin 'brave man dies' poetry and to Brian Bremen for being my Virgil to scholarship about Ezra Pound during the period of writing and publication of *Hugh Selwyn Mauberley.* My thoughts on the intertextuality between Dylan and Dalton Trumbo were first developed in preparing for a talk at Boston University, "Personal Agency and the Big Switch 1962–64: Thucydides, Bob Dylan and Stanley Kubrick", February 27, 2017, available on-line at http://www.wbur.org/worldofideas/2017/03/05/palaima. My thanks to Herb Golder, Chris Walsh, Christopher Ricks and Richard Thomas for their comments at the time. Elizabeth Vandiver at the last minute graciously offered me permission to include her evidence of absence of any connection between Pound and Owen through 1920; and Danni Corfield, project archivist (Random House) The Museum of English Rural Life and Special Collections University of Reading, soon afterward provided key information on the publication date of Sassoon's 1920 edition of Owen's poems (both *infra* n. 10 and 11). Kevin S. Lee suggested several stylistic improvements, as did the editors. Alain Zaramian pointed me to Lindo 1971. I am solely responsible for all shortcomings in this final version.

https://doi.org/10.1515/9783110545708-014

of what we might call common or popular intellectual currency; and it has been made so by the likes of Wilfred Owen and Ezra Pound and Tim O'Brien[1]– and Bertolt Brecht.[2]

When Horace's pronouncement is used, in whole or part, by these and other modern authors, even those of us who can trace the sentiments and thoughts triggered by the line back to Pindar or Tyrtaeus or Callinus or Homer or to popular Greek funerary epigrams[3] do not flip through all the metaphorical files in our personal memory folders in order to extract the essence of what particular authors in particular contexts are trying to convey. Owen's own non-elite social and educational background make it likely that for him Horace's phrase (and the poem in which it was placed) was the end all and be all.[4] Owen probably had smaller Latin and much lesser Greek than Ben Jonson attributed to Shakespeare.[5] Still, when correctly assessed, Owen had something like Shakespeare's "knowledge of the classics": "substantially that of an extremely clever Elizabethan grammar-school boy...used to brilliant effect".[6] Moreover, they both viewed the ancient authors they knew as trustworthy mentors for advice on "how to live in the present".[7]

For the acutely class-conscious Owen, his asserted intertexual relationship to Horace gave him the courage and authority to declare and depict otherwise taboo truths about man's inhumanity to man. His famous poem "Dulce Et Decorum Est" in its entirety ironically glosses the Horatian line –from the once able-bodied soldiers transformed into beggars and hags in the first two lines,

> Bent double, like old beggars under sacks,
> Knock-kneed, coughing like hags, we cursed through sludge,

1 Palaima and Tritle 2013, 728–730, 733f.

2 Most 2013, 459.

3 Brown 2016, 276–278, 282–284. See generally Lindo 1971, although he argues for poems of Tyrtaeus as the hypotext for Horace.

4 Vandiver 2010, 393–404 discusses the use, in whole or part, of the Horatian tag line by Henry Newbolt and minor writers as "evocative of the entire ethos of service and sacrifice that was the background assumption of so much of the poetry" written in response to World War I and proposes (394f.) that Owen's use of the Horatian line in original Latin "can be read as a direct response to the concluding Latin lines of [Newbolt's] 'Clifton Chapel'".

5 Vandiver 2010, 114–118.

6 Burrow 2013, 20.

7 Burns 2014/15, 69.

to the eight-line closing sentence:

> If you could hear, at every jolt, the blood
> Come gargling from the froth-corrupted lungs,
> Obscene as cancer, bitter as the cud
> Of vile, incurable sores on innocent tongues,–
> My friend, you would not tell with such high zest
> To children ardent for some desperate glory,
> The old Lie: Dulce et decorum est
> Pro patria mori.

It gives voice to the realities of war as experienced by middle- and working-class soldiers who dutifully provided ample supplies of their own flesh and blood to the butchery of trench warfare and rarely spoke up for themselves. Owen's Horatian title historically heats up the ironies in what he calls "the old lie". The quantity of the senselessly made dead and the quality of the sheer evil of the experience of trench warfare, what Owen boils down to "War and the pity of War", are captured forever in an economical 28-line word photograph, in four fewer lines than Horace's original.

Owen's is a clear case of one-to-one quotation used ultra-explicitly, both truncated in his title and used entire in the closing line of his poem. By contrast, Pound in *Hugh Selwyn Mauberley* IV (= Pound 1926, 190) might have been channeling Callinus to judge by his thinking that some of those who fought believed "the old lie" *pro domo*. The phrase *pro domo* adds the idea behind Callinus fr. 1.7 παίδων κουριδίης τ' ἀλόχου to Horace's *pro patria* and Callinus's own γῆς πέρι. Pound also manipulates the Horatian line as he spotlights its component parts—the two key adjectives by quotation marks—then negates them:

> These fought, in any case,
> and some believing,
>   pro domo, in any case ...
>   ...
> some in fear, learning love of slaughter;
> Died some, pro patria,
>   non "dulce" non "et decor" ...

It has recently been proposed that Pound used Owen's poem, and not Horace's ode, as his model here. According to Rachel Potter (2012, 196):

> In *Hugh Selwyn Mauberley*, [Pound] traces a recent history of poets ranging from Swinburne to Wilfred Owen. Through rhythmical and linguistic echoes and partial quotations the poem recreates the idioms of different writers. Owen's "Dulce et Decorum Est", for instance, is half quoted:

> Died some, pro patria,
> Non 'dulce' non 'et decor' ...
>
> Pound is careful to preserve the life and tone of Owen's poetic voice so that Owen's words become the means with which the poem represents the language and suffering of war.

However, Pound's *Hugh Selwyn Mauberley* was printed in June 1920 by the Ovid Press, London; and the first publication of "Dulce Et Decorum Est" was also in 1920 in Sassoon's edition of Owen's collected poems by Chatto & Windus. End-of-year reviews of the Sassoon edition (e. g., in *The Guardian*, 29 December 1920) make it most likely that Owen's "Dulce Et Decorum Est" appeared too late for Pound to have read it in published form before he wrote *Mauberley*, if he even would have been inclined to read it in this period of upheaval and at the time of his impending departure for France.

Pound's classical orientation and preoccupations also make Owen an unlikely model. Pound's clear interests in classical authors, including Roman elegiac poets, from 1914 through 1920, suggest he *was* using Horace as his model text.[8] Pound's *Homage to Sextus Propertius* was finished in 1917, although not published until 1919; and Pound's *Mauberley* is structured so as to use Greek quotations and tags in Greek in the first part and in Greek transliterated into the Roman alphabet in the second part.[9] Classical figures and allusions in the poem like Homer, Pindar, Sappho, Catullus, Capaneus, Penelope and the actual Greek words of the Sirens, reinforce how immersed Pound was in classical texts. There is no mention in standard studies of *Mauberley* or of Pound's years in London that Pound had any contact with, awareness of, or interest in Owen or Sassoon.[10] Stock binding orders from the Chatto and Windus archives would seem to

---

8 Espey (1955, 88 f.) specifically links *Mauberley* IV with Horace 3.2.13 and also with a nod in the direction of Cicero's *De Domo Sua*. R.E. Thomas (1983) traces succinctly Pound's familiarity and preoccupation with Horace from his freshman year at University of Pennsylvania onward.

9 Nadel (2005, introduction).

10 Froula, 1983; Espey 1955; Wilhelm 1990. Vandiver (forthcoming) sums it up this way: "The title page of the first edition of *Hugh Selwyn Mauberley* gives the date as 'June 1920'. A notice of the book appears in the *TLS* of 1 July 1920, p. 427. [Sassoon's edition of] Owen's *Poems* appears in the *TLS* list of 'New Books and Reprints' on 16 December 1920, p. 862, and is favorably reviewed in *TLS* of 6 January 1921, p. 6; thus it seems clear that Owen's *Poems* (including the first publication of 'Dulce et Decorum Est') was not published before late November or early December 1920".

provide definitive proof. The publisher received the first of the 300 bound copies of Sassoon's edition of Owen's poems on November 18, 1920.[11]

An interesting intertextual detail is that Pound truncates Horace's *decorum* to a different Latin word, *decor.* He does not opt for the more common noun and more culturally important Roman value term *decus.* A simple reason may be the sound pattern that *decor* creates with the bitterly damning lines soon to follow:

> Daring as never be<u>fore</u>, wastage as never be<u>fore</u>.
> Young blood and high blood,
> Fair cheeks, and fine bodies;
>
> fortitude as never be<u>fore</u>
>
> frankness as never be<u>fore</u>,[12]

O'Brien, who declares that what he calls Horace's "do-or-die aphorism" is an "epitaph for the insane", uses it, like Owen, as a title.[13] Owen truncates. Pound recites and negates. O'Brien cuts it into pieces and strews its parts in the headings of chapters two, twelve and nineteen of his thoughtful first novel *If I die in a combat zone, box me up and ship me home.* In pieces, they will have the most force in replacing "the old lie" with the truth. O'Brien's intertextual strategy is simple and in line with Owen's. He is telling readers: just be aware that an old Roman poet once used this line of Latin to brainwash young men into thinking they owe it to their families, their parents, and their country to get themselves slaughtered for at best no good reason.

By contrast with such straightforward cases of direct quotation or manipulation of an original passage in its original language, part of intertextual artistic virtuosity lies in making sure that the relationship between the passage at hand and the passage being pointed at (the model) is not pedantically 1:1, so that a-b-c-d in the passage being read does not equate with A-B-C-D in the target or model passage. Still, in order to appreciate what Richard Thomas calls "the

---

11 Danni Corfield (*supra* p. 147, personal communication 09/01/17) confirms Vandiver's reasoning (*supra* n. 10) with information from the Chatto & Windus archives (CW B/2/6) stock book binding orders, 1916–1928, p. 349. The company received 300 bound copies of the book for distribution between November 18 and December 22, 1920, 266 of these between November 30 and December 3.

12 It is also possible that Pound read Latin words in *echthlipsis* as Latin schoolmasters of the period (Allen and Greenough 1903, 434, § 642; 411, § 612f) instructed. He most likely would have said, heard and remembered the first part of Horace's line as *dulc' et decor' est.*

13 Palaima 2000 (8–10), for this and the discussion here following.

art of reference", a critic is called upon to indicate (pun intended) in some detail, as I have just done in brief, how the author's passage interacts with and relates to the passage(s) to which the author is pointing. An expert critic nowadays may be the only person capable of identifying and explicating the target passages in ancient Greek and Latin authors and how they work across barriers of time, space, cultures and languages.

Intertextuality then is an art, not a science. It is an art that, when involving classical texts and writers, requires exegesis that is often so complex as to seem to call for the application of the principle of Occam's razor. If a proposed allusion or reference requires so much explanation, can it possibly be true? The answer, of course, is yes. The amount of explication needed is a product of the imbalance between the ancients and ourselves. Ancient writers waded in the streams of Greek and Latin literary tradition from an early age, and swam in them throughout their lives. We artificially and now relatively late in our secondary education familiarize ourselves with selections of ancient texts and fragments. Imagine being able to think and respond to the world with Virgil's or Horace's brains and the stores of Greek literature they had in their heads when they were at the height of their powers. The process of doing this might well short-circuit our own minds.

Here in tribute to Richard Thomas and his interests in the "art of reference" in the works of Augustan poets and of Bob Dylan, I am taking up three examples, one from Virgil, one from Horace and one from Dylan, that will drive home what I consider the paramount achievement of Richard's scholarship. We will see, to paraphrase Richard, that these three great song poets were not "playing" with their models, but sending their readers back to them, whether "through memory or physically", so that they may bring back meaning and understanding from the model texts. These then enrich the response of readers to the realities of the human condition as these three master artists saw it and then represented it.

1 Virgil and Homer

The passage that I have selected from Virgil was taken up by Richard Thomas in his programmatic treatment of the origins in the period of Alexandrian poetry of what he calls "the art of reference" rather than allusion.[14] It well illustrates "the sophistication and subtlety with which the art was practiced" and supports Thomas's claim that we are seeing from the Alexandrians onward the effects on the

14 Thomas 1986.

ars poetica of writers and poets becoming scholars as well. To look back here already—something the title of Pennebaker's groundbreaking documentary film of Dylan's 1965 tour of England suggests we not do—along a sliding scale from scholar-writer to popular writer, i.e., from authors more capable of meaningfully alluding to Greek and Latin texts to those who are less capable, we would list Pound, Owen and O'Brien in that order. Here my own sensibilities are those of a scholar, or perhaps a pedant or *pedant* or *pedante*, in arguing, in the literal sense, about the details that underscore the geniuses at work.

Thomas identifies a significant intertextual connection between Virgil's *Georgics* 1.104–110 and Homer's *Iliad* 21.257–262.[15] Virgil links what appears to be "a very mundane and technical passage" of "a man in the act of irrigation" by means of a "long acknowledged close translation" to a simile of a farmer at work at irrigation used by Homer during the climactic combat between Achilles in full berserker mode and the river god Scamander:

Quid dicam, iacto qui semine comminus arva
insequitur cumulosque ruit male pinguis harenae
deinde satis fluvium inducit rivosque sequentis
et, cum exustus ager morientibus aestuat herbis,
ecce supercilio clivosi tramitis undam
elicit? illa cadens raucum per levia murmur
saxa ciet, scatebrisque arentia temperat arva.

Why say anything about the man who, having flung his seed grain, closes quarters
with his ploughed plots and tears down the built up low heaps of thick enemy sand
and then leads in upon his crops a torrent and then streams as reinforcements
and, when his land, consumed by drought, seethes with dying shoots, blades, stalks,
look! along the ridge of the sloping footpath a wave of water
he orders forward? As it cascades, that wave raises a hoarse murmur
throughout the smooth rocks and it sates the parched fields as it surges.

ὡς δ' ὅτ' ἀνὴρ ὀχετηγὸς ἀπὸ κρήνης μελανύδρου
ἂμ φυτὰ καὶ κήπους ὕδατι ῥόον ἡγεμονεύῃ
χερσὶ μάκελλαν ἔχων, ἀμάρης ἐξ ἔχματα βάλλων·
τοῦ μέν τε προρέοντος ὑπὸ ψηφῖδες ἅπασαι
ὀχλεῦνται· τὸ δέ τ' ὦκα κατειβόμενον κελαρύζει
χώρῳ ἔνι προαλεῖ, φθάνει δέ τε καὶ τὸν ἄγοντα

As when from a dark-water spring a man who knows the art of irrigation
leads a current of water along a course through his plants and garden plots
wielding a mattock in his hands, shoveling the small check dams out of his ditch;
when the water flows forth freely, all the stones and pebbles along the bottom

15 Thomas 1986, 178 f.; 1988, 84 f.

are swept along in a mass and, as it streams down quickly, the water murmurs
on the steep terrain and overtakes even the irrigator.

What is ingenious here in the two passages is a kind of chiasmus. Virgil ramps up, as Thomas explains, through the rush of his initial word choice (*iacto*, *insequitur*, *ruit* and especially *comminus* in lines 104 and 105) the militarily aggressive aspects of a farmer's fieldwork, describing him as joining "in hand to hand combat" (*comminus*) with nature's defense works. Homer inserts into the very crescendo of Achilles' most energetic and violent use of his own perfected martial skills—his furious *aristeia*, a merciless killing spree unmatched in Homer —a simile stripped almost literally of everything that could have military associations.[16]

Thomas notices that Virgil leaves out the "mattock" (μάκελλαν) that Homer's ἀνὴρ ὀχετηγὸς (literally a "man in the act of conducting or drawing off water through piping or another kind of man-made conduit", i.e., a man without any hint of even a metaphorical military association) uses in his work. If we carry forward from Homer the artistic effect of this intentional omission in Virgil's passage, it is also fair to say that we carry back from Virgil's passage a heightened realization of how stripped of warfare the *Iliad* simile is. There is nothing in Homer's simile to suggest the psychologically unhinged martial violence in the extended *aristeia* that surrounds it. In other words, this is Virgilian intertextuality that even profits Homerists by enriching their understanding of the model text.

Thomas speaks of *Georgics* 1.104–110 being a "close translation" of *Iliad* 21.257–262 that makes the adaptation "noticeable and beyond dispute".[17] There is no disputing that "what Virgil expects of his reader is recollection of the *context* of the Homeric simile", as Virgil's opening cascade of military words makes clear. What we might improve upon is explaining just how Virgil makes sure our minds will go back to this Homeric passage. Virgil, however, is here adapting the source passage in the *Iliad* to his own purposes. Noting differences between the two passages will help us appreciate the art of Virgil's particular translation and exactly how the allusion to Homer is activated.

---

16 Only ἔχματα taken as the "buttressing support mound" for fortification towers (*Il.* 12.260) or as itself a bulwark against attack (ἐπηλυσίης: *h. Merc.* 37) appears in a military context. But ἔχματα also can mean the heaped-up stones used as props for ships: *Il.* 14.410 ἔχματα νηῶν. Its meaning is further softened by its other uses in natural settings, e.g., ἔχματα γαίης, of the earth which holds fast the roots of a tree, Ap. Rhod. 1.120.

17 Thomas 1986, 178.

For example, missing from Virgil's passage is any overt reference to a particular human agent doing the irrigation work. There is no Latin equivalent to ἀνὴρ ὀχετηγὸς (*Il.* 21.257) at the opening of the corresponding simile in the Georgics and no equivalent to τὸν ἄγοντα at its close. There is only the unspecified antecedent of *qui* in line 104.

In making the case for the unmistakable intertextual connection, Thomas cites two pieces of evidence:

(1) *supercilio clivosi tramitis* closely renders χώρῳ ἔνι προαλεῖ while

(2) the noun *scatebris* matches the Homeric verb κελαρύζει in sense and in rarity.

To what degree are these claims true? Do they need to be modified? Would the pairings taken in isolation be considered true equivalents of one another? We proceed *hysteron proteron.*

If I had to put my own money down, I would wager that Virgil wrote *murmur* to close his penultimate line as a match for κελαρύζει, which likewise closes Homer's penultimate line. κελαρύζει *is* a rare word. It is glossed by Hesychius: κελαρύζει· ἠχεῖ 'sounds, echoes' and φωνεῖ 'speaks loudly and clearly'; κελαρύξεται (*sic*): μετὰ φωνῆς ἠχήσει 'will sound with a clear voice'; cf. κέλωρ· φωνή 'voiced sound'. These glosses specify that the word conveys a "sound" effect.[18] Likewise κελάρυσμα is used by Oppian to connote "murmuring" (Beekes 2010:1, 667 *s.* κελαρύζω). *scatebris*, however, has to do with the "movement" of water (de Vaan 2008, 543 *s.* scatō, ere). It means "to gush forth, swarm". It has Indo-European cognates meaning "to jump". A good semantic parallel is found in our English word "spring". In its connotation of sudden and forceful movements of water, it matches the participial noun phrase τὸ δέ τ' ὦκα κατειβόμενον in Homer, the verbal form here (κατείβομαι "I am flowing down, overflowing") capturing in other uses a quick downward flowing of water, even an overflow. The emphasis of *scatebris* on the welcome "surgings forth", rather than any sound effect, better suits Virgil's use in his magnificent closing clause. Through the hard work of the unidentified farmer, nature now takes its man-made course: "that wave falling through smoothed rocks raises a murmuring (*murmur*) and sates the parched fields with its surges (*scatebris*)".

Likewise, it is perhaps too strong a claim that *supercilio clivosi tramitis* "closely renders" χώρῳ ἔνι προαλεῖ. The Latin phrase specifies the locus from which the unnamed farmer will lure forth the water: the hilly ridge (metaphorically *supercilium*, the "eyebrow") along which a walking path (*trames*) has long

18 See also κελαρύζειν· ἰδίωμα ψόφου 'a kind of soft noise'.

been worn. In Homer, the swiftly downward flowing stream murmurs on a landscape that itself literally "leaps forth" (προαλής, in likely relationship to the root of the verb ἅλλομαι 'I leap, bound, spring', implying a steep decline). The rapid force of the flow overtakes even the irrigator, as the Scamander will overtake Achilles. Virgil's anonymous farmer by contrast sets up a consistent course of water flow that will deliver the nourishing water in periodic surges, gush after gush after gush.

The takeaway is that we are not dealing here with a direct, one-to-one correspondence, with elements in the same order. Virgil is sending us back to the Homeric hypotext in a way that allows us to apply our observations to both the simile in the *Iliad* and the derivative simile in the *Georgics*. Virgil does not closely translate Homer, because he has a different message to communicate. Moreover, he is already a mature poet, and, like Ezra Pound, a scholar poet.

2 Horace *Odes* 3.2. and Tyrtaeus and Callinus

Above, we considered an intertextuality where two specific passages are clearly related, though in very few straightforward one-to-one correspondences. They add meaning to one another through what they explicitly say and what they do not say. Now we move to a case where models are claimed, although none is fully satisfactory. Here we are dealing with the famous Horatian line (*Carm.* 3.2.13) from which we have already looked forward in time. Now we look back.

Nisbet and Rudd's commentary (2004, 26 f.) on this line is a convenient starting point because it constitutes a kind of *opinio communis:*

> 13. **dulce et decorum est pro patria mori:** *decorum* in the sense of 'noble' or 'glorious' can be paralleled from all periods, *OLD* 3; in this heroic context it is enough to cite Tyrt. 10.1 f. τεθνάμεναι γὰρ καλὸν ἐνὶ προμάχοισι πεσόντα / ἄνδρ' ἀγαθὸν περὶ ᾗ πατρίδι μαρνάμενον, Callinus 1.6 ff. ... But here it has the additional sense of 'right and proper', *OLD* 4; in philosophy the pleasant and the honourable are sometimes opposed, but here they are compatible. In view of the patriotic commonplaces in 13 and 14, *dulce* might be expected to provide a conventional sentiment, perhaps echoing Simonides (14n.), yet no exact parallel is available that antedates Horace.

The exact flavor that *dulce* imparts to the Horatian line and the reception it received from the likes of Owen and Pound bothered Nisbet to such a degree that he "at one time considered [emending to] 'dulci decorum est pro patria mori'" since "it would produce a more rational and nobler sentiment", citing as a parallel *Acts of the Pagan Martyrs* II.41 ff. Musurillo: κλέος σοί ἐστιν ὑπὲρ γλυκυτάτης πατρίδος τελευτῆσαι. And he had the integrity to admit later that his proposed solution was unnecessary given that "the ethos of most societies, including our own, has often been different from the individualism that now prevails in the West".

In discussing Pindar's debt to Homer and to martial elegies together with commonplaces in the sentiments expressed in funerary epigrams that celebrate those who have died in battle for their *polis*, Christopher Brown makes the point that literary poems, including passages like *Iliad* 15.494–499 and Alcaeus (an Horatian favorite in *Odes* 1–3) fr. 400 Voigt,[19] and inscribed song poems commemorating the dead "cluster around the idea of a noble death in battle, focusing on the τιμή and κλέος that will accrue to the fallen hero and his family."[20] When Pindar takes up a similar theme in his seventh *Isthmian*, he is then "not anchored to verbal parallels" but is likely "drawing on themes of the genre represented by fragments of Callinus and Tyrtaeus rather than echoing specific passages". There was a common pool "of poems suitable for performance in any polis" that would be used at symposia and in composing or selecting funerary epigrams.

This sounds very much like what Bob Dylan probably felt and thought upon discovering the long and rich traditions of American, British, Scottish, and Irish folk songs and different regional and period varieties of American blues music. They have been for him ever since ample reservoirs from which he has drawn in large and small doses. In some cases, there is a specific inspiration or model in the mind of the author of a new work. In other cases, there is only a dipping into the deep pool of themes and images, phrases, and rhymes.

Can we determine which process is at work with *dulce et decorum est pro patria mori?* Let us keep in mind that scholars of this poem have always been concerned with death and patriotism, and thus with finding a source that says it is a fine or noble thing to die for your country.[21] That is why Tyrtaeus has long been adduced as the principal model. For example, Paul Shorey's 1900 students' series edition of the *Odes* and *Epodes*, offers "the old lie" directly to young school boys by posing a rhetorical question:[22]

---

19 τὸ γὰρ / Ἄρευι κατθάνην κάλον. Brown pers. communication 08/17/17.

20 Brown 2016, 276 and note 14.

21 While recognizing that Horace *Odes* 3.2.14 and 3.2.25 f. can be traced back to fragments of Simonides and that "the idea in *Odes* 3.2.13" "certainly finds expression as far back as Homer" and "traces of it are found in Alcaeus and Callinus", Lindo 1971 argues on the basis of other scattered allusions to Tyrtaeus that Horace in *Odes* 3.2.13 also is indebted to Tyrtaeus. Here we argue for specific consecutive lines of Callinus as the intertext for the specific, and now rightly famous, line of Horace.

22 Shorey 1900, 307.

13. **dulce**, etc. And if he (the young Roman lion) dies, why 'how can man die better?'

Shorey compares in Greek only Tyrtaeus fragment 10. In Latin he points to Cicero, *Phil.* 14.31: *O fortunata mors, quae naturae debita pro patria est potissimum reddita!* School commentary and scholarly commentary then both are satisfied to find a parallel that speaks of dying for one's country. Perhaps we can look at this another way.

For starters, consider structural parallels. Horace's line has three components, here listed in the order in which scholars have sought them: (1) death/dying; (2) for the good of your country; and (3) a predicated description of the social significance of (1 + 2).

Horace, *Carm.* 3.2.13:

(3) dulce et decorum est (2) pro patria (1) mori

Tyrtaeus fr. 10.1 f.:

(1) τεθνάμεναι γὰρ (3) καλὸν ἐνὶ προμάχοισι πεσόντα
ἄνδρ' ἀγαθὸν (2) περὶ ῇ πατρίδι μαρνάμενον,

Callinus fr. 1.5–8:

καί τις (1) ἀποθνηίσκων ὕστατ' ἀκοντιστάτω
(3) τιμῆέν τε γάρ ἐστι καὶ ἀγλαὸν ἀνδρὶ μάχεσθαι
(2) γῆς πέρι καὶ παίδων κουριδίης τ' ἀλόχου
δυσμενέσιν.

Tyrtaeus' two lines have the advantage of mentioning (1) dying, (2) on behalf of the πατρίς (*patria*), and (3) that it is καλὸν "beautiful, fine, noble". But Callinus has those elements, too; and Callinus is parallel to Horace in having a two-adjective phrase define (3) the social implications of the action of dying for one's country: his τιμῆέν τε γάρ ἐστι καὶ ἀγλαὸν would seem to parallel Horace's *dulce et decorum est*.

If we imagine that Horace has Callinus 1.5–8 or something like it even vaguely in mind, we then have to ask whether *decorum* would come close to conveying the social significance of τιμῆεν. τιμῆεν quite literally means "made up of τιμή". Semantically τιμή comes to mean something like 'honor', but etymologically it denotes the 'payment' by other members of society to an individual for actions performed in service to their society.[23] τιμῆεν then puts in a Vorticist line-initial spotlight what every Greek male from Bronze Age epic verse onwards strives for: the public honor he acquires for publicly recognized actions that benefit the social groups in which he lives. This, or its Roman equivalent, seems to be what *decorum* in its longstanding meaning of "noble" or "glorious" would convey to Horace's reader.

Decorum, with its connection to *decet* and *decus*, would be a fine word to capture some of the other social implications of τιμῆεν (Callinus) and even of καλόν (Tyrtaeus). The word *decus* means originally "ornament, adornment" evolving to "dignity, propriety". It has a sense like the related Greek adjective ἀριδείκετος, meaning something like "distinctive". It conveys the same sense of "conspicuously and socially commendable" that Old and Middle Irish *dech* conveys: "the best, preeminent" (= *decus*), and that Latin *dig-nus* "estimable, valued" (< **dec-nos*) conveys, too.[24] Compare the passage from the Old Irish wisdom-text *Tecosca Cormaic* (*TC*) or *The Instructions of King Cormaic Mac Airt* where we are instructed that it is best in royal social settings to treat poets with reverence and dignity:[25]

> *'A húi Chuind, a Chormaic,' ol Carpre, 'cid as dech do rig?' 'Ni handsa", ol Cormac. 'Dech dó [...] armitiu filed.'*
>
> "O grandson of Conn, O Cormac", said Cabre, "what is best for a king?" "Not hard to tell", said Cormac. "Best for him [...is] honouring poets". (*TC*, § 1)

However, given (1) the developmental shift noted by Ernout and Meillet to *decet* with a meaning of "il convient" "it suits or befits" and equivalent to Greek πρέπει is "conspicuously fit, beseems, suits," as *decens* is equivalent to πρέπων and εὐπρεπής, and (2) that "*decorum* traduit [translates] πρέπον Cicero, *Or.* 70", *decorum* seems closer to another aspect of ἀγλαόν, the visual:[26] πρέπει means "be distinguished, shine forth, show itself clearly to be" and in primary usage refers to things taken in by sight.

The meaning conveyed by ἀγλαός is that something (a prize, arms, water, leaves on a tree) is "splendid, shining, gleaming, bright and beautiful" and thereby "gives delight", that is, it appeals to feeling and to sight. In its sense of delighting, I associate ἀγλαόν in Callinus with *dulce* in Horace. *Dulce*

---

23 The adjectival suffix is 'material' here and is felt to be so from our Linear B documentation, where the suffix *–went* is well attested, onwards into historical Greek.

24 Walde / Hofmann 1938, 330 f. *s. decet.*

25 Fogarty 2016, 222.

26 Ernout / Meillet 1939, 256 f. *s. decet.*

comes from the same Indo-European root as Greek γλυκύς, although not unproblematically—some posit that *dulcis* and γλυκύς come from a common loan word. Both convey that something is pleasing, gives pleasure. Szemerenyi associated ἀγλαός with ἀγάλλομαι "I glory or take delight in" and ἄγαλμα, literally the end product of the act of "glorifying, delighting, honoring".[27]

Still there is here no pedantic 1:1 correspondence between the two Latin and the two Greek adjectives. *Decorum* would seem to convey the sense of social propriety and due social recognition found in ἀγλαόν, but without its brilliance and forceful impact. *Decorum* has both an aesthetic sense (good in appearance) and a moral sense (conveying a somewhat weaker form of *honor*). Horace, in my view, has found a way of reducing the intensity of the combined force of τιμῆεν and ἀγλαόν and making them fit into the smaller field that is available for individual human action in the Roman culture of Horace's time. *dulce* at root appeals to taste. I think Horace uses *dulce* because *decorum* cannot live up even to καλόν (Tyrtaeus) in its force and social significance. It is really needed to make *decorum* work, if Callinus is the model text. And it also then produces the two-part description that is distinctive in Callinus.

Finally, we should add an observation made by Christopher Brown concerning the effects that Horace has achieved by transforming Callinus. Regardless of what pool of Greek ἀνὴρ ἀγαθός poetry Horace drew it from, if any, "the expression *dulce et decorum* is", as Brown observes, "unusual": "the alliteration is likely significant, and might, in addition to adding trenchancy, evoke earlier Republican Latin, which would suit the Roman odes with their preoccupation with old time Roman values and paradigms of Republican virtue such as Regulus".[28]

3 Bob Dylan and Songs of War and Other Things

When we turn here now to Bob Dylan, it is, I hope, with insights gained as to how our understanding of the scholarly sensibilities of song-poets and the inspirational resources they seek to acquire and place into their poetic and creative tool kits determine what kinds of poetic art they are likely to practice and what kinds of intertextual relationships we are likely to find. In the last stages of his career, with the critical scrutiny that has accompanied receiving major public honors like the Kennedy Center Honor (1997), the Academy Award for Best Orig-

27 Szemerényi 1964, 155.

28 Brown pers. communication 08/17/17 with reference to Leumann / Hofmann / Szantyr 1965, 2.701.

inal Song (2001), the Pulitzer Prize special citation (2008), the Presidential Medal of Freedom (2012) and the Nobel Prize in Literature (2016), Bob Dylan is now seen to be what he has always been, intellectually omnivorous and opportunistically creative. He is also constrained in ways that remind us of Pound and especially Owen, but also set him apart, not only from them, but I sincerely believe from any "poet" in the long Western tradition. He is *sui generis*.

Dylan's relationship to his models and his use of them, conscious and unconscious, has been problematized in the last quarter century by the economically driven preoccupation with the personal ownership of ideas, including the words and images that express them. Imagine what we would now have of Virgil and Horace, or even of Pound and Owen, if intellectual property copyright lawyers had been acting on behalf of first the estates of Homer, Hesiod, Callinus, Tyrtaeus, Pindar, and Alcaeus and then the estates of Horace and Virgil. Given famous modern cases of plagiarism uncovered in the work of such notables writing about war and human beings in times of war as Doris Kearns Goodwin, Christopher Hedges, and Stephen E. Ambrose, it is perhaps inevitable that Dylan's unabashed ways of "loving" his models and "stealing" from them have drawn similar "gotcha" attention.

In thinking through how to approach this contribution and then writing it, it has become clear to me what singular factors were at work in Dylan's coming to be a major figure in American history and culture of the last six decades. Dylan has had the advantage of all the advances in travel and communication, in preservation through recording, in intensified research into all aspects of ethnomusicology, in computer applications to song production, dissemination, preservation and recovery, that have taken place in the post-WW II United States.

Dylan's provincial world was changed, as he himself tells us, when he heard in Minneapolis in the winter of 1959, the Smithsonian recordings of Woody Guthrie.[29] But three years later in December 1962, he flew to London and absorbed British and Scottish folk ballads directly from masters like Martin Carthy. Much later (May 3, 2006 to April 1, 2009) in the 101 hour-long broadcasts of his Theme Time Radio program, Dylan explored the Croesus-like treasure rooms of American popular music. His Croesus was producer Eddie Gorodetsky, whose music collection contains a true myriad of records and fourteen myriads of digital files.

These resources and possibilities would have been unavailable to Dylan during his gestational stage and later, if he had been born in a town like Duluth and

29 Dylan 2004, 244f., recalls thinking after hearing the Guthrie songs, "'So this is the game'. I could sing all these songs, every single one of them, and they were all I wanted to sing. It was like I had been in the dark and someone had turned on the main switch of a lightning conductor".

raised in one like Hibbing even twenty-five years earlier. The challenge with understanding intertexuality in Dylan's song poems then is unlike the challenge that the poems of Owen or Pound, Virgil or Horace present to us. The volume of potential influences upon Dylan is staggering, almost immeasurable, and is matched now by the volume of documentation and hypothesizing about from where or whom Dylan got what. Richard Thomas's own book on Dylan, *Why Bob Dylan Matters*,[30] concentrates, although not exclusively, on Dylan's love and theft of Virgil and Ovid and makes us aware of how similar Dylan is to Virgil in his ways of writing song poems and his disposition towards society. There Richard gives us a plain-spoken definition of intertextuality that makes sense of what Dylan is doing: "the process by which poets, songwriters, painters, composers or artists of any genre produce new meaning through the creative reuse of existing texts, images or sound".[31]

Dylan is like Owen in not continuing his formal education much beyond what we call the secondary level. Owen aspired to learning Latin and hoped to master Greek, because mastery of those languages was key to the social status he wished to attain. Dylan, from a solidly comfortable middle-class background, never expressed anxieties about foregoing the economic and social prerogatives that a college degree brought with it in the late fifties and early sixties. Nor did he care for the approaches to learning adopted in university classrooms or feel he was missing out on much.

To me the quintessential *exemplum*, almost Plutarchian in having a small personal act speak for the nature of the man, of where Dylan stands in relationship to literary and song traditions, is offered to us in his Nobel Prize acceptance speech. There he tells the audience, arguably among the world's most culturally distinguished people, that when he received the "surprising news" of having been awarded the Nobel Prize in literature, "I began to think about William Shakespeare, the great literary figure". Who but someone whose passions for what he does are so all-absorbing would so ingenuously feel, and then act upon, the need to explain to the highly educated crowd assembled, and to all who he knew would read his words later, that William Shakespeare was "a great literary figure"?

Owen wanted desperately to be on the inside, and criticized those controlling the British military machine and the unquestioning multitude who lent their support to the whole endeavor with deep human feelings of compassion and exceptional capacities to "see" other human beings. Sassoon's mentorship

---

30 Thomas 2017.
31 Thomas 2017, 131.

gave Owen a validation that seemed to reassure him that some few persons of high cultural standing shared and perhaps even surpassed his own deep moral questioning of the senseless deaths and destruction of normal human lives.

Owen, however, truly did internalize the pity of War and expressed his strong emotions as ones he thought other human beings had capacities to share, once they were alerted to them. *The Guardian*'s reviewer of the Sassoon edition of Owen's poems aptly characterizes his empathy: "Others have shown the disenchantment of war, have unlegended the roselight and romance of it, but none with such compassion for the disenchanted or such sternly just and justly stern judgment on the idyllisers". It was not for Owen to realize how unmoved by human suffering all the targets of Sassoon's white-heat anger and vitriolic contempt could be, even if forced to take notice of it. Owen's stern justice and just sternness might derive from his belief that acceptance is the only option for those who live far down in the hierarchy of power.

Pound was masterful at facilitating and promoting those he respected and championed, although he remained ever an outsider, living as an expatriate in London and Paris and towns in Italy for thirty-seven years of his adult prime. The equivalent of folk singers like Woody Guthrie or Pete Seeger in his criticisms of the *status quo*, he truly lived small. He still means a lot to a very few *cognoscenti*, but there are too many terrorist bombs in his poetry for his works ever to become widely used school texts, like the writings of Horace, Owen or Tim O'Brien in various periods.

Dylan somehow has managed to find a pocket where he can be an outsider to whom people on the inside, at all levels of society and all measures of access to power and the resources that make for power, are willing to listen. When we are interpreting Virgil and Horace on war and on people of power, we need to keep in mind that the author and singer of songs about the insanities of war in our culture, about our racism, and about the effects of our merciless capitalism—songs like "John Brown", "Masters of War", "Ballad of Hollis Brown", "George Jackson", "Clean-Cut Kid", "The Lonesome Death of Hattie Carroll", "The Groom's Still Waiting at the Altar", and "Workingman's Blues #2"—could be described by President Jimmy Carter in 2015 as someone whose words "are more precise... and permanent than anything said by a president of the United States", who must sometimes have to stand naked. And President Barack Obama in 2010 welcomed Dylan's firm outsider posture: "You want him to be a little skeptical about the whole enterprise".

Part of Dylan's secret might be his Owen-like capacity to see human beings and to write and sing true criticism in a way that can be heard and felt even by powerful people. While not as humorous as Clarence Darrow's "I have never killed anyone, but I have read some obituary notices with great satisfaction" and its many variants during Darrow's career, Dylan gives us a clue as to how he can write in "Masters of War" in 1963 "And I hope that you die / and your death'll come soon" and "I'll stand o'er your grave / 'Til I'm sure you're dead" and not be viewed as an extremist. It goes a long way to explaining also why his many insightful criticisms can be readily accepted. In the liner notes to *The Freewheelin' Bob Dylan*, he writes about "Masters of War": "I've never really written anything like that before. I don't sing songs which hope people will die, but I couldn't help it with this one. The song is a sort of striking out, a reaction to the last straw, a feeling of what can you do?" Notice here that Dylan palms the death wish off on the "song", probably with some measure of truth given his own ambivalence about topical songs even while he was writing and singing them.

We should also emphasize that Dylan took on war, racism, and economic disparity when significant numbers of Americans were worried about these very problems and human injustices. "Masters of War" was written during the winter of 1962–1963 and recorded and released in April-May, 1963. President Eisenhower had warned the American people in his televised farewell speech on January 17, 1961 about the "military-industrial complex". The Cuban Missile Crisis in October, 1962 had Americans and the rest of the world terrified. As Dylan himself explains,[32] "["Masters of War"] was an easy thing to do. There were thousands and thousands of people just wanting that song, so I wrote it up". What Dylan came up with was what Oliver Trager concisely labels as "[a]n angry, stark, and vengeful piece of righteous and poetic vitriol".[33]

Dylan in "Masters of War", like Owen in "Dulce et Decorum Est", uses the title phrase strategically in making his point. Dylan uses the phrase only one time: in the very first line of his long song poem. By writing and singing "Come you masters of war", Dylan avoids the hackneyed apostrophe, "O, you masters of war". Instead, he issues the kind of invitation we find in hymns like "O Come, O Come, Emmanuel!" and "O, Come, All Ye Faithful" where people are summoned to bear witness. Dylan also uses this formulaic phrasing in true folk songs that he wrote himself or in others that he transformed and performed: "Come gather 'round people / Wherever you roam"; "Come around you rovin' gamblers and a story I will tell"; "Come you ladies and you gentlemen, a-listen

32 Heylin 2009, 118.

33 Trager 2004, 418 f. And it is non-topical enough to be applied to any and all wars, as Dylan used it (Corcoran 2002, 146–148) on national television at the height of the Gulf War in 1991.

to my song".[34] He may have been inspired subliminally by the refrain in the Piedmont blues classic released on record by Sonny Terry in 1962, "Jump, Little Children". Dylan would also have had readily accessible in his memory banks Robert Johnson's sermon to a wayward woman: "You better come on in my kitchen / It's goin' to be rainin' outdoors". He could have even channeled Clarence Quick's 1957 (written in 1956) hit doo-wop song "Come Go With Me". Still the question remains how did Dylan come up with such an original phrase as "masters of war"?

Dalton Trumbo published his famous novel about World War I and its terrifying human costs, *Johhny Got His Gun,* in 1939. As Trumbo explains in the preface to the second edition released in 1959,[35] his book first came out on September 3, "ten days after the Nazi-Soviet Pact, two days after the start of World War II". A bad case of bad timing. He wrote it in response to what enthusiasm for war at the start of World War I by "idyllisers" had wrought:

> It was an August made palpitant and breathless by the pre-nuptial nights of young gentlemen-officers and the girls they left permanently behind them. One of the Highland regiments went over the top in its first battle behind forty kilted bagpipers, skirling away for all they were worth—at machine guns.
>
> Nine million corpses later, when the bands stopped and the serenities started running, the wail of bagpipes would never again sound quite the same. It was the last of the wars; and *Johnny Got His Gun* was probably the last American novel written about it before an entirely different affair called World War II got under way.

The reprint in 1959 was so popular that a mass paperback edition was released in 1959–1960 by Ace Star (title K-109) Books and selling for 50 cents.[36] It proclaimed on its back cover that "a great pre-World War II (*sic*) best seller becomes a best-seller again" and on its front that it is "a book that can never be forgotten by anyone who ever reads it".

Dylan gives us insight into his reading habits in radio interviews of the period. For example, he tells Studs Terkel in a WFMT radio interview April 26, 1963[37] that he read Robert Gover's *One Hundred Dollar Misunderstanding* about

34 Ricks, 2003, 264f. and n. 2. Dylan's "North Country Blues", "Rambling, Gambling Willie", and "Hard Times in New York Town", all with traditional roots in tune, words and/or subject matter. Gray 2006, 541–543 discusses the influence of 19th-century American poets, especially Henry Wadsworth Longfellow, on Dylan's poetic craft. See Dylan 2004, 37. Hayden Pelliccia suggests that Dylan is indebted here to the opening of Longfellow's "Paul Revere's Ride": "Listen, my children, and you shall hear", a poem he likely learned in childhood.

35 Trumbo 1959a, 1f.

36 Trumbo 1959b.

37 Terkel 2005, 204.

"this straight-A college kid, you know, fraternity guy, and a fourteen-year old Negro prostitute". If we read what Michael Gray characterizes as Gover's "cult bohemian novel", we can trace the impact it had on Dylan's own sensibilities about race and social and economic barriers and hatreds, about capturing the phrasings and mannerisms of the characters with which he peoples his song poems, and even his ways of spelling the words he sings and writes down as lyrics.[38]

My point here is that Dylan was reading the 'in' popular literature of the time. He absorbed it and reused it creatively. Wilentz (2010, 81f.) emphasizes clear intertexts between Dylan's "Desolation Row" and Jack Kerouac's novel *Desolation Angels*, in specific phrases, not just the title of the song and the title of the book. For example, Kerouac describes a character David D'Angeli based on contemporary poet Philip Lamantia as "the perfect image of a priest". Dylan in the seventh stanza of "Desolation Row" writes: "The Phantom of the Opera / In a perfect image of a priest".

Several Dylanologists have drawn connections between Dylan's work and Dalton Trumbo's. Sean Wilentz rightly thinks that Dylan's fictional anti-war song "John Brown" is "a ballad reminiscent of Dalton Trumbo's anti-war novel of 1939, *Johnny Got His Gun*".[39] But Wilentz does not discuss the re-release of *Johnny Got His Gun* and its enormous popularity at around the time Dylan arrived and was establishing himself in New York, the period when he was reading the likes of Gover and was writing and singing 'anti-war' songs like "John Brown" and eventually "Masters of War". Seth Rogovoy thinks that the reference to "picket[ing] the movie *Exodus*" in Dylan's "Talkin' John Birch Paranoid Blues" might be his "very knowing and sophisticated reference to the movie's screenwriter, Dalton Trumbo", who was blacklisted during the McCarthy period as one of the "infamous 'Hollywood 10'".[40] These observations show that serious Dylanologists suspect that Trumbo was on the young movie-loving Dylan's radar screen.[41]

The wildly popular second edition of Trumbo's classic sorrow-of-war book, mass-circulated in paperback, I believe is Dylan's model for the title and the ferociously angry energy—surprising even to Dylan himself—of his classic anti-war song, which, like Trumbo's novel, can be applied to war after war after war.

38 See Gray (2006, 270 s. Gover, Robert) for Gover's account of meeting and having dinner and drinking with Dylan and Dylan playing "Masters of War" for him.

39 Wilentz 2010, 152, n. 1. Entries for Trumbo and *Johnny Got His Gun* are missing from the index in Wilentz, 2010, 377–396.

40 Rogovoy 2009, 38.

41 Trumbo is not mentioned in Gray 2006.

Read the closing paragraphs of *Johnny Got His Gun* and take in the cascades of words. With his minimally punctuated flow of words and phrases, Trumbo matches Dylan's catalogue of what terrible effects on normal human lives—and on our natural hopes for living humanly throughout our lives—the plans and directives of Eisenhower's Military-Industrial-Complex leaders have. Dylan excoriates the "masters of war" in direct address with anaphoric "you" and depersonalized "you that". Trumbo uses "you" and "you who" in the same intense way. I here underline significant intertextual phrases and themes. Take in Trumbo's equivalent of Dylan's angry, stark, righteous and poetic vitriol:[42]

> If you make a war if there are guns to be aimed if there are bullets to be fired if there are men to be killed they will not be us. They will not be us the guys who grow wheat and turn it into food the guys who make clothes and paper and houses and tiles the guys who build dams and power plants and string the long moaning high tension wires the guys who crack crude oil down into a dozen different parts who make light globes and sewing machines and shovels and automobiles and airplanes and tanks and guns oh no it will not be us who die. It will be you.
>
> It will be you—you who urge us on to battle you who incite us against ourselves you who would have one cobbler kill another cobbler you who would have one man who works kill another man who works you who would have one human being who wants only to live kill another human being who wants only to live. Remember this. Remember this well you people who plan for war. Remember this you patriots you fierce ones you spawners of hate you inventors of slogans. Remember this as you have never remembered anything else in your lives.
>
> We are men of peace we are men who work and we want no quarrel. But if you destroy our peace if you take away our work if you try to range us one against the other we will know what to do. If you tell us to make the world safe for democracy we will take you seriously and by god and by Christ we will make it so. We will use the guns you force upon us we will use them to defend our very lives and the menace to our lives does not lie on the other side of a nomansland that was set apart without our consent it lies within our own boundaries here and now we have seen it and we know it.
>
> Put the guns into our hands and we will use them. Give us the slogans and we will turn them into realities. Sing the battle hymns and we will take them up where you left off. Not one not ten not ten thousand not a million not ten millions not a hundred millions but a billion two billions of us all the people of the world we will have the slogans and we will have the hymns and we will have the guns and we will use them and we will live. Make no mistake of it we will live. We will be alive and we will walk and talk and eat and sing and laugh and feel and love and bear our children in tranquility in security in decency in peace. You plan the wars you masters of men plan the wars and point the way and we will point the gun.

42 Trumbo 1959a, 308 f.

Listen to “Masters of War”. Go back to *Johnny Got His Gun* as an intertext. Do what Richard Thomas says the art of reference invites us to do. Take in all its emotional and intellectual content. Listen to “Masters of War” in your head, particularly these lines:[43]

Come you masters of war
You that build all the guns
You that build the death planes
You that build the big bombs

You put a gun in my hand
And you hide from my eyes
And you turn and run farther
When the fast bullets fly

You fasten the triggers
For the others to fire
Then you set back and watch
When the death count gets higher

Imagine like Dylan and like Trumbo, the satisfyingly “stern justice” the deaths of those masters of men “who fasten the triggers for others to fire” would bring. And you will rank Dylan among the accomplished masters of the “love and theft” of source texts.

43 Bob Dylan, “Masters of War” © 1963 by Warner Bros. Inc.; renewed 1991 by Special Rider Music.

Works Cited

Journals are abbreviated as in *L'Année Philologique*. References to ancient authors and texts generally follow the conventions of the *OCD* (Hornblower, S. / Spawforth, A. / Eidinow, E. (eds.) (2012), *The Oxford Classical Dictionary* (4th ed.), Oxford). Other works cited by abbreviation are:

AE =	*L'Année Épigraphique.*
CEG =	*Hansen, P.A. (ed.) (1983–1989), Carmina Epigraphica Graeca, Berlin.*
CIL =	*Corpus Inscriptionum Latinarum.*
CLE =	*Bücheler, F. / Lommatzsch, E. (1895–1926), Carmina Latina Epigraphica, Leipzig.*
GVI =	*Peek, W. (1955), Griechische Vers-Inschriften, Berlin.*
IMEGR =	*Bernand, É. (ed.) (1969), Inscriptions métriques de l'Égypte gréco-romaine. Recherches sur la poésie épigrammatique des Grecs en Égypte. Annales littéraires de l'Université de Besançon 98, Paris.*
IosPE =	*Latyschev, V. (ed.) (1885–1901) Inscriptiones antiquae orae septentrionalis Ponti Euxini graecae et latinae, St. Petersburg.*
KL =	*Keil, H. (ed.) (1857–1880), Grammatici Latini, Leipzig.*
OLD =	*Glare, P.G.W. (ed.) (1968–1982), Oxford Latin Dictionary, Oxford.*
SGO =	*Merkelbach, R. / Stauber, J. (eds.) (1998–2004), Steinepigramme aus dem griechischen Osten, Berlin.*
SH =	*Lloyd-Jones, H. / Parsons, P. (eds.) (1983), Supplementum Hellenisticum, Berlin.*
TLL =	*Thesaurus Linguae Latinae.*

The following works are cited by author and date.

Adams, J.N. (1982), *The Latin Sexual Vocabulary*, London.

Adams, J.N. (2003), *Bilingualism and the Latin Language*, Cambridge.

Agrell, P. (2004), "Wed or Unwed? Ambiguity in *Aeneid* 4", in: *PVS* 25, 95–110.

Ahl, F. (1985), *Metaformations: Soundplay and Wordplay in Ovid and Other Classical Poets*, Ithaca, NY.

Ahl, F. (trans.) (2007), *Virgil, Aeneid*, Oxford.

Alden, M. (2000), *Homer beside Himself: Para-Narratives in the* Iliad, Oxford.

Allen, J. H. / Greenough, J. B. (1903), *A New Latin Grammar*, Boston / London.

Ancona, R. (1994), *Time and the Erotic in Horace's Odes*, Durham / London.

Anderson, R.D. / Parsons, P.J. / Nisbet, R.G.M. (1979), "Elegiacs by Gallus from Qaṣr Ibrîm", in: *JRS* 69, 125–155.

Anderson, W.S. (1981), "Servius and the 'Comic Style' of *Aeneid* 4", in: *Arethusa* 14, 115–125.

André, J.M. (1966), *L'otium dans la vie morale et intellectuelle romaine: des origines à l'époque augustéenne*, Paris.

Auden, W.H. (1948), *The Dyer's Hand and Other Essays*, London.

Austin, R. G. (ed.) (1955), *P. Vergili Maronis Aeneidos Liber Quartus*, Oxford.

Barber, E. A., (ed.) (1960), *Sexti Properti Carmina*, 2nd ed., Oxford.

Barchiesi, A. (1981), "Notizie sul 'nuovo Gallo'", in: *A&R* 26, 153–166.

https://doi.org/10.1515/9783110545708-015

Barchiesi, A. (1994), "Immovable Delos: *Aeneid* 3.73–98 and the Hymns of Callimachus", in: *CQ* 44, 438–443.
Barchiesi, A. (2005), "The Search for the Perfect Book: A PS to the New Posidippus", in: K. Gutzwiller (ed.), *The New Posidippus: A Hellenistic Poetry Book*, Oxford, 320–342.
Barsby, J. (ed.) (1999), *Terence, Eunuchus*, Cambridge.
Beekes, R. (2010), *Etymological Dictionary of Greek*, 2 vols., Leiden / Boston.
Biles, Z.P. / Olson, S.D. (eds.) (2015), *Aristophanes, Wasps*, Oxford.
Bleisch, P. (1999), "The Empty Tomb at Rhoeteum: Deiphobus and the Problem of the Past in *Aeneid* 6.494–547", in: *ClAnt* 18, 187–226.
Bowie, A.M. (1998), "*Exuvias effigiemque:* Dido, Aeneas and the Body as Sign", in: D. Montserrat (ed.), *Changing Bodies, Changing Meanings: Studies on the Human Body in Antiquity*, London, 57–79.
Bowie, E. L. (1986), "Early Greek Elegy, Symposium and Public Festival", in: *JHS* 106, 13–35.
Bowra, C.M. (1957), "Melinno's Hymn to Rome" in: *JRS* 47, 21–28.
Boyd, B.W. (1983), "*Cydonea Mala:* Virgilian Word-Play and Allusion", in: *HSPh* 83, 169–174.
Boyd, B.W. (1984), "*Parva seges satis est:* The Landscape of Tibullan Elegy in 1.1 and 1.10", in: *TAPhA* 114, 273–280.
Boyd, B.W. (1997), *Ovid's Literary Loves: Influence and Innovation in the* Amores, Ann Arbor.
Bradley, K.R. (2001), "Imagining Slavery: The Limits of the Plausible" [Review of W. Fitzgerald (2000), *Slavery and the Roman Literary Imagination*], in: *JRA* 14, 473–477.
Bradley, K.R. (2015), "The Bitter Chain of Slavery", in: *DHA* 41, 149–176.
Breed, B.W. (2006), *Pastoral Inscriptions: Reading and Writing Virgil's* Eclogues, London.
Bright, D.F. (1971), "A Tibullan Odyssey", in: *Arethusa* 4, 197–214.
Bright, D.F. (1978), *Haec mihi fingebam: Tibullus in His World*, Leiden.
Brink, C.O. (1963), *Horace on Poetry, I: Prolegomena to the Literary Epistles*, Cambridge.
Brink, C.O. (1969), "Horatian Notes: Despised Readings in the Manuscripts of the *Odes*", in: *PCPhS* 15, 1–6.
Brown, C.G. (2016) "Warding Off a Hailstorm of Blood: Pindar on Martial Elegy", in: L. Swift / C. Carey (eds.), *Iambus and Elegy: New Approaches*, Oxford, 273–290.
Brown, E.L. (1963) *Numeri Vergiliani: Studies in 'Eclogues' and 'Georgics'*, Brussels.
Bundy, E.L. (1972), "The 'Quarrel between Kallimachos and Apollonios' Part I: The Epilogue of Kallimachos's 'Hymn to Apollo'", in: *California Studies in Classical Antiquity* 5, 39–94.
Burns, T.W. (2014/5), "Small Latin and Less Greek" [Review of C. Burrow (2013), *Shakespeare and Classical Antiquity*], in: *Claremont Review of Books* 15, 69–73.
Burrow, C. (2013), *Shakespeare and Classical Antiquity*, Oxford.
Burton, J.B. (1995), *Theocritus's Urban Mimes: Mobility, Gender, and Patronage*, Berkeley / Los Angeles.
Buscaroli, C. (ed.) (1932), *Virgilio: Il libro di Didone*, Milan / Genoa / Rome / Naples.
Busch, S. (1999), *Versus balnearum: Die antike Dichtung über Bäder und Baden im römischen Reich*, Stuttgart / Leipzig.
Cairns, F. (1977), "Horace on other people's love affairs (*Odes* I 27; II 4; I 8; III 12)", in: *QUCC* 24, 121–147.
Cairns, F. (1979), *Tibullus: A Hellenistic Poet at Rome*, Cambridge.
Cairns, F. (1989), *Virgil's Augustan Epic*, Cambridge.
Cairns, F. (1997), "Ancient 'etymology' and Tibullus: On the Classification of 'Etymologies' and on 'Etymological Markers'", in: *PCPhS* 42, 24–59.

Cairns, F. (2003), "The 'Etymology' in Ovid 'Heroides' 20.21–32", in: *CJ* 98, 239–242.
Cairns, F. (2006), *Sextus Propertius: The Augustan Elegist*, Cambridge.
Cairns, F. (2016), *Hellenistic Epigrams: Contexts of Exploration*, Cambridge.
Cameron, A. (1995), *Callimachus and his Critics*, Princeton.
Campbell, D.A. (1967), *Greek Lyric Poetry: A Selection of Early Greek Lyric, Elegiac and Iambic Poetry*, Basingstoke / London.
Campbell, D.A. (ed.) (1982), *Greek Lyric*, Vol. I, Cambridge, MA.
Canali, L. (trans.) / Paratore E. (ed.) (1978), *Virgilio, Eneide*, vol. 2, Milan.
Carey, J. (ed.) (1969), *Andrew Marvell: A Critical Anthology*, Harmondsworth.
Casali, S. (2006), "The Making of the Shield: Inspiration and Repression in the *Aeneid*", in: *G&R* 53, 185–204.
Casali, S. (2007), "Killing the Father: Ennius, Naevius and Virgil's Julian Imperialism", in: W. Fitzgerald / E. Gowers (eds.), *Ennius Perennis: The Annals and Beyond*, Cambridge, 103–128.
Casali, S. (2010), "The Development of the Aeneas Legend", in J. Farrell / M. Putnam (eds.), *A Companion to Vergil's Aeneid and its Tradition*, Chichester / Malden, MA, 37–51.
Cheney, P. / Hardie, P. (eds.) (2015), *The Oxford History of Classical Reception in English Literature, Volume 2: 1558–1660*, Oxford.
Clark, M.E. (1983), "Horace, *Ars Poetica* 75–78: The Origin and Worth of Elegy", in: *CW* 77, 1–5.
Clausen, W.V. (ed.) (1994), *A Commentary on Virgil, Eclogues*, Oxford.
Clausen, W.V. (2002), *Virgil's* Aeneid: *Decorum, Allusion, and Ideology*, Leipzig.
Coleman, R. (ed.) (1977), *Vergil, Eclogues*, Cambridge.
Conington, J. (ed.) (1884), *The Works of Virgil, vol. 2: Aeneid I–VI*, 4th ed. rev. by H. Nettleship, London.
Connors, C. (1994), "Ennius, Ovid and Representations of Ilia", in: *MD* 32, 99–112.
Conte, G.G. (1986), *The Rhetoric of Imitation: Genre and Poetic Memory in Virgil and Other Latin Poets*, C. Segal (trans.), Ithaca, NY.
Conte, G.B. (1989), "Love without Elegy: The *Remedia amoris* and the Logic of a Genre", G. Most (trans.), in: *Poetics Today*, 10, 441–469.
Conte, G.B. (2007), *The Poetry of Pathos: Studies in Vigilian Epic*, Oxford.
Cooley, A.E. / Cooley, M.G.L. (2013), *Pompeii and Herculaneum: A Sourcebook*, London.
Corcoran, N. (2002), "Death's Honesty", in: N. Corcoran (ed.), *Do You, Mr. Jones?: Bob Dylan with the Poets and Professors*, London, 143 f.
Courtney, E. (1987), "Quotation, Interpolation, Transposition", in: *Hermathena* 143, 7–18.
Courtney, E. (ed.) (1993), *The Fragmentary Latin Poets*, Oxford.
Courtney, E. (ed.) (1995), *Musa Lapidaria: A Selection of Latin Verse Inscriptions*, Atlanta.
Crowther, N.B. (1978), "Horace, Catullus, and Alexandrianism", in: *Mnemosyne* 31, 33–44.
Cunningham, I.C. (ed.) (1987), *Herodas, Mimiambi*, Leipzig.
D'Arms, J.H. (1970), *Romans on the Bay of Naples*, Cambridge, MA.
Damschen, G. (2004), "Das lateinische Akrostichon: neue Funde bei Ovid sowie Vergil, Grattius, Manilius und Silius Italicus", in: *Philologus* 148, 88–115.
Danielewicz, J. (2015), "One Sign after Another: The Fifth ΛΕΠΤΗ in Aratus' *Phaen.* 783–4?", in *CQ* 65, 387–390.
Davies, M. (1986), "Alcaeus, Thetis and Helen", in: *Hermes* 114, 257–262.
Davies, M. (ed.) (1991), *Sophocles, Trachiniae*, Oxford.

Davis, G. (1991) *Polyhymnia: The Rhetoric of Horatian Lyric Discourse*, Berkeley / Los Angeles.
Davis, G. (2005), "From Lyric to Elegy: The Inscription of the Elegiac Subject in *Heroides* 15 (Sappho to Phaon)", in: W. Batstone / G. Tissol (eds.), *Defining Genre and Gender in Latin Literature: Essays Presented to William S. Anderson on His Seventy-Fifth Birthday*, New York, 175–191.
Davis, P. (2011), "Marvell and the Literary Past", in: D. Hurst / S. N. Zwicker (eds.), *The Cambridge Companion to Andrew Marvell*, Cambridge, 26–45.
Day Lewis, C. (trans.) (1966), *The* Eclogues, Georgics *and* Aeneid *of Virgil*, Oxford.
de Grazia, M. (2010), "Anachronism", in: B. Cummings / J. Simpson (eds.), *Cultural Reformations: Medieval and Renaissance in Literary History*, Oxford, 13–32.
de La Cerda, I.L. (ed.) (1612), *P. Virgilii Maronis priores sex libri Aeneidos argumentis, explicationibus, notis illustrati auctore Ioanne Ludovico de la Cerda Toletano Sociatatis Iesu*, Lyon.
de Vaan, M. (2008), *Etymological Dictionary of Latin and the Other Italic Languages*, Leiden / Boston.
Degani, E. / Burzacchini, G. (1977), *Lirici greci: antologia*, Bologna.
Desmond, M. (1994), *Reading Dido: Gender, Textuality, and the Medieval* Aeneid, Minneapolis, MN.
Du Quesnay, I. (1979), "From Polyphemus to Corydon: Virgil, *Eclogue* 2 and the *Idylls* of Theocritus", in: D. West / A.J. Woodman (eds.) *Creative Imitation and Latin Literature*, Cambridge, 35–70.
Dylan, B. (2004), *Chronicles: Volume 1*, New York.
Edwards, M.W. (1991), *The Iliad: A Commentary, Volume 5, Books 17–20*. Cambridge.
Eliot, T.S. (1951), *Selected Essays*, 3rd ed. enlarged, London.
Elliott, J. (2013), *Ennius and the Architecture of the* Annales, Cambridge.
Ellis, R. (ed.) (1889), *A Commentary on Catullus*, 2nd ed., Oxford.
Enk, P.J. (ed.) (1918), *Gratti Cynegeticon Quae Supersunt*, Zutphen.
Ernout, A. / Meillet, A. (1939), *Dictionnaire étymologique de la langue latine: histoire des mots*, Paris.
Erskine, A. (2001), *Troy between Greece and Rome: Local Tradition and Imperial Power*, Oxford.
Eskuche, G. (1890), "Die Elisionen in den 2 letzten Füssen des lateinsichen Hexameters, von Ennius bis Walahfridus Strabo", in: *RhM* 45, 236–64, 385–418.
Espey, J.J. (1955), *ezra pound's mauberley* [sic], Berkeley / Los Angeles.
Everett, B. (1979) "The Shooting of the Bears: Poetry and Politics in Andrew Marvell" in: R.L. Brett (ed.), *Andrew Marvell: Essays on the Tercentenary of his Death*, Oxford, 62–103.
Fairclough, H.R. (trans.) (1916), *Virgil, vol. 1*, London / New York; rev. by G. P. Goold (1999), Cambridge, MA.
Fantham, E. (1979), "The Mating of Lalage: Horace, *Odes* 2.5", in: *LCM* 4, 47–52.
Fantham, E. (1993), "Ceres, Liber, and Flora: Georgic and Anti-Georgic Elements in Ovid's *Fasti*", in *PCPhS* 38, 39–56.
Fedeli, P. (ed.) (1985), *Properzio, Il libro terzo delle elegie*, Bari.
Fedeli, P. (ed.) (2005), *Properzio, Elegie Libro II: Introduzione, testo, e commento*, Cambridge.
Feeney, D. (1983), "The Taciturnity of Aeneas", *CQ* 33, 204–219 (= Harrison, S.J. (ed.), *Oxford Readings in Vergil's* Aeneid, Oxford 1990, 166–190.

Feeney, D. / Nelis, D. (2005) "Two Virgilian Acrostics: Certissima Signa?", in *CQ* 55, 644–646.
Feeney, D. (2007), *Caesar's Calendar: Ancient Time and the Beginnings of History.* Berkeley / Los Angeles.
Feldherr, A. (1999), "Putting Dido on the Map: Genre and Geography in Vergil's Underworld", in: *Arethusa* 32, 85–122.
Finglass, P.J. (ed.) (2011), *Sophocles, Ajax*, Cambridge.
Fitzgerald, W. (2000), *Slavery and the Roman Literary Imagination*, Cambridge.
Fo, A. (trans.) (2012), *Publio Virgilio Marone, Eneide*, Turin.
Fogarty, H. (2016), "'Dubad nach innsci': Cultivation of Obscurity in Medieval Irish Literature", in: M. Boyd (ed.), *Ollam: Studies in Gaelic and Related Traditions in Honor of Tomás Ó Cathasaigh*, Lanham, MD, 211–224.
Forbiger, A. (ed.) (1873) *P. Vergili Maronis Opera*, 4th ed., vol. 2, Leipzig.
Fordyce, C. J. (1961), *Catullus: A Commentary*, Oxford.
Fowler, D. P. (1983), "An Acrostic in Vergil (*Aeneid* 7.601–4)?", in: *CQ* 33, 298.
Fraenkel, E. (1950), *Aeschylus, Agamemnon*, 3 vols., Oxford.
Fraenkel, E. (ed.) (1957), *Horace*, Oxford.
Franklin, J.L., Jr. (1991), "*Literacy and the Parietal Inscriptions of Pompeii*", in J.H. Humphrey (ed.), *Literacy in the Roman World*, 77–98.
Franklin, J.L., Jr. (1996/7), "Vergil at Pompeii: A Teacher's Aid", in: *CJ* 92, 175–184.
Fraser, P.M. (1972), *Ptolemaic Alexandria*, 3 vols., Oxford.
Freis, R. (1983) "The Catalogue of Pindaric Genres in Horace 'Ode' 4.2", *ClAnt* 2, 27–36.
Freudenburg, K. (1996), "Verse-Technique and Moral Extremism in Two Satires of Horace (*Sermones* 2.3 and 2.4)", in: *CQ* 46, 196–206.
Froula, C. (1983), *A Guide to Ezra Pound's Select Poems*, New York.
Fuhrer, T. (1988), "A Pindaric Feature in the Poems of Callimachus", in: *AJPh* 109, 53–68.
Fulkerson, L. (2004), "*Omnia Vincit Amor:* Why the *Remedia* Fail", in: *CQ* 54, 211–223.
Gagliardi, D. (1993), "Orazio e gli amori ancillari: per l'interpretazione di *Carm.* II, 4", in: G. Bruno (ed.), *Letture orazione*, Venosa, 91–97.
Galinsky, G. K. (1969), *Aeneas, Sicily and Rome*, Princeton.
Garrod, H. W. (1910), "On the Meaning of Ploxinum", in: *CQ* 4, 201–204.
Gerber, D. E. (1997), "Elegy", in: Gerber, D. E. (ed.), *A Companion to the Greek Lyric Poets, Mnemosyne*, 89–129.
Geymonat, M. (2004), "Capellae at the End of the *Eclogues*", in *HSPh* 102, 315–318.
Gigante, M. (1979), *Civiltà delle forme letterarie nell'antica Pompei*, Naples.
Gigante, M. (1995), *Philodemus in Italy: The Books from Herculaneum*, D. Obbink (trans.), Ann Arbor.
Gildenhard I. (2007), "Virgil vs. Ennius, or: The Undoing of the Annalist", in: W. Fitzgerald / E. Gowers (eds.) *Ennius Perennis: The Annals and Beyond*, Cambridge, 73–102.
Giordano, C. (1966), "Le iscrizioni della casa di M. Fabio Rufo", in: *Rendiconti dell' Accademia di Archeologia, Lettere e Belle Arti di Napoli* 41, 73–89.
Goldberg, S. (1999). [Review of J. Barsby (ed.) (1999), *Terence, Eunuchus*], in: *BMCRev* 1999.06.23.
Golden, M. (2011), "Slavery and the Greek family", in K. R. Bradley / P. Cartledge (eds.), *The Cambridge World History of Slavery, vol. I: The Ancient Mediterranean World*, Cambridge, 134–152.

Goldschmidt N. (2013), *Shaggy Crowns: Ennius'* Annales *and Virgil's* Aeneid, Oxford
Gomme, A. W. (1957), "Interpretations of Some Poems of Alkaios and Sappho", in: *JHS* 77, 255–266.
Goold, G.P. (ed.) (1977), *Ovid I, Heroides and Amores*, Cambridge, MA.
Goold, G.P. (ed.) (1983), *Catullus*, London.
Gover, R. (1961), *One Hundred Dollar Misunderstanding*, New York.
Gow, A.S.F. (ed.) (1950), *Theocritus*, 2 vols., Cambridge.
Gow, A.S.F. / Page, D. L. (eds.) (1965), *The Greek Anthology: Hellenistic Epigrams*, 2 vols., Cambridge.
Gow, A.S.F. / Page, D. L. (eds.) (1968), *The Greek Anthology: The Garland of Philip*, 2 vols., Cambridge.
Gowers, E. (2002), "Blind Eyes and Cut Throats: Amnesia and Silence in Horace *Satires* 1.7", in: *CPh* 97, 145–161.
Gowers, E. (2012), *Horace, Satires, Book I.* Cambridge.
Gray, M. (2006), *The Bob Dylan Encyclopedia*, New York / London.
Green, R.P.H. (1986), "Conubium in the *Aeneid*", in: C. Deroux (ed.), *Studies in Latin Literature and Roman History* IV, Bruxelles, 393–421.
Grishin, A.A. (2008), "*Ludus in undis:* An Acrostic in *Eclogue* 9", in: *HSPh* 104, 237–240.
Grishin, A.A. (2009), *Acrostics in Virgil's Poetry: The Problem of Authentication*, MA Thesis, Harvard University.
Günther, H.-C. (2013), "The First Collection of Odes: *Carmina* I–III", in: H.-C. Günther (ed.), *Brill's Companion to Horace*, Leiden, 211–406.
Gutzwiller, K. (1996) "The Evidence for Theocritean Poetry Books", in M.A. Harder / R.F. Regtuit, / G.C. Wakker (eds.), *Theocritus, Hellenistica Groningana 2*, Groningen, 119–148.
Gutzwiller, K.J. (1998), *Poetic Garlands: Hellenistic Epigrams in Context*, Berkeley / Los Angeles.
Halperin, D.M. (1983), *Before Pastoral: Theocritus and the Ancient Tradition of Bucolic Poetry*, New Haven.
Hammond, P. (2006), *The Making of Restoration Poetry*, Cambridge.
Harder, A. (ed.) (2012), *Callimachus, Aetia: Introduction, Text, Translation, and Commentary*, 2 vols., Oxford.
Hardie, P. (1993), *The Epic Successors of Virgil: A Study in the Dynamics of a Tradition*, Cambridge.
Hardie, P. (1998), *Virgil*, Oxford.
Hardie, P. (2012), *Rumour and Renown: Representations of 'Fama' in Western Literature*, Cambridge.
Harris, W.V. (1989), *Ancient Literacy*, Cambridge, MA.
Harrison, E.L. (1989), "The Tragedy of Dido", in: *EMC* 33, 1–21.
Harrison, S.J. (ed.) (1990), *Oxford Readings in Vergil's* Aeneid, Oxford.
Harrison, S.J. (ed.) (1991), *Vergil, Aeneid 10: With Introduction, Translation, and Commentary*, Oxford.
Harrison, S.J. (2002), "Ovid and Genre: Evolutions of an Elegist", in: P. Hardie (ed.), *The Cambridge Companion to Ovid*, Cambridge, 79–94.
Harrison, S.J. (2007), *Generic Enrichment in Vergil and Horace*, Oxford.

Harrison, S.J. (2013), "Author and Speaker(s) in Horace's *Satires* 2", in: A. Marmodoro / J. Hill (eds.), *The Author's Voice in Classical and Late Antiquity*, Oxford, 153–171.
Harrison, S.J. (2015), [Review of D. Seider (2013), *Memory in Vergil's Aeneid: Creating the Past*], in: *Mnemosyne* 68, 166–170.
Harrison, S.J. (2017) *Horace, Odes Book II*, Cambridge.
Harvey, A.E. (1955), "The Classification of Greek Lyric Poetry", in: *CQ* 5, 157–175.
Hawkins, S. (2014) "Catullus 60: Lesbia, Medea, Clodia, Scylla", in: *AJPh* 135, 559–567.
Headlam, W. / Knox, A.D. (eds.) (1922), *Herodas, The Mimes and Fragments*, Cambridge.
Helbig, W. (1868), *Wandgemälde der vom Vesuv verschütteten Städte Campaniens*, Leipzig.
Henkel, J.H. (2009), *Writing Poems on Trees: Genre and Metapoetics in Vergil's Eclogues and Georgics*, Dissertation, The University of North Carolina at Chapel Hill.
Henkel, J.H. (2014), "Vergil Talks Technique: Metapoetic Arboriculture in *Georgics* 2", in: *Vergilius* 60, 33–66.
Henry, J. (1878), *Aeneidea*, vol. 2, London.
Heylin, C. (2009), *Revolution in the Air: The Songs of Bob Dylan, 1957–1973*, Chicago.
Heyne, C.G. (ed.) (1832), *P. Virgilius Maro varietate lectionis et perpetua adnotatione illustratus a C.G. Heyne. Editio quarta curavit G. P. E. Wagner*, vol. 2, Leipzig / London.
Heyworth, S.J. (2007a), *Cynthia: A Companion to the Text of Propertius*, Oxford.
Heyworth, S.J. (ed.) (2007b), *Sexti Properti Elegi*, Oxford.
Hill, D.L. (ed.) (1980), *The Renaissance; Studies in Art and Poetry: The 1893 Text, Walter Pater*, Berkeley / Los Angeles.
Hilton, J. (2013), "The Hunt for Acrostics by Some Ancient Readers of Homer", in: *Hermes* 141, 88–95.
Hinds, S. E. (1983), "Carmina Digna. Gallus P. Qaşr Ibrîm 6–7 Metamorphosed", in: *Papers of the Liverpool Latin Seminar* 4, 43–54.
Hinds, S. E. (1987), *The Metamorphosis of Persephone: Ovid and the Self-Conscious Muse*, Cambridge.
Hinds, S. E. (1992), "*Arma* in Ovid's *Fasti* Part 1: Genre and Mannerism", in: *Arethusa* 25, 81–112.
Hinds, S. E. (2000), "Essential Epic: Genre and Gender from Macer to Statius", in: M. Depew / O. Obbink (eds.), *Matrices of Genre: Authors, Canons, and Society*, Cambridge, MA, 221–244.
Hollis, A.S. (ed.) (2007), *Fragments of Roman Poetry c. 60 BC–AD 20: Edited with an Introduction, Translation, and Commentary*, Oxford.
Horsfall, N. (1986), "The Aeneas legend and the *Aeneid*" in: *Vergilius* 32, 8–17.
Horsfall, N. (1991), *Virgilio: l'epopea in alambicco*, Naples.
Horsfall, N. (ed.) (1995), *A Companion to the Study of Virgil*, Leiden.
Horsfall, N. (ed.) (2006), *Virgil, Aeneid 3: A Commentary*, Leiden.
Horsfall, N. (ed.) (2013), *Virgil, Aeneid 6: A Commentary*, Berlin.
Horsfall, N. (2016), *The Epic Distilled: Studies in the Composition of the* Aeneid, Oxford.
Höschele, R. (2016), "Unplumbed Depths of Fatuity?" Philip of Thessaloniki's Art of Variation", in: R. Sistakou / A. Rengakos (eds.), *Dialect, Diction, and Style In Greek Literary and Inscribed Epigram*, Berlin, 105–118.
Hunter, R.L. (1996), *Theocritus and the Archaeology of Greek Poetry*, Cambridge.
Hunter, R.L. (ed.) (1999), *Theocritus: A Selection*, Cambridge.

Huskey, S.J. (2005), "In Memory of Tibullus: Ovid's Remembrance of Tibullus 1.3 in *Amores* 3.9 and *Tristia* 3.3", in: *Arethusa* 38, 367–386.
Hutchinson, G. O. (2008) *Talking Books: Readings in Hellenistic and Roman Books of Poetry*, Oxford.
Huyck, J. (1987), "Vergil's Phaethontiades", in: *HSPh* 91, 217–228.
Jacques, J.-M. (1960), "Sur un acrostiche d'Aratos (*Phén.* 783–787)", in: *REA* 62, 48–61.
James, S.L. (2003), *Learned Girls and Male Persuasion: Gender and Reading in Roman Love Elegy*, Berkeley / Los Angeles.
Janko, R. (ed.) (1994), *The Iliad: A Commentary: Volume 4, Books 13–16*, Cambridge.
Janko, R. (ed.) (2011), *Philodemus, On Poems, Books 3–4: With the Fragments of Aristotle, On Poets*, Oxford.
Jocelyn, H.D. (1980), "Horace, *Odes* 2.5", in: *LCM* 5, 197–200.
Kania, R. (2016), *Virgil's Eclogues and the Art of Fiction: A Study of the Poetic Imagination*, Cambridge.
Kannicht, R. (1969), *Euripides, Helena*, 2 vols., Heidelberg.
Katz, J.T. (2000), "Egnatius' Dental Fricatives (Catullus 39.20)", in: *Classical Philology* 95, 338–348.
Katz, J.T. (2016) "Another Vergilian Signature in the *Georgics*?", in: P. Mitsis / I. Ziogas (eds.), *Wordplay and Powerplay in Latin Poetry*, Berlin, 69–86.
Kayachev, B. (2016a), *Allusion and Allegory: Studies in the Ciris*, Berlin.
Kayachev, B. (2016b), "Catullus 64.291: A Textual Note", in: *CQ* 66, 790–794.
Keegan, P. (2014), *Graffiti in Antiquity*, London.
Keith, A.M. (1992), "*Amores* 1.1: Propertius and the Ovidian Programme", in: C. Deroux (ed.) *Studies in Latin Literature and Roman History VI*, Brussels, 327–344.
Keith, A.M. (2000), *Engendering Rome: Women in Latin Epic*, Cambridge.
Keith, A.M. (2008), *Propertius: Poet of Love and Leisure*, London.
Keith, A.M. (ed.) (2011), *Latin Elegy and Hellenistic Epigram: A Tale of Two Genres at Rome*, Newcastle upon Tyne.
Kennedy, D.F. (1983), "Shades of Meaning: Virgil, *Eclogue* 10.75–77", in: *LCM* 8, 124.
Kennedy, D.F. (1993), *The Arts of Love: Five Studies in the Discourse of Roman Love Elegy*, Cambridge.
Kenney, E.J. (1958), "Nequitiae Poeta", in: N.I. Herescu (ed.), *Ovidiana: Recherches sur Ovide, publiées à l'occasion du bimillénaire de la naissance du poète*, Paris, 201–209.
Kenney, E.J. (ed.) (1961), *P. Ovidi Nasonis, Amores, Medicamina faciei femineae, Ars amatoria, Remedia amoris*, 2nd ed. 1994, Oxford.
Kenney, E.J. (1962), "The Manuscript Tradition of Ovid's *Amores*, *Ars Amatoria*, and *Remedia Amoris*", in: *CQ* 12, 1–31.
Kenney, E.J. (1983), "Virgil and the Elegiac Sensibility", in: *ICS* 8, 44–59.
Kiessling, A. / Heinze, R. (eds.) (1930), *Q. Horatius Flaccus: Oden und Epoden*, Berlin.
Kirstein, R. (2002), "Companion Pieces in the Hellenistic Epigram", in: R.F. Retguit / G.C. Wakker (eds.), *Hellenistic Epigrams*, Groningen, 117–121.
Knox, P.E. (1984), "Sappho, fr. 31 LP and Catullus 51: A Suggestion", in: *QUCC* 46, 97–102.
Knox, P.E. (1986), *Ovid's Metamorphoses and the Traditions of Augustan Poetry*, Cambridge.
Knox, P.E. (ed.) (1995), *Ovid's Heroides: Select Epistles*, Cambridge.
Knox, P.E. (2014), "Ovidian Myths on Pompeian Walls", in: C. Newlands / J. Miller, (eds.), *A Handbook to the Reception of Ovid*, Chichester, 36–54.

Knox, P.E. (2015), "Virgil's Catullan One-Liner", in H.-C. Günther (ed.), *Virgilian Studies: A Miscellany Dedicated to the Memory of Mario Geymonat*, Studia Classica et Mediaevalia, Nordhausen, 287–320.

Koch, J.T. (2006), *Celtic Culture: A Historical Encyclopedia*, 5 vols., Santa Barbara, CA.

Köhnken, A. (1981), "Apollo's Retort to Envy's Criticism: (Two Questions of Relevance in Callimachus, Hymn 2, 105FF.)", in: *AJPh* 102, 411–422.

Korenjak, M. (2009), "ΛΕΥΚΗ: was bedeutet das erste 'Akrostichon'?", in: *RhM* 152, 392–396.

Krevans, N. (1993), "Ilia's Dream: Ennius, Virgil and the Mythology of Seduction" in: *HSPh* 95, 257–271.

Kronenberg, L. (2009), *Allegories of Farming from Greece and Rome: Philosophical Satire in Xenophon, Varro, and Virgil*, Cambridge.

Krostenko, B.A. (2001), *Cicero, Catullus, and the Language of Social Performance*, Chicago.

Kyriakou, P. (1996), "A Variation of the Pindaric Breakoff Formula in *Nemean* 4", in: *AJPh* 117, 17–35.

La Penna, A. / Grassi, C. (eds.) (1971), *Virgilio, Le opere: Antologia*, Florence.

Leach, E.W. (1964), "Georgic Imagery in the *Ars amatoria*", in *TAPhA* 95, 142–154.

Leach, E.W. (1978), "Vergil, Horace, Tibullus: Three Collections of Ten", in: *Ramus* 7, 79–105.

Lee-Stecum, P. (1998), *Powerplay in Tibullus: Reading Elegies Book 1*, Cambridge.

Lee-Stecum, P. (2013), "Tibullus in First Place", in T.S. Thorsen (ed.), *The Cambridge Companion to Latin Love Elegy*, Cambridge, 68–82.

Leishman, J.B. (1966), *The Art of Marvell's Poetry*, London.

Leumann, M. / Hofmann, J.B. / Szantyr, A. (1965), *Lateinische Syntax und Stilistik*, Munich.

Levitan, W. (1979), "Plexed Artistry: Aratean Acrostics", in: *Glyph* 5, 55–68.

Lindo, L.I. (1971), "Tyrtaeus and Horace, *Odes* 3.2", in: *CPh* 66, 258–260.

Lissberger, E. (1934), *Das Fortleben der Römischen Elegiker in den Carmina Epigraphica*, Tübingen.

Lombardo, S. (trans.) (2005), *Virgil, Aeneid*, Indianapolis / Cambridge.

Lowrie, M. (1994), "Lyric's *Elegos* and the Aristotelian Mean: Horace, *C.* 1.24, 1.33, and 2.9", in: *CW* 87, 377–394.

Ludwig, W. (1957), "Zu Horaz, *C.* 2,1–12" in: *Hermes* 85, 336–345.

Lyne, R.O.A.M. (1978), *Ciris: A Poem Attributed to Vergil*, Cambridge.

MacKinnon, J.K. (1971), "Heracles' Intention in His Second Request of Hyllus: *Trach.* 1216–51", in: *CQ* 21, 33–41.

Maiuri, A. (1964), *Pompei ed Ercolano fra case e abitanti*, Milan.

Mallory, J. P. / Adams, D. Q. (1997), *Encyclopedia of Indo-European Culture*, London.

Maltby, R. (1991), *A Lexicon of Ancient Latin Etymologies*, Leeds.

Maltby, R. (1993), "The Limits of Etymologising", in: *Aevum(ant)* 6, 257–275.

Maltby, R. (ed.) (2002), *Tibullus, Elegies: Text, Introduction and Commentary*, Cambridge.

Mandelbaum, A. (trans.) (1971), *The* Aeneid *of Virgil*, New York.

Mankin, D. (ed.) (1995), *Horace, Epodes*, Cambridge.

Martindale, C. (2013), "Reception—A New Humanism? Receptivity, Pedagogy, the Transhistorical", in: *Classical Receptions Journal* 5, 169–183.

Mayer, R. (2012), *Horace, Odes Book I*, Cambridge.

McCallum, S.L. (2015) "*Heu Ligurine:* Echoes of Vergil in Horace *Odes* 4.1", in: *Vergilius* 61, 29–42.

McCartney, E. S. (1927), "Modifiers That Reflect the Etymology of the Word Modified, with Special Reference to Lucretius", in: *CPh* 22, 184–200.
McKeown, J. C. (1987), *Ovid, Amores: Text, Prolegomena and Commentary in Four Volumes, Vol. 1: Text and Prolegomena*, Liverpool.
McNelis C. / Sens A. (2016), *The* Alexandra *of Lycophron*, Oxford.
Meyer, E.A. (2009), "Writing Paraphernalia, Tablets, and Muses in Campanian Wall Painting", in: *AJA* 113, 569–597.
Michalopoulos, A. (2001), *Ancient Etymologies in Ovid's Metamorphoses: A Commented Lexicon*, Leeds.
Milnor, K. (2014), *Graffiti and the Literary Landscape in Roman Pompeii*, Oxford.
Mitsis, P. (2010), "Achilles Polytropos and Odysseus as Suitor: *Iliad* 9.307–429", in: P. Mitsis / C. Tsagalis (eds.), *Allusion, Authority, and Truth: Critical Perspectives on Greek Poetic and Rhetorical Praxis*, Berlin, 51–76.
Moles, J.L. (1984), "Aristotle and Dido's *hamartia*", *G&R* 31, 45–55.
Moles, J.L. (1987), "The tragedy and guilt of Dido", in: M. Whitby / P. Hardie / M. Whitby (eds.), *Homo Viator: Classical Essays for John Bramble*, Bristol, 153–161.
Monti, R. (1981), *The Dido Episode and the* Aeneid: *Roman Social and Political Values in the Epic*, Leiden.
Morgan, L. (2011), *Musa Pedestris: Metre and Meaning in Roman Verse*, Oxford.
Most, G.W. (2003), "Epinician Envies", in: D. Konstan / K. Rutter (eds.), *Envy, Spite and Jealousy: The Rivalrous Emotions in Ancient Greece*, Edinburgh, 123–142.
Most, G.W. (2013), "Horace", in: A. Grafton / G.W. Most / S. Settis (eds.), *The Classical Tradition*, Cambridge, MA, 454–460.
Mouritsen, H. (2011), *The Freedman in the Roman World*, Cambridge.
Munari, F. (ed.) (1951), *P. Ovidi Nasonis Amores, Testo, Introduzione, Traduzione e Note*, Florence.
Murgatroyd, P. (1980), "Horace's Xanthias and Phyllis", in: *CQ* 30, 540.
Myers, M.Y. (2013), "Vergil's Underworld and the Afterlife of Love Poets", paper delivered at the *Symposium Cumanum*, "Aeneid Six and Its Cultural Reception", Villa Vergiliana, Cumae and the University of Naples Federico II, Italy, 6/25/2013.
Mynors, R.A.B. (ed.) (1958), *C. Valerii Catulli Carmina*, Oxford.
Mynors, R.A.B. (ed.) (1969), *P. Vergili Maronis Opera*, Oxford.
Nadel, I.B., (ed.) (2005), *Ezra Pound, Early Writings: Poems and Prose*, New York.
Nagel, A. / Wood, C.S. (2010), *Anachronic Renaissance*, New York / Cambridge, MA.
Nagle, B.R. (1980), The Poetics of Exile: Program and Polemic in the *Tristia* and *Epistulae ex Ponto of Ovid*, Bruxelles.
Nappa, C. (2005), *Reading after Actium: Vergil's* Georgics, *Octavian, and Rome*, Ann Arbor, MI.
Nappa, C. (2007), "Catullus and Vergil", in: M.B. Skinner (ed.), *Blackwell's Companion to Catullus*, Malden, MA / Oxford, 377–398.
Nelis, D. (2001), *Vergil's* Aeneid *and the* Argonautica *of Apollonius Rhodius*, Leeds.
Neri, C. (2003), *Erinna: Testimonianze e Frammenti*, Bologna.
Newton, J.M. (1972), "What Do We Know About Andrew Marvell?", in: *The Cambridge Quarterly* 6, 33–42, 125–143.
Nilsson, N.O. (1952), *Metrische Stildifferenzen in den Satiren des Horaz*, Uppsala.
Nisbet, R.G.M. / Hubbard, M. (eds.) (1970), *A Commentary on Horace:* Odes, *Book I*, Oxford.

Nisbet, R.G.M. / Hubbard, M. (eds.) (1978), *A Commentary on Horace:* Odes, *Book II*, Oxford.

Nisbet, R.G.M. / Rudd, N. (eds.) (2004), *A Commentary on Horace:* Odes, *Book III*, Oxford.

Norbrook, D. (1999), *Writing the English Republic: Poetry, Rhetoric and Politics 1627–1660*, Cambridge.

Norden, E. (ed.) (1981), *P. Vergilius Maro, Aeneis Buch VI*, 7th ed., Stuttgart.

Notopoulos, J.A. (1939), "The Name of Plato", in: *CPh* 34, 135–145.

Notopoulos, J.A. (1942), "Plato's Epitaph", in: *AJPh* 63, 272–293.

Nünlist, R. (1998), *Poetologische Bildersprache in der frühgriechischen Dichtung*, Stuttgart / Leipzig.

O'Brien, Tim (1973), *If I Die in a Combat Zone, Box Me Up and Ship Me Home*, New York.

O'Hara, J.J. (1990), *Death and the Optimistic Prophecy in Vergil's* Aeneid, Princeton.

O'Hara, J.J. (1993), "Medicine for the Madness of Dido and Gallus: Tentative Suggestions on *Aeneid* 4", in: *Vergilius* 39, 12–24.

O'Hara, J.J. (1996a) *True Names: Vergil and the Alexandrian Tradition of Etymological Wordplay*, Ann Arbor. Expanded edition, 2017.

O'Hara, J.J. (1996b), "Vergil's Best Reader? Ovidian Commentary on Vergilian Etymological Wordplay", in: *CJ* 91, 255–276 (= Knox, P.E. (ed.) *Oxford Readings in Ovid*, Oxford 2007, 100–122).

O'Hara, J.J. (ed.) (2011), *Vergil, Aeneid Book 4*, Newburyport, MA.

Oliensis, E. (1998), *Horace and the Rhetoric of Authority*, Cambridge.

Page, D.L. (ed.) (1941), *Select Papyri, Volume III: Poetry*, Cambridge MA.

Page, D.L. (ed.) (1955), *Sappho and Alcaeus: An Introduction to the Study of Lesbian Poetry*, Oxford.

Page, D.L. (ed.) (1981), *Further Greek Epigrams*, Cambridge.

Page, T.E. (ed.) (1894), *The* Aeneid *of Virgil: Books I-VI*, London.

Page, T.E. (ed.) (1920), *Q. Horatii Flacci Carminum, Liber II*, London.

Palaima, T.G. (2000), "Courage and Prowess Afoot in Homer and the Vietnam of Tim O'Brien", in: *Classical and Modern Literature* 20, 1–22.

Palaima, T. / Tritle, L. (2013), "The Legacy of War in the Classical World", in: B. Campbell / L. Tritle (eds.), *The Oxford Handbook of Warfare in the Classical World*, Oxford, 726–742.

Palmer, A. (1883), *The Satires of Horace*. London / New York.

Paratore, E. (ed.) (1947), *Virgilio, Eneide, libro quarto*, Roma.

Paschalis, M. (1997), *Virgil's* Aeneid: *Semantic Relations and Proper Names*, Oxford.

Pasquali, G. (1920), *Orazio lirico*, Florence.

Pease, A.S. (ed.) (1935), *P. Vergili Maronis Aeneidos Liber Quartus*, Cambridge, MA.

Pelliccia, H. (2011), "Unlocking *Aeneid* 6.460: Plautus' *Amphitryon*, Euripides' *Protesilaus* and the Referents of Callimachus' *Coma*", in: *CJ* 106, 149–219.

Pelliccia, H. (2017) "What Counts as a Wife?", in: K.M. Coleman (ed.), *Albert's Anthology*, Cambridge, MA, 151–154.

Perkell, C. (1997), "The Lament of Juturna: Pathos and Interpretation in the Aeneid", *TAPhA* 127, 257–286.

Perret, J. (ed.) (1977), *Virgile, Énéide, livres I–IV*, Paris.

Pichon, R. (1966), *Index verborum amatorium*, Hildesheim (= Paris, 1902).

Pierce, K.F. (1997), "The Portrayal of Rape in New Comedy", in: S. Deacy / K.F. Pierce (eds.), *Rape in Antiquity: Sexual Violence in the Greek and Roman Worlds*, London, 163–184.

Platnauer, M. (1951), *Latin Elegiac Verse: A Study of the Metrical Usages of Tibullus, Propertius and Ovid*, Cambridge.
Porter, J.I. (2017), "Reception, Receptivity, and Anachronism in Marius the Epicurean" in: C. Martindale / S. Evangelista / E. Prettejohn (eds.), *Pater the Classicist: Classical Scholarship, Reception, and Aestheticism*, Oxford, 149–162.
Potter, R. (2012), *Modernist Literature*, Edinburgh.
Pound, E. (1920), *Hugh Selwyn Mauberley*, London.
Pound, E. (1926), *Personae: Collected Shorter Poems*, New York.
Prettejohn, E. (2017), *Modern Painters, Old Masters: The Art of Imitation from the Pre-Raphaelites to the First World War*, New Haven / London.
Putnam, M.C.J. (1986), *Artifices of Eternity: Horace's Fourth Book of Odes*, Ithaca, NY.
Putnam, M.C.J. (2005), "Virgil and Tibullus 1.1", in: *CPh* 100, 123–141.
Quinn, K. (1963), *Latin Explorations: Critical Studies in Roman Literature*, London.
Ramírez de Verger, A. (ed.) (2003), *P. Ovidius Naso, Carmina Amatoria*, Munich.
Ramsay, W. (1859), *A Manual of Latin Prosody*, Oxford.
Rancière, J. (1996), "Le Concept d'anachronisme et la vérité de l'historien", *L'Inactuel: Psychanalyse et Culture* 6, 53–68.
Reckford, K.J. (1999), "Only a Wet Dream? Hope and Skepticism in Horace, Satire 1.5", *AJPh* 120, 525–554.
Reed, J.D. (1997), "Ovid's Elegy on Tibullus and Its Models", in: *CPh* 92, 260–269.
Richmond, J.A. (ed.) (1962), *The Halieutica Ascribed to Ovid*, London.
Ricks, C. (2003), *Dylan's Visions of Sin*, New York.
Rogovoy, S. (2009), *Bob Dylan: Prophet, Mystic, Poet*, New York.
Ross, D.O. (1975), *Backgrounds to Augustan Poetry: Gallus, Elegy and Rome*, Cambridge.
Rudd, N. (1976), "Dido's culpa", in: N. Rudd, *Lines of Enquiry: Studies in Latin Poetry*, Cambridge, 32–53 (= Harrison, S.J. (ed.) *Oxford Readings in the Roman Novel*, Oxford 1999, 145–166).
Rudd, N. (1980), "Achilles or Agamemnon? A Note on Horace *Epistles* 1.2.13", in: *CPh* 75, 68 f.
Rudd, N. (1989), *Horace, Epistles Book II and Epistle to the Pisones ('Ars Poetica')*, Cambridge.
Rüpke, J. (2012), *Religion in Republican Rome: Rationalization and Ritual Change*, Philadelphia.
Rutherford, I. (1997), "Odes and Ends: Closure in Greek Lyric Poetry", in: D.H. Roberts / F.M. Dunn / D.P. Fowler (eds.), *Classical Closure: Reading the End in Greek and Latin Literature*, Princeton, 43–61.
Sassoon, S. (1920), *Poems by Wilfred Owen with an Introduction by Siegfried Sassoon*, London.
Saylor, C. (1986), "Some Stock Characteristics of the Roman Lover in Vergil, *Aeneid* IV", in: *Vergilius* 32, 73–77.
Scarcia, R. (trans.) (2002), *Virgilio, Eneide*, Milan.
Schlegel, C. (2010), "Horace and the Satirist's Mask: Shadowboxing with Lucilius", in: G. Davis (ed.), *A Companion to Horace*, Malden, MA / Oxford, 253–270.
Schmid, W. (1974), *Catullus: Ansichten und Durchblicke*, Göppingen.
Scodel, R. (2003), "Two Epigrammatic Pairs: Callimachus' Epitaphs, Plato's Apples", in: *Hermes* 131, 257–268.
Seider, A. (2013), *Memory in Vergil's Aeneid: Creating the Past*, Cambridge.

Sens, A. (ed.) (1997), *Theocritus, Dioscuri (Idyll 22)*, Göttingen.
Sens, A. (2003), "Asclepiades, Erinna, and the Poetics of Labor", in: P. Thibodeau / H. Haskell (eds.), *Being There Together*, Afton, MN, 78 – 87.
Sens, A. (2005), "The Art of Poetry and the Poetry of Art: The Unity and Poetics of Posidippus' Statue-Poems", in: K.J. Gutzwiller (ed.), *The New Posidippus: A Hellenistic Poetry Book*, Oxford, 206 – 225.
Sens, A. (ed.) (2011), *Asclepiades of Samos, Epigrams and Fragments*, Oxford.
Shackleton Bailey, D.R. (ed.) (1985), *Horatius, Opera*, Stuttgart.
Sharland, S. (2009), "Soporific Satire: Horace, Damasippus and Professor Snore (Stertinius) in *Satire* 2.3", in: *ACD* 113 – 131.
Shorey, P. (ed.) (1900), *Horace, Odes and Epodes*, Boston.
Sider, D. (ed.) (1997), *The Epigrams of Philodemos*, New York.
Simeone, W. (1952), "A Probable Antecedent of Marvell's Horatian Ode", in: *Notes and Queries* 197, 316 – 318.
Skinner, M. B. (2003) *Catullus in Verona: A Reading of the Elegiac Libellus, Poems 65 – 116*, Columbus, OH.
Skutsch, O. (1956), "Zu Vergils Eklogen", in: *RhM* 99, 193 – 201.
Skutsch, O. (1985), *The* Annals *of Q. Ennius*, Oxford.
Smith, K.F. (ed.) (1913), *The Elegies of Albius Tibullus*, New York.
Smith, N. (ed.) (2003), *The Poems of Andrew Marvell*, London.
Smith, P. (1981), "Aineiadai as Patrons of *Iliad* XX and the *Homeric Hymn to Aphrodite*", *HSPh* 85, 17 – 58.
Solin, H. (1975), "Die Wandinschriften im sogenannten Haus des M. Fabius Rufus", in: B. Andreae / H. Kyrieleis (eds.), *Neue Forschungen in Pompeji*, Recklinghausen, 243 – 272.
Solodow, J.B. (1986), "*Raucae, tua cura, palumbes:* Study of a Poetic Word Order", in *HSPh* 90, 129 – 153.
Somerville, T. (2010), "Note on a Reversed Acrostic in Vergil *Georgics* 1.429 – 1.433", in: *CPh* 105, 202 – 209.
Spal, A. (2016), *Poesie, Erotik, Witz: Humorvoll-spöttische Versinschriften zu Liebe und Körperlichkeit in Pomeji und Umgebung*, Berlin.
Stroh, W. (1971), *Die römische Liebeselegie als werbende Dichtung*, Amsterdam.
Sutherland, E.H. (1997), "Vision and desire in Horace, *C.* 2.5", in: *Helios* 24, 23 – 43.
Sutherland, E.H. (2002), *Horace's Well-Trained Reader: Toward a Methodology of Audience Participation in the* Odes, Frankfurt am Main.
Syfret, R.H. (1961), "Marvell's 'Horatian Ode'", *The Review of English Studies* 12, 160 – 172.
Syndikus, H.P. (2001), *Die Lyrik des Horaz: eine Interpretation der Oden, Band I: erstes und zweites Buch*, Darmstadt.
Szemerényi, O. (1964), *Syncope in Greek and Indo-European and the Nature of Indo-European Accent*, Naples.
Tarán, L. (1984), "Plato's Alleged Epitaph", in: *GRBS* 25, 63 – 82.
Tarrant, R.J. (2016), *Texts, Editors, and Readers: Methods and Problems in Latin Textual Criticism*, Cambridge.
Terkel, S. (2005), *And They All Sang: Adventures of an Eclectic Disc Jockey*, New York / London.
Thomas, R.E. (1983), "Pound and Horace's *Ode* 3.30", in: *Helix* 13 – 14, 57 – 59.

Thomas, R.F. (1979), "On a Homeric Reference in Catullus", in: *AJPh* 100, 475 f.
Thomas, R.F. (1981), "Cinna, Calvus, and the Ciris", in: *CQ* 31, 371–374 (= Thomas, R.F., "Intertextuality Observed", *Reading Virgil and His Texts: Studies in Intertextuality*, Ann Arbor 1999, 300–303).
Thomas, R.F. (1982), "Catullus and the Polemics of Poetic Reference (Poem 64.1–18)", in: *AJPh* 103, 144–164 (= Thomas, R.F., "Preparing the Way: Catullan Intertextuality", in: *Reading Virgil and His Texts: Studies in Intertextuality*, Ann Arbor 1999, 12–32).
Thomas, R.F. (1983), "Virgil's Ecphrastic Centerpieces", in: *HSPh* 87, 175–184 (= Thomas, R.F., "Intertextuality Observed", in: *Reading Virgil and His Texts: Studies in Intertextuality*, Ann Arbor 1999, 310–320).
Thomas, R.F. (1986), "Virgil's Georgics and the Art of Reference", in: *HSPh* 90, 171–198 (= Thomas, R.F., *Reading Virgil and His Texts: Studies in Intertextuality*, Ann Arbor 1999, 114–141).
Thomas, R.F. (ed.) (1988), *Virgil, Georgics*, 2 vols., Cambridge.
Thomas, R.F. (1992), "The Old Man Revisited: Memory, Reference, and Genre in Virg., *Geo.* 4.116–148", in: *MD* 29, 35–70 (=Thomas, R.F., *Reading Virgil and His Texts: Studies in Intertextuality*, Ann Arbor 1999, 173–205).
Thomas, R.F. (1995), "*Vestigia ruris:* Urbane Rusticity in Virgil's *Georgics*", in *HSPh* 97, 197–214 (= Thomas, R.F., *Reading Virgil and His Texts: Studies in Intertextuality*, Ann Arbor 1999, 229–245).
Thomas, R.F. (1998). "Voice, Poetics, and Virgil's Sixth Eclogue", in J. Jasanoff / H. Melchert / L. Oliver (eds.), *Mír Curad: Studies in Honor of Calvert Watkins*, Innsbruck, 669–676 (= Thomas, R.F., *Reading Virgil and His Texts: Studies in Intertextuality*, Ann Arbor 1999, 288–296).
Thomas, R.F. (1999), *Reading Virgil and His Texts: Studies in Intertextuality*, Ann Arbor.
Thomas, R.F. (2001), *Virgil and the Augustan Reception*, Cambridge.
Thomas, R.F. (ed.) (2011), *Horace, Odes Book IV; and Carmen Saeculare*, Cambridge.
Thomas, R.F. (2017), *Why Bob Dylan Matters*, New York.
Thomson, D.F.S. (ed.) (1997), *Catullus*, Toronto.
Tomlinson, C. (1993), "Some Aspects of Horace in the Twentieth Century", in: C. Martindale / D. Hopkins (eds.), *Horace Made New: Horatian Influences on British Writing from the Renaissance to the Twentieth Century*, Cambridge, 240–257.
Trager, O. (2004), *Keys to the Rain: The Definitive Bob Dylan Encyclopedia*, New York.
Tränkle, H. (1960), *Die Sprachkunst des Properz und die Tradition der Lateinische Dichtersprach*, Wiesbaden.
Treggiari, S. (1981), "Concubinae", in: *PBSR* 49, 59–81.
Treggiari, S. (1985), "*Iam proterva fronte:* Matrimonial Advances by Roman Women", in: J.W. Eadie / J. Ober (eds.), *The Craft of the Ancient Historian: Essays in Honor of Chester Starr*, Lanham, MD, 343–352.
Trumbo, D. (1939), *Johnny Got His Gun*, Philadelphia.
Trumbo, D. (1959a), *Johnny Got His Gun*, New York.
Trumbo, D. (1959b), *Johnny Got His Gun*, New York.
Vandiver, E. (2010), *Stand in the Trench, Achilles: Classical Receptions in British Poetry of the Great War*, Oxford / New York.
Vandiver, E. (forthcoming), "Classics, Empire, and War", in: K. Haynes (ed.), *Oxford History of Classical Receptions in English Literature vol. 5: 1880-*, Oxford.

Varone, A. (2002), *Erotica Pompeiana: Love Inscriptions on the Walls of Pompeii*, Rome.
Vaughn, J.W. (1981), "Theocritus Vergilianus and Liber Bucolicon", in: *Aevum* 55, 47–68.
Vlassopoulos, K. (2010), "Athenian slave names and Athenian social history", in: *ZPE* 175, 113–144.
Voigt, E.-M. (ed.) (1971), *Sappho et Alcaeus*, Amsterdam.
Wachter, R. (1998), "'Oral Poetry' in ungewohntem Kontext: Hinweise auf mündliche Dichtungstechnik in den Pompejanischen Wandinschriften", in: *ZPE* 121, 73–89.
Walde, A. / Hofmann, J.B. (1938), *Lateinisches Etymologisches Wörterbuch*, Heidelberg.
Watson, L.C. (ed.) (2003), *A Commentary on Horace's* Epodes, Oxford.
Webb, R.H. (2009), *Ekphrasis, Imagination and Persuasion in Ancient Rhetorical Theory and Practice*, Aldershot.
West, D. (trans.) (1991), *Virgil, The Aeneid*, London.
West, D. (1998), *Horace, Odes II: Vatis Amici*, Oxford.
West, M.L. (1974), *Studies in Greek Elegy and Iambus*, Berlin.
Wheeler, A.L. (1911), "Erotic Teaching in Roman Elegy and the Greek Sources. Part II", in: *CPh* 6, 56–77.
White, S.A. (1994), "Callimachus on Plato and Cleombrotus", in: *TAPA* 124, 135–161.
Whitman, C. H. (1958), *Homer and the Heroic Tradition*, Cambridge, MA.
Wilentz, S. (2010), *Bob Dylan in America*, New York.
Wilhelm, J.J. (1990), *Ezra Pound in London and Paris 1908 • 1925*, University Park / London.
Williams, G. (1968), *Tradition and Originality in Roman Poetry*, Oxford.
Williams, G. (1995), "*Libertino patre natus:* True or False?", in: S.J. Harrison (ed.), *Homage to Horace: A Bimillenary Celebration*, Oxford, 296–313.
Williams, R.D. (ed.) (1972), *The* Aeneid *of Virgil*, London.
Wills, J. (1997), [Review of J.J. O'Hara (1996), *True Names: Vergil and the Alexandrian Tradition of Etymological Wordplay*], in: *BMCRev* 97.12.17.
Wilson, A.J.N. (1969), "Andrew Marvell: *An Horatian Ode upon Cromwell's Return from Ireland:* The Thread of the Poem and its Use of Classical Allusion", *Critical Quarterly* 11, 325–341.
Wiseman, T.P. (1969), *Catullan Questions*, Leicester.
Wiseman, T.P. (1979), *Clio's Cosmetics: Three Studies in Greco-Roman Literature*, Leicester.
Wolfe, D.M. (ed.) (1953–1982), *The Complete Prose Works of John Milton*, 8 vols., New Haven, CT.
Worden, B. (1987), "Andrew Marvell, Oliver Cromwell, and the Horatian Ode", in: K. Sharpe / S.N. Zwicker (eds.), *Politics of Discourse: The Literature and History of Seventeenth-Century England*, Berkeley / Los Angeles, 147–180.
Wordsworth, C. (1837), *Inscriptiones Pompeianae, or Specimens and Facsimiles of Ancient Inscriptions Discovered on the Walls of Buildings at Pomepeii*, London.
Zetzel, J.E.G. (1980), "Horace's *Liber Sermonum:* The Structure of Ambiguity", in: *Arethusa* 13, 59–77.

Notes on Contributors

Barbara Weiden Boyd is Henry Winkley Professor of Latin and Greek at Bowdoin College (Brunswick, Maine). She is the author or editor of several books on Ovid, most recently *Ovid's Homer: Authority, Repetition, and Reception* (Oxford University Press, 2017), as well as of numerous articles on Virgil, Ovid, and Augustan poetry. Her career as a scholar of Augustan poetry began, like Richard's, at the University of Michigan, where she learned that the keenness of his philological mind could be matched only by his warm friendship and camaraderie. She is grateful to be able to call him a friend.

Brian W. Breed is Associate Professor and Chair of the Department of Classics at the University of Massachusetts Amherst. He has recently been a co-editor of *Lucilius and Satire in Second-Century BC Rome* (Cambridge 2018). His current work is focused on Roman poetry in the years of the second triumvirate.

Sergio Casali teaches Latin language and literature at the University of Rome "Tor Vergata". He has published a commentary on Ovid, *Heroides* 9 (Florence, 1995), one on *Aeneid* 2 (Pisa, 2017), and various articles on Roman poetry. He is now working on a commentary on *Aeneid* 4 for Cambridge University Press.

Julia Dyson Hejduk is the Reverend Jacob Beverly Stiteler Professor of Classics at Baylor University. She has published books and articles on Virgil, Ovid, and other Latin authors, most recently the edited volume *Happy Golden Anniversary, Harvard School!* (*Classical World* 101.1 [2017]). She is currently working to bring acrostic conversations in Latin poetry into the light.

Peter E. Knox was Richard's first student at Harvard and is now the Eric and Jane Nord Family Professor and Director of the Baker-Nord Center for the Humanities at Case Western Reserve University. His teaching and scholarship focus primarily on Hellenistic poetry and Roman poetry of the late Republic and Early Empire, especially Ovid.

Leah Kronenberg was fortunate enough to have Richard Thomas as an advisor for both her undergraduate thesis and graduate dissertation. She is the author of *Allegories of Farming from Greece and Rome: Philosophical Satire in Xenophon, Varro and Virgil* (Cambridge, 2009) and various articles on Republican and Augustan literature. She is currently Associate Professor of Classical Studies at Boston University.

Charles Martindale is emeritus Professor of Latin at the University of Bristol. He is especially interested in Latin poetry, aesthetics, reception, and English/Classics literary relations. He co-edited *Classics and the Uses of Reception* with Richard Thomas (2006); is general editor, with David Hopkins, of the 5-volume *Oxford History of Classical Reception in English Literature*; has co-edited *Pater the Classicist* (2017), with Stefano Evangelista and Elizabeth Prettejohn, and is currently revising his *Cambridge Companion to Virgil*, with Fiachra Mac Góráin.

Charles McNelis is a Professor of Classics at Georgetown University. His research primarily concerns Latin poetry, Hellenistic poetry, and the interplay between them. Though never a

https://doi.org/10.1515/9783110545708-016

student of Richard Thomas, he has been deeply influenced by him both directly and through his students, including two of the editors of this volume. He counts himself fortunate to be part of that educational genealogy, and to be Richard's friend.

James J. O'Hara is the author of *Death and the Optimistic Prophecy in Vergil's Aeneid* (Princeton 1990), *True Names: Vergil and the Alexandrian Tradition of Etymological Wordplay* (Ann Arbor 1996, expanded edition 2017), *Inconsistency in Roman Epic: Studies in Catullus, Lucretius, Vergil, Ovid and Lucan* (Cambridge 2007), *Vergil: Aeneid Book 4* (Focus/Hackett 2011) and *Vergil: Aeneid Book 8* (Focus/Hackett 2018). He was educated at the College of the Holy Cross and the University of Michigan, and is the George L. Paddison Professor of Latin at the University of North Carolina, Chapel Hill.

Tom Palaima is Robert M. Armstrong Professor of Classics at the University of Texas at Austin. A MacArthur fellow for his work with all aspects of writing systems of the Bronze Age Aegean, he teaches honors and graduate seminars on the human response, individual and collective, to experiences of war and violence. These include Songs as Social Commentary and Bob Dylan: History and Imagination.

Hayden Pelliccia was an assistant professor at Harvard from 1985–9 and has taught at Cornell ever since then.

David O. Ross taught at Yale and the University of Michigan, retiring in 2000, and has been since then teaching at Groton School, in happy seclusion.

Alexander Sens is Markos and Eleni Tsakopoulos Kounalakis Chair of Hellenic Studies at Georgetown University. His interest in Greek poetry of the late Classical and early Hellenistic periods developed out of his time as Richard's student. He is currently working on a commentary on select Hellenistic epigrams and on a Loeb edition of Nicander, Lycophron, and Aratus.

Index of Passages Discussed

Alcaeus
fr. 42 85 f.

Greek Anthology
AP 7.13 105–108
AP 7.525 102 f.
AP 7.60 103 f.
AP 7.712 106
AP 9.251 108–111
AP 9.256 111–113
AP 11.321 109 f.
AP 11.322 109 f.

Callinus
fr. 1.5–8 149, 158–160

Catullus
17.14–20 19–23
64.288–91 23 f.

CIL
IV.1173 (*CLE* 946) 35–40
IV.1520 (*CLE* 354; Courtney 96) 32–34
IV.1824 (*CLE* 947; Courtney 89) 39 f.
IV.1898 (*CLE* 948; Courtney 90) 38–40
IV.4091 (*CLE* 945; Courtney 88) 35–40

Dylan, Bob
"Masters of War" 163–168

Ennius
Annales
28 f. Skutsch 7–9
44–46 Skutsch 9–12

Homer
Iliad
1.29–31 81 f.
1.111–115 82
9.338–343 80 f.
13.459–461 7
19.295–300 80 f.
20.182–184 7
20.300–308 5 f.
21.257–262 153–156
Odyssey
11.421–423 82
Homeric Hymn to Aphrodite
196 f. 11

Horace
Ars Poetica
75–78 57
Epistles
2.1.173–176 69 f.
Odes
1.33.1–4 54 f.
2.4 75–88
2.5 75–88
2.9.9–12 56
3.2.13 156–160
4.2.22–24 114 f.
Satires
1.2.28–30 66
1.2.68–72 66 f.
1.3.25–28 67 f.
1.3.38–48 68–70
1.5.27–31 67 f.
1.5.34–36 71
1.10.67–73 63, 70
2.2.33–37 71 f.
2.3.43–45 72
2.3.296–299 72 f.

Lucan
1.239–243 141 f.

Marvell, Andrew
"A Horatian Ode Upon Cromwell's Return from Ireland" 131–146
"Damon the Mower"
57–60 142 f.
"The First Anniversary of the Government under His Highness the Lord Protector"
7–12 137 f.

https://doi.org/10.1515/9783110545708-017

"Tom May's Death"
49–52 139

Milton, John
"On the late Massacre in Piedmont"
1–5 144

Plutarch
Flamininus
12.6 3 f.

O'Brien, Tim
If I die in a combat zone, box me up and ship me home 151

Ovid
Amores
2.1.5 f. 29 f.
3.9.1–6 58 f.
3.11.35 f. 32–34
Metamorphoses
2.370 25
Remedia amoris
169–98 89–99

Owen, Wilfred
"Dulce Et Decorum Est" 148 f.

Pound, Ezra
Hugh Selwyn Mauberley IV 149–152

Propertius
1.1.5 32–34
1.6.12 36–40
1.7.11–14 29 f.
2.23.12 36–40

Sophocles
Ajax
487–505 82–84

Tecosca Cormaic
§ 1 159

Theocritus
2 117–129

Tibullus
1.2 117–129

Trumbo, Dalton
Johnny Got His Gun 165–168

Tyrtaeus
fr. 10.1 f. 158–160

Virgil
Aeneid
3.94–98 12–14
4.165–172 41–49
6.440–476 51–62
6.650 13 f.
6.692–94 61 f.
Eclogues
2 117–129
6.62 f. 17–27
Georgics
1.104–10 153–156

Yeats
"Easter, 1916"
74–80 144 f.

Index Rerum

Achilles 4–8, 58 f., 77, 80 f., 86, 97 f., 153 f., 156
acrostics see wordplay
addressee 58, 76, 87, 108
Aeneas 3–15, 32, 41–49, 51, 61 f., 97 f.
aesthetics 8, 63, 112, 160
Agamemnon 81–83
Alcaeus 57, 85 f., 157, 161
allusion see intertextuality, reference
Amaryllis 122
anachronicism 132 f., 146
Anacreon 76
anagrams see wordplay
Anchises 8, 10 f., 13–15, 32, 61
Antiphanes 109–113
Apollonius of Rhodes 17, 51, 55, 59, 125 f.
apposition, inserted 97
Aratus 21 f.
Artemidorus 123
Asclepiades 106 f.

baskania see resentment
'break-off' formula 101
Briseïs 77, 80 f.
bucolic poetry 90–99, 118, 120, 123 f., 126 f., 143

Callimachus 4, 30, 61, 68, 73, 90, 101–105, 107–110, 112–114, 138
– *Aetia* prologue 103, 107 f., 112
Callinus 148 f., 156–161
Carthy, Martin 161
Cassandra 81 f.
Catullus 17–27, 33, 47, 51, 54, 56 f., 59–61, 86, 91, 142 f., 150
Celtic 18–20, 24
Chryseïs 81 f.
Cinna 56 f., 126
Cisalpine Gaul 18–20, 26
closure 101–115
Clytemnestra 82
contextualism 131
Corydon 98, 121 f., 127 f.
Cycnus 23, 25
Cynthia 30, 91, 94

Daphnis 120, 122 f.
Dardanus 6 f., 12 f.
Darrow, Clarence 163 f.
Delia 125–127
Delos 4, 12
Delphi 3 f., 14
Delphis 120, 122
didactic 93–95, 98 f.
Dido 41–49, 51, 59–61
Donatus 97
double entendre see wordplay
Dylan, Bob 152 f., 157, 160–168
– 'Ballad of Hollis Brown' 163
– 'Clean-Cut Kid' 163
– 'George Jackson' 163
– 'Hard Times in New York Town' 165
– 'John Brown' 163, 166
– 'Masters of War' 163 f., 165–168
– 'North Country Blues' 165
– 'Rambling, Gambling Willie' 165
– 'Talkin' John Birch Paranoid Blues' 166
– *The Freewheelin' Bob Dylan* 164
– 'The Groom's Still Waiting at the Altar' 163
– 'The Lonesome Death of Hattie Carroll' 163
– 'Workingman's Blues #2' 163

ecphrasis 97 f.
Eisenhower, Dwight D. 164, 167
elegy 29–40, 47, 51–62, 76, 81, 89–92, 99, 118, 126–128, 150, 157
Ennius 4 f., 7–15, 17, 31, 73
envy 101–115 see resentment
epitaphs 102 f., 113, 151
Eridanus 18, 25
Erinna 105–109, 113
etymology 17, 19, 51–62, 135, 158
– etymological signpost 52, 58, 60
– gloss by adjective 55 f., 58

https://doi.org/10.1515/9783110545708-018

– Ovidian comment on Virgilian 58
– suppression of terms in 56
euphemism 39, 68–70
Euripides 17, 53 f., 82
Eurysaces 83
Eustathius 21
Evenus 108–110, 112
Exodus (film) 166

Flamininus, Titus Quinctius 3, 15

Gallus, C. Cornelius 26, 29–40, 89, 94, 97–99, 127
genre 26, 30, 51 f., 55–60, 62, 65, 69 f., 91 f., 95, 101, 103, 113 f., 117–124, 126–128, 136, 143, 157, 161 f.
– generic signpost 60
Gorodetsky, Eddie 161
Gover, Robert 165 f.
Guthrie, Woody 161, 163

Helen 80, 85 f.
Heliades 17, 23–26
Heracles 19
Hesiod 93 f., 161
Hesychius 19, 155
historicism 131 f.
Homer 4–5, 79, 11–15, 17 f., 20–24, 55, 59, 80 f., 97, 120, 126, 131 f., 148, 150, 152–157, 161
– *Iliad* 4–9, 11–14, 20 f., 23, 80, 97, 153 f., 156 f.
– *Odyssey* 24, 59, 82, 125
Horace 33, 46, 51, 53–58, 60, 63, 65–73, 76, 78 f., 82–87, 90 f., 114, 118, 133–139, 141–145, 147–152, 156–163
– *Ars Poetica* 57
– *Epodes* 76, 157
– *Odes* 54, 56, 58, 75, 77, 79–81, 84, 86 f., 91, 114, 135 f., 138, 156 f.
Horatianism 131–146
hunting 93 f., 137

iambos 76
Ilia 9–11
imitation 91, 97 f., 118, 123–125, 132, 134 f., 143
impotence 19
impropriety 76
insects, as metaphor for hostile critics 108–113
intertextuality see allusion, reference

Johnson, Robert 165
Juturna 62

Kinbote, Charles see allusion

leisure 89–99
Leonidas 105–107, 113
Liguria, Ligurians 19 f., 23, 25
London 150, 161, 163
– Dylan in 161
– Pound in 150, 163
love madness, *dementia* 121, 127 f.
Lucretius 22, 52, 59, 64, 68, 93, 96

magic 118, 120, 122,125 f., 128
marriage 81, 83
– in Trojan family 8–9
– 'marriage' of Dido and Aeneas 41–49
– to Hades 105 f.
– to non-Athenian ξένοι 84
Marvell 130–136
medicine 19, 67
for curing love 89, 92, 99
Meleager 105, 123, 128
metapoetics 25 f., 69, 97, 126, 143
meter 39, 57, 63–73, 127
– Priapean meter 19
mime 87, 118–120
morality 73, 79
music 54, 157, 161
– American 157, 161
– Folk 157, 161, 163 f.

O'Brien, Tim 148, 151, 153, 163
Orpheus 26, 56 f.
Ovid 17, 25, 29–34, 37, 39 f., 43, 51–53, 58–60, 73, 89–99, 142 f., 162
– *Amores* 29, 32–34, 52, 58 f., 90
– *Metamorphoses* 40, 73
– *Remedia amoris* 37, 89–99

otium see leisure
Owen, Wilfred 147–151, 153, 156, 161–164

paraclausithyron 54, 125 f.
Parcae 10, 86
pastoral poetry see bucolic poetry
Peleus 23, 85 f.
Peneus 23
Pericles 83 f.
– citizenship law of 83
Phaethon 17 f., 23–25
Phaethontiades 17 f., 23–25 see Heliades
Philip 108–110
Phoenix 82
Phthonos see envy
Pindar 101, 114 f., 148, 150, 157, 161
Po River 18, 25 f.
poetry books 113
– authorial design in 117–129
Pound, Ezra 148–151, 153, 156, 161–163
Priam 6 f., 13 f., 82, 85
Propertius 29–34, 36 f., 39 f., 60, 65, 90 f., 94, 125, 127, 142, 150
prophecy
– in Ennius 9–11, 14 f.
– in Homer 4–7, 9, 14 f.
– in *Homeric Hymn to Aphrodite* 11
– in Virgil 4 f., 12–15
propriety 159 f. see impropriety
puns see wordplay

Quick, Clarence 165

rape 9 f., 62, 79, 81, 87
readers 17 f., 21, 29–31, 40, 62 f., 73, 85, 89, 96, 102, 109, 117–119, 124, 128 f., 140, 147, 151 f.
reception 85, 101–104, 110 f., 113, 133, 147, 156
reference see allusion, intertextuality
resentment 101–113 see envy

Sassoon, Siegfried 150 f., 162 f.
satire 63, 65, 70, 73, 86
schema Cornelianum see apposition, inserted
Shakespeare 134 f., 143, 148, 162
Silenus 17
Simaetha 120–122, 125 f.
slaves 77, 79, 80–84, 86 f.
– slave-girl (*ancilla*) 77, 79, 84
– names of 87
– romantic/sexual relationship between master/mistress and 77–88
solecism 63, 71
Sophocles 82 f.
sphragis 87, 104, 111, 113

Tarentum, Old Man of 18
Tecmessa 77 f., 83 f.
Telamon 83
Terry, Sonny 165
Teucer 83
Theocritus 17 f., 23 f., 117–126, 128, 143
Thestylis 121 f.
Thetis 23, 58, 85 f.
Thomas, Richard 5, 8, 17–18, 21–24, 26 f., 42, 51, 77, 95, 98, 114, 126–129, 131, 147, 151–155, 162, 168
Tibullus 31, 33, 47, 55, 58–60, 90 f., 117 f., 120, 124–128
Tityrus 17, 121 f.
transhistoricism 132, 134, 145
trees 17–27, 93 f., 111–113, 154, 159
– alder 17–27
– poplar 17–27
Troy, ruling house of 5–14, 85.
Trumbo, Dalton 165–168
Tyro 9, 11
Tyrtaeus 148, 156–161

Valgius 56 f.
Virgil 4 f., 8 f., 12–15, 17 f., 21–27, 30–32, 41–43, 45 f., 48 f., 52 f., 56–61, 65, 82, 90, 92, 94–99, 117 f., 120–128, 132, 135, 140, 143, 147, 152–156, 161–163
– *Aeneid* 4 f., 8, 12–15, 17 f., 21, 25, 31 f., 38, 40 f., 51 f., 54, 57–60, 97 f., 132, 134
– *Eclogues* 26, 96–99, 118, 121–124, 126–128
– *Georgics* 1, 7, 22, 25 f., 51 f., 55–57, 65, 90, 92, 94–99, 128, 153–156

witches 125 f.

wordplay 21f., 25f., 32, 51–54, 56, 58, 69, 134, 142, 152
- acrostics 21f., 24
- anagrams 22
- *double entendre* 76
- pun 22, 25, 32, 69, 134f., 142
wound of love 59, 61